A WORLD TO MAKE

A WORLD TO MAKE

Development in Perspective

Edited by
Francis X. Sutton

Transaction Publishers
New Brunswick (U.S.A.) and London (U.K.)

Library of Congress Catalog Number: 89-20349
ISBN: 0-88738-813-2
Printed in the United States of America

Library of Congress Cataloging-in-Publication Data

A World to make: development in perspective/edited by Francis X. Sutton.
    p. cm.
    "Originally published as a special issue of Daedalus, winter 1989"–Verso. t.p.
    Papers from a colloquium held May 19-20, 1988, at the American Academy of Arts and Sciences in Boston, Mass.
    ISBN 0-88738-813-2
    1. Economic development–Congresses. 2. Economic development–Social aspects–Congresses. I. Sutton, Francis X. (Francis Xavier)
    HD73.W695   1990   89-20349
    338.9–dc20   CIP

Contents

Contributors to This Volume

Edmar L. Bacha
Professor of Economics
Catholic University, Rio de Janeiro, Brazil

David E. Bell
Clarence Gamble Professor of Population Sciences and International Health
Harvard University, Cambridge, Massachusetts

Peter D. Bell
President
The Edna McConnell Clark Foundation, New York, New York

Nancy Birdsall
Chief, Population and Human Resources Division, Brazil Department
World Bank, Washington, D.C.

McGeorge Bundy
Professor of History
New York University, New York, New York

Gelia T. Castillo
Professor of Rural Sociology
University of the Philippines at Los Banos College, Laguna, Philippines

Lincoln C. Chen
Taro Takemi Professor of International Health
Harvard University School of Public Health, Boston, Massachusetts

Hollis B. Chenery
Thomas D. Cabot Professor of Economics Emeritus
Harvard University, Cambridge, Massachusetts

Kamla Chowdhry
Chairman
Vikram Sarabhai Foundation, New Delhi, India

Clifford Geertz
Harold F. Linder Professor of Social Science
Institute for Advanced Study, Princeton, New Jersey

John D. Gerhart
Deputy Vice President, Developing Countries Programs
The Ford Foundation, New York, New York

VII

James P. Grant
Executive Director
United Nations Children's Fund, New York, New York

Stanley Heginbotham
Deputy Director, International Affairs Programs
The Ford Foundation, New York, New York

Abiola Irele
Professor of French, University of Ibadan, Ibadan, Nigeria
Visiting Professor, The Ohio State University, Columbus, Ohio

Susan P. Joekes
Fellow, Institute of Development Studies
University of Sussex, Brighton, England

Tom G. Kessinger
President
Haverford College, Haverford, Pennsylvania

Charles P. Kindleberger
Ford International Professor of Economics Emeritus
Massachusetts Institute of Technology, Cambridge, Massachusetts

Arthur Kleinman
Professor of Medical Anthropology and Psychiatry
Harvard Medical School and Harvard University, Cambridge, Massachusetts

Paul R. Krugman
Professor of Economics
Massachusetts Institute of Technology, Cambridge, Massachusetts

Robert A. LeVine
Roy E. Larsen Professor of Education and Human Development
Harvard University, Cambridge, Massachusetts

John P. Lewis
Professor of Economics and International Affairs
Princeton University, Princeton, New Jersey

D. Anthony Low
Smuts Professor of the History of the British Commonwealth
President, Clare Hall
University of Cambridge, Cambridge, England

Charles William Maynes
Editor, *Foreign Policy*
Washington, D.C.

William H. McNeill
Robert A. Millikan Distinguished Service Professor Emeritus of History
University of Chicago, Chicago, Illinois

Mohamed Naciri
Professor
Institut Agronomique et Vétérinaire de Hassan II, Rabat, Morocco

Dwight H. Perkins
Director, Harvard Institute for International Development
Harold Hitchings Burbank Professor of Political Economy
Harvard University, Cambridge, Massachusetts

Cranford Pratt
Professor of Political Science
University College, University of Toronto, Toronto, Canada

Kenneth Prewitt
Vice President of Programs
The Rockefeller Foundation, New York, New York

Michael Roemer
Institute Fellow, Harvard Institute for International Development
Harvard University, Cambridge, Massachusetts

Jeffrey D. Sachs
Professor of Economics
Harvard University, Cambridge, Massachusetts

Amartya Sen
Lamont University Professor of Economics
Harvard University, Cambridge, Massachusetts

Soedjatmoko
Former Rector
United Nations University, Tokyo, Japan

Alfred Stepan
Dean, School of International and Public Affairs
Columbia University, New York, New York

Francis X. Sutton
Retired Deputy Vice President
The Ford Foundation, New York, New York

Judith Tendler
Professor, Department of Urban Studies and Planning
Massachusetts Institute of Technology, Cambridge, Massachusetts

Miguel Urrutia
Manager, Economic and Social Development Department
Inter-American Development Bank, Washington, D.C.

F. Champion Ward
Former Vice President for Education and Research
The Ford Foundation, New York, New York

George Zeidenstein
President
The Population Council, New York, New York

Introduction

I T HAS BEEN MORE THAN FORTY YEARS since World War II came to an end and a new era in world history began. Despite wars, disasters, and multitudes still in desperate poverty, this has been an era of unprecedented advance in the world's well-being. Statistics show that both rich nations and poor have prospered as never before: lives have been lengthened, education and the uses of modern science and technology have spread astoundingly, and new horizons and opportunities have opened up for vast populations.

So positive a view of the past forty years is not as common nowadays as it might be or as it was some years ago. The years following World War II were full of the anxiety and tension of the Cold War. But they were also times of optimism and a self-confident readiness to address the new challenge of a global concern with the well-being of human beings, East and West, North and South. Future historians may well see these years as the time when an equal regard for people everywhere began. No longer were there to be different standards for the treatment of different races and peoples. Colonialism and "civilizing missions" were put to an end, and human rights were made universal in the 1948 United Nations Declaration. Poverty, ignorance, and disease were not to be accepted as our inescapable mortal lot but to be viewed as evils removable by human effort. In the vision that inspired President Truman's Point IV, scientific and technical knowledge was to be shared and applied to conquer them. Nations everywhere assumed the responsibility of attacking these evils in their own countries, and an international obligation of the richer nations to help the poorer was proclaimed. *Development* is the word that came to describe these obligations and efforts. It quickly became a major feature of international relations, nations being classified as "developing" or "developed," the poor nations to try bettering themselves and the richer, developed nations to help them without intruding on their sovereignty.

"Development" became the label that framed the hopes and aspirations of multitudes in the developing countries, guided their nation-building efforts, and inspired the international enterprise of development assistance. It has been a major subject of domestic and foreign policy and has been served by small armies of professionals and experts in nearly every field of practical endeavor through which modern societies function—in education, health, industry, agriculture, administration, and research.

What development has meant in all its political, social, economic, and technical diversity has never been easy to grasp and has been subject to change and controversy throughout the decades. Since the late 1960s a particularly sharp divergence of conceptions has been evident. Doubts about the success of old policies have arisen, and Third World voices denouncing the whole international structure in which development was conceived have called for a new international economic order. In the Western world, declining trust in government and the resurgence of neoclassical market economics brought critical doubts about the "statism" of development aid programs. Perhaps more importantly, a worried or pessimistic view of the state of the world came to prevail, despite the efforts of an amiable American president to make us feel better. In retrospect, the years before seemed to have been less troubled by social problems and economic uncertainties (the French call them *les années heureuses*). Whether or not the shift in mood was justified by experience and events, it had evident impact on the self-confidence with which the problems of the world, and certainly the development of poor countries, were addressed.

This issue of *Dædalus* grows out of an effort to take stock of what development has been and what, after such great changes, it has become. The effort was stimulated by the retirements of two professors from Harvard University—David E. Bell and Hollis B. Chenery, who have devoted most of their distinguished careers to development. Both have been engaged in its theory and analysis as well as its practice, Bell as administrator of the U.S. Agency for International Development and head of the Ford Foundation's international division, and Chenery as vice-president of the World Bank. A colloquium on development was planned that would bring together an array of scholars and practitioners of development that would be representative of various disciplines and parts of the world. The articles in this issue were prepared as papers for the colloquium, which was held at the American Academy of Arts and Sciences on May 19 and 20, 1988. They are supplemented by a liberal use of oral presentations—the remarks of commentators and the discussions that followed the presentation of papers, all of which were recorded, transcribed, and edited by the *Dædalus* staff.

The aspiration of the colloquium was to view development in its broad, historical complexity as an organizing principle of governments and international relations, as a set of ideas or ideologies, and as a series of programs and practices. To do so required that we reach beyond the community of development specialists for the perspectives of others. In one of its most fundamental aspects, development has been an effort at deliberate control of the course of human affairs, and it seemed appropriate to set our consideration of it in the longer perspective that Professor William McNeill provides in his article, "Control and Catastrophe in Human Affairs." Bravely venturing into the domain of economists, McNeill sketches a sequence of widening efforts to control the cycles of boom and bust through corporate organization in the years between the 1873 crash and the Great Depression of the 1930s, followed after World War II by economic management on a nationwide scale that brought new prosperity until at least the 1970s. He suggests that the success of corporate management in the earlier period depended on the existence of a large and unorganized sector of small buyers and sellers and that the breakdown in the 1930s came after this sector had diminished in importance. Similarly, he says (as many Third World spokesmen have loudly complained) that the successes of national economic management in the West and Japan after World War II depended on a Third World much less well organized than the First World. The present debt crisis may herald a breakdown (a "catastrophe") on a wider scale, corresponding to the widened scale of control since World War II.

In his article McNeill also discusses political cycles of control and catastrophe, and Anthony Low's article gives a concise but sweeping view of political and social change in Asia and Africa since World War II. In a somewhat different mode Peter Bell gives a similar view of Latin America in his commentary. Low argues quite properly that the sort of efforts at control and improvement that we have come to call development had a history reaching back at least to the nineteenth century. Indeed, one can trace such beginnings in the long historical process of governments creating more rationalized and purposeful efforts to cope with the problems their countries faced— part of Max Weber's "process of rationalization." But as I argue in my article, the idea and practice of development crystallized in the 1950s and 1960s into a new kind of ideological orthodoxy that guided the actions of governments, the United Nations, and other international organizations. Governments in developing nations were unquestionably the prime agents of development. John Lewis remarks in his article that "it is a safe guess" that if a conference on development had been held in 1950, "no one would have been asked to write an essay on 'government and national economic development.' Such a topic would have been thought the subject of the whole conference."

This central role for government was encouraged both by the jealous regard for sovereignty in newly independent nations and by a prevailing conviction that development required national planning. The influence of the Soviet Union as an apparently successful example of planned development was widespread, and although the Western world was sometimes ambivalent toward national planning, it generally agreed that this was what the developing nations needed. Whatever else development was, it included economic development, and the flourishing of a new subject—development economics—provided rationales and guides for planning. As Lewis and I stress in our articles, development was infused with the revived visions of economic growth that dominated public agendas in the 1950s after rather curious neglect in previous decades. However varied they were, the developing countries were viewed as similar in their need to make economic growth the central strategy of development.

In the course of the colloquium we came to call this set of ideas the Old Testament. It is now certainly in shreds. Edmar Bacha, the Brazilian economist, said it died with American hegemony. What happened to it and what gropings toward a New Testament have been made are the subjects of a great part of this issue of *Dædalus*. Clearly, many things did not work out as they were written in the Old Testament. The hopes of planned and controlled development have been disappointed in major ways. Abiola Irele's *cri de coeur* about the state of education and access to modern knowledge in his own Nigeria and Africa in general was undoubtedly the most poignant expression of these disappointments. But they are also present in Mohamed Naciri's account of fumbling or disastrous efforts to control the growth of cities and the progress of rural areas in Morocco, Iran, Cambodia, and elsewhere. The difficulty of controlling population growth had less prominence in the papers and discussion than it might have had. But Kamla Chowdhry and Dr. Soedjatmoko set forth alarms about the threats to the environment that now make "sustainable" development a popular cry.

Some of what has gone awry may have been due to overweening confidence in the old ideas and in the competence of governments. Hollis Chenery modestly conceded that planning has not been very successful and saw a retreat from hopeful long perspectives to a preoccupation with short-run problems. The old conception that carefully planned and insulated economies are good for developing countries is now nearly universally abandoned. As Paul Krugman bluntly writes, "In 1955 the Soviet Union was widely perceived as a model of (national) economic transformation; in 1988 its place has been taken by Taiwan and Korea." But the erosion of old faiths came from more than strategies of economic management. James Grant, the head of UNICEF, recalled the rise of a "basic needs" approach to development in the 1970s as a response to criticisms that the old approaches were making the rich richer and the poor poorer. In the Old Testament view, development was the progress of nations. The 1970s brought passionate concern about equity and distribution, the new concern for women and children that development economist Susan Joekes spoke of, and means were sought to help the "poorest of the poor." As Robert McNamara said in his valedictory at the World Bank, development came to have two aims, the relief of "absolute poverty" competing with national economic growth.

There is not only complexity of purpose to complicate present views of the developing countries. Their variety can no longer be blurred to treat them all together. In his article Krugman argues that they once had a common role in the world economy as primary exporters and capital importers, but in addressing the present scene he proposes a four-part classification: inward-looking primary exporters, wards of the international community, new manufacturing exporters, and problem debtors. There was much critical discussion of this classification but general agreement that uniformity was gone. David Bell pointed out that the practice of aid had long ago led to classifications. The need to recognize regional and political variety stood out so strongly that we heard Edmar Bacha and anthropologist Clifford Geertz declaring in the concluding session that the old ascendancy of economists was gone and calling for more political science or interdisciplinary marvels of comprehension.

The intense discussion of the debt problem in the colloquium left no doubt, however, about the critical importance of international economics for both the developing countries and their creditors. International economist Jeffrey Sachs and Edmar Bacha, as commentators on Krugman's paper, were joined in debate by the dean of Columbia's School of International and Public Affairs, Alfred Stepan, who commented on a paper by Charles William Maynes, the editor of *Foreign Policy*, on American foreign policy toward the Third World (published elsewhere and not included here). Development has historically been a joint international concern driven by economic and political interests, and there was little doubt that it must continue to be so. The debt problem has brought serious threats to the banking system of the Western world; Jeffrey Sachs echoed William McNeill in pointing out that the risks involved have been pushed more onto the debtor countries than onto their creditors. And the arresting of development by the repayment of debt now burdens the world economy as poor countries' imports have shrunk.

An economic basis for continued international interest in the development of poor countries thus clearly continues to exist, and it is reinforced by political interests. Despair at the sense of losing ground in the capacity to acquire and use the modern knowledge essential to development was expressed by Irele and Soedjatmoko (who was unfortunately struck by illness at the last moment and could not be present at the colloquium). They linked it to the turbulent and deteriorating state of the universities in the Third World. One of the hopes of development has been that nations everywhere would share in the advancement and use of modern knowledge, and bitterness at continued dependency contributes to political instability and international tensions. In his concluding remarks, McGeorge Bundy seconded the call from Irele and Soedjatmoko for new efforts to sustain first-class universities in the Third World, in their own and the world's interest. And in these days of acute concern with environmental problems on a world scale, Soedjatmoko argues that they will not be satisfactorily met without developing countries having the capacity to contribute to their solution.

Development as an international cooperative enterprise has necessarily been a matter of political relations between governments. Weakened faith in the capacities and benevolent actions of governments has in recent years pushed much development assistance away from government toward the private sector. Current enthusiasm for private voluntary organizations found expression in Kamla Chowdhry's article, and the rising importance of private schools was noted by the Aga Khan aide, Robert Edwards, in the rather somber discussions of education. But today's popularity of markets and privatization did not sweep away recognition of the continuing indispensability of government actions. The discussion of "food and freedom" by economics professor Amartya Sen, based on a paper published elsewhere, includes strong evidence that the role of government is critical to ensuring basic food supplies and warding off famine. With government planning, India has been able to stave off starvation in circumstances where per capita supplies were lower than in African countries that have had famines. In "Thoughts on Good Health and Good Government" Nancy Birdsall explores cautiously the possibilities of "market" solutions meeting health needs in developing countries, but with the presumption that governments will continue to bear the prime responsibility. John Lewis argues that excessive faith in governments has now swung to too little faith, and he rises to some passion in criticizing the current popularity of privatization. The general conclusion that development must continue to be the business of governments and their international relations was firmly accepted.

How much development is or can be infused with moral energy to help the poor and unfortunate kept appearing in the discussion, sometimes despairingly, as when Canadian political scientist Cranford Pratt cried, "Where is the old moral passion?" Fatigue in providing aid, the weakening of Cold War motivations, and ambivalence toward the Third World were cited as reasons for having little hope of increasing concessional aid from the United States. There were, however, some at the colloquium like John Lewis, who in his article argues that aid is now especially needed and cheap in terms of U.S. budgets. The outlook for more channeling of aid through international agencies was thought to be poor, whatever its merits.

Against the sweeping generality and coherence of the Old Testament, canonical order and orthodoxy seem lacking in present thinking about development. There was no radical foe of development at the colloquium, but authors were cited who call for discarding the whole idea in favor of some untarnished alternative. In the conclusions of the colloquium there were glimmerings of a New Testament with clear antecedents in the Old and recognition of the variety and complexity of the contemporary world, which the Old Testament helped bring forth. Clifford Geertz thought the New not so different from the Old, and the sociologist from the Philippines, Gelia Castillo, reminded everyone that the earlier need for institutional and human development continues as before. The old vision of a world transformed by the spread of modern knowledge persists, with anxiety over the capacities of universities and research in the Third World to make this spread possible. And the present tendency of international economics to overshadow development economics only accentuates the older awareness that the economy of any country is engaged in a world economy.

The need to recognize the diversity of the developing countries was repeatedly emphasized, as was the difficulty of doing so in any coherent way. The distinctiveness and cultural identity of peoples and nations is a principle of the Old Testament that may only now be getting proper respect. We can hardly fail to notice it nowadays, for Third World countries have learned to speak for themselves and insist that the world attend to their views. The necessity of development is axiomatic to them, and they will see to it that efforts to bring forth a polyglot New Testament such as this issue of *Dædalus* adumbrates are not neglected.

Francis X. Sutton

William H. McNeill

Control and Catastrophe in Human Affairs

C ATASTROPHE OBVIOUSLY PLAYS A BIG ROLE in human affairs, manifesting itself in social relations, profoundly affecting both economics and politics. The historical record, indeed, seems to amount to little else than one catastrophe after another, if we mean by catastrophe some sequence of events that disrupts established routines of life and inflicts suffering or death on many.

Ever since civilization arose, leaving decipherable records that allow us to understand something of what people have experienced, catastrophes have been chronic and all but continual. Famine, epidemic, and/or war have affected nearly every participant in civilized society at some time. Despite all the skills we now command, a life immune from exposure to one or more of these catastrophes remains unusual. Perhaps we should recognize that risk of catastrophe is the underside of the human condition—a price we pay for being able to alter natural balances and to transform the face of the earth through collective effort and the use of tools.

A simple example from water engineering may make this situation obvious. In my lifetime the Army Corps of Engineers began to control Mississippi floods by building an elaborate system of levees along the river's lower course. This had the undesired effect of concentrating sediment on the river bottom between the levees. As a result, the water level now rises each year, and the levees have to be raised higher from time to time. Under this regimen, sooner or later the mighty Mississippi will break its banks and inflict far greater damage

1

on the surrounding landscape than if there were no levees and the river were free to overflow each spring and deposit sediment across the breadth of its natural floodplain, as it did in my childhood. Chinese engineers, who began to confine the Yellow River between levees as long ago as 600 B.C., have witnessed this sort of catastrophe several times in recorded history. The superior earth-moving resources of modern technology do not seem at all likely to be able to compensate—indefinitely—for the increasing instability of a river being artificially lifted higher and higher above the adjacent floodplain.

Intelligence and ingenuity in this and innumerable other cases run a race with all the nasty eventualities that interfere with human hopes and purposes; it is far from clear which is winning. Both intelligence and catastrophe appear to move in a world of unlimited permutation and combination, provoking an open-ended sequence of challenge and response. Human history thus becomes an extraordinary, dynamic equilibrium in which triumph and disaster recur perpetually on an ever-increasing scale as our skills and knowledge grow.

This sort of pattern is readily apparent in economics. To begin with, the great human advances were technological. Because they required the concerted effort of thousands of persons, cooperation was achieved by obedience to the commands of a ruler, backed ultimately by the threat of force. Catastrophes had their place in these early command economies, since the armies assembled for war, or for work on some vast construction project, were vulnerable to epidemic disease. Also, crops could always fail and provoke famine. Civilized communities learned to live with such disasters by supporting family systems that encouraged the high birthrates needed to replace these population losses.

For the first 4,000 years of civilized history, private initiatives remained marginal though important. Merchants and other adventurers carried skills, ideas, and goods across political boundaries; sporadic diffusion of civilization resulted. Still, for millennia, producing for distant markets, depending on goods brought from afar, was too risky to sustain ordinary human life. Luxuries and a few critical strategic materials—copper and tin primarily—did in fact travel long distances, but that was all.

Beginning about 1000 A.D. improved transportation changed the situation fundamentally. Articles of common consumption began to enter trade networks—wool, cotton, salt, timber, fish, grain, and the like—on unprecedented scale, and large numbers of people became dependent on food and other commodities brought from afar. Thus the market first supplemented and then supplanted the age-old pattern of obedience to the command of a leader as the regulator of everyday activity for increasing numbers of ordinary people in the thickly populated parts of Eurasia. With this advance (and it was an enormous advance, creating new wealth by allowing specialized production to achieve all the economies that Adam Smith analyzed so persuasively in *The Wealth of Nations*) came a new form of catastrophe—the occasional paralyzing financial crisis.

Periodic crashes of the credit system on which long-distance trade depended began to show up at least as early as the fourteenth century and have continued into our own time. Economic activity has altered in very diverse ways since the fourteenth century, but an irregular four- to five-year alternation between boom and bust has persisted throughout all such changes. The pattern has upset innumerable lives by benefiting a few and hurting the great majority, whose means of livelihood have temporarily collapsed because of panic.

Economists of the late nineteenth and the twentieth centuries have devoted much effort to figuring out how and why this pattern has continued. Since about 1950, countermeasures have softened the impact of what may now be called old-fashioned credit crises, thanks, in large part, to the theoretical understanding economists have been able to work out. The prestige they enjoy in our society today rests on this achievement, even though defects in their foresight have recently become so conspicuous as to call the adequacy of accepted theories into question.

Questions have arisen because, in addition to the four- to five-year business cycles, other, longer-term changes of behavior create larger and more recalcitrant rhythms of economic expansion and downturn in the market. Recent examples are the crash of 1873 and the hard times that prevailed thereafter until the 1890s, and the decade of depression that followed the 1929 crash.

In each case, hard times were followed by a boom that dimmed the effect of the familiar, short-term crises for a generation or so. In retrospect, one may see why. The surge in wealth during the first three decades of the twentieth century probably occurred because of new forms of management and control invented in the aftermath of the 1873 crash. Alfred Chandler's book *The Visible Hand* explains what happened with magnificent precision and insight. In brief, a few ambitious captains of industry built up large corporations that soon dominated the manufacture and sale of such commodities as steel, chemicals, sewing machines, and automobiles. They took full advantage of economies of scale that the latest machinery permitted, and organized a smooth assembly-line flow of all the factors of production—raw material, fuel, labor, and, when appropriate, parts produced elsewhere. Vertical integration allowed a single manager to decide how much raw material was needed and how much or how many end products to offer for sale. If need be, he could cut back production to maintain prices or expand production and lower prices so as to sell more.

When a few such corporations were able to dominate their markets, economies of scale lowered costs very sharply, and such lowered costs were passed on to consumers, at least in part. Both corporate profits and ordinary living standards rose accordingly, but critical advantages remained in the hands of corporation managers. Big corporations were cushioned against short-term credit crises by their managers' ability to adjust output to sales and to fix the prices at which they chose to sell to outsiders. As long as such outsiders were numerous and unorganized, industrial corporation managers could make their plans and reality match up with unprecedented accuracy. The business cycle was not eliminated, but it became catastrophic only for small producers and for those employees who lost their jobs in bad times. In well-managed corporations, however, technical and financial planning foresaw and guarded against temporary inconveniences arising from the ups and downs of the business cycle.

Thus, as long as most of the population farmed and could revert to a quasi-subsistence mode of life in times of credit collapse, corporate management of large-scale industrial production could avert most of the costs of the business cycle from themselves while improving ordinary citizens' lives by cheapening old products and creating new consumer goods. This achievement transformed industrial society profoundly between the 1880s and the 1930s.

Yet corporate management of production and sales had its limitations. A big corporation selling to a government or to another equally well-managed corporation had trouble fixing its sale prices at will.

Managers' power to control results was weakened when a large proportion of total output went to other corporations or to the government, for such purchasers were liable to bargain hard over prices and attach other conditions to delivery and payment. As more and more of the business world achieved corporate organization, such dealings multiplied, and the effective autonomy of individual corporations diminished accordingly. To flourish freely and realize their managers' plans exactly, corporations needed a matrix of unorganized buyers and sellers with whom to do business. But the rapid proliferation of corporate business organization that resulted from spectacular early successes had the effect of thinning that unorganized matrix, whereupon corporate managers began to encounter intractable new problems. The perils of the marketplace thus crept back into corporate boardrooms.

The result was the crash and stubborn depression of the 1930s. Dismissing workers and cutting back production while holding prices steady, or nearly steady, did not work when the agricultural, family, and small-firm segment of the economy ceased being able to sustain the shock of credit crunch. Instead, corporate policies intensified the depression, since dismissing workers diminished purchasing power, and that meant fewer sales, dictating further cutbacks in employment and further reduction of available purchasing power. The prevailing corporate policies for surviving bad times therefore created a vicious circle for which there was no ready cure. In time, even the biggest and best-managed corporations began to feel the pinch. Managers had not counted on or prepared for prolonged depression. Their method of guarding against ordinary credit collapses simply intensified the big crash when it came.

Thus, market catastrophe, bigger and more stubborn than before, was able to threaten even the largest corporations, and for a full decade no one in the United States knew what to do, in spite of numerous New Deal efforts to blunt the human costs of the depression. Only in Germany did a brutal new political regime prove itself capable of curing unemployment, but, as we all know, Nazi economic success in the 1930s swiftly provoked a new and far greater political catastrophe in the 1940s.

Nonetheless, economic management on a nationwide scale was sufficiently perfected during World War II to provide the basis for a swift postwar recovery followed by a boom that lasted into the

1970s. New concepts—the gross national product (GNP), for example—and new statistical measuring rods were created to allow skills that had been developed for the management of big corporations to direct the economic effort of entire nations. During the war, the new managers—government officials, often recruited from private industry to begin with—handled the nation and all available material resources as a single firm had been accustomed to treat the labor and raw materials required for large-scale industrial production and had the additional advantage of controlling money and credit within very broad limits.

The nation-as-firm was not completely sovereign, since economic and strategic planning transcended national boundaries on both Allied and Axis sides. But transnational implementation remained shaky, especially among the Axis powers, and after the war it was the national unit of management that prevailed, using macroeconomic concepts and statistical data introduced initially for war mobilization. The Soviet Union was both precocious and backward. Socialist planning had been introduced as early as 1928, but Soviet economic managers remained more reliant on command and compulsion than Western countries, where control of credit became crucial. In Western Europe, on the other hand, transnational integration revived and was carried further than elsewhere, but the constituent national units of the European Economic Community retained veto power over common policies, and each government continued to exercise credit and other controls independently, though not without extensive mutual consultation.

The nationwide scale of economic management that emerged from the depression of the 1930s and World War II seems very like the enlarged corporate scale of management that emerged from the crash of 1873 and the depressed decades that followed. And the limits of this new way of minimizing exposure to the perils of the marketplace may well turn out to be similar. One can see already that the spectacular economic success achieved by the leading Western countries and by Japan after 1950 occurred in the context of a much less well-organized Third World. How important that context was for the increase in living standards and GNP of the leading industrial countries is debatable. But it is hard to doubt that raw material suppliers in the Third World and that immigrant laborers coming from poor and mainly agricultural countries bore a disproportionate share of the costs of the fluctuations in the business cycle that persisted in spite of all the deliberate countermeasures that Keynesian and post-Keynesian economists devised. The well-managed industrial nations, like the large, prosperous corporations of the early twentieth century, were effectually insulated from such disturbances by the policies of their managers. The brunt of such catastrophes passed off onto others.

Whether such parallels will provoke another general economic crisis is unclear. It seems possible, for the world's finances are surely in disarray. Third World debt is largely unrepayable, even if the poor nations were willing to try to pay. The financial difficulties facing countries like Poland, Mexico, and Brazil are more significant, since their debts are much larger. United States indebtedness, both governmental and private, is most critical of all and seems sure to result in the disguised repudiation of inflation.

Probably no one knows just what the effect of wholesale debt repudiation would be on the financial system of the world. But it looks as though the economically well-managed nations of the postwar era were in imminent danger of losing the safety valve they enjoyed as long as they acted within the context of poorer, less well-organized trading partners who accepted the prices and terms of trade offered to them in return for an escalating series of loans— loans that now threaten to become unsupportable. In 1929, private citizens who bought cars and other goods on what were then new-fangled installment plans were in much the same situation as the world's poor countries are today. But since debtor nations are not nearly so numerous as persons in debt, the parallel should not be pressed too far.

All I wish to suggest is that twice in the past century a very successful response to one sort of market catastrophe, making simple recurrence of the old sort of breakdown unlikely or impossible, has shifted the burden of malfunction onto less well-organized participants in the economic exchange network, and when the disadvantaged became unable to bear the burden, then market catastrophe engulfed even the better-organized, larger units of management, creating a new and more baffling crisis in the system as a whole.

Should we then accept the conservation of catastrophe as a reality in human affairs? The hypothesis strikes me as worth exploring. As long as a majority of the participants in the market system could fall back on local subsistence from agriculture when credit collapsed, periodic crises were not threatening to the economic system as a whole. When, however, a large number of persons severed connection with rural subsistence agriculture, business cycles became far more life threatening and new forms of organization had to be invented to minimize the danger. Public relief was the first response; the rise of big corporations and more extended management of economic processes, industry by industry, was another. But, now it appears that these new organizational forms of production and distribution may eventually encounter stumbling blocks, triggering new forms of crisis.

One cannot say for sure that the quantity or severity of the resulting market catastrophe was the same as what arose in earlier times when small-scale actors dominated the scene. Fewer breakdowns, lasting longer and being more difficult to recover from, may add up to about the same total of human suffering and dislocation. On the other hand, they may not. Comparing radically different standards of living in different times and places is difficult. Perhaps, therefore, the notion of the conservation of catastrophe ought only to be entertained as a rhetorical reminder of the refractory character of human behavior even when managed with all the rationality and foresight of which we are capable.

*   *   *

Refractoriness to rational management is not limited to economics. The tendency toward conservation of catastrophe seems rather more evident in the political than in the economic field, for the better organized a government is at home and the better it is able to keep the peace domestically, the more capable it is of waging war abroad. Even if periods of peace make outbreaks of violence less frequent, their scale, when they do occur, is certain to increase.

Yet amidst the incessant tumult of political struggles that dominate the historical record, we detect one clear pattern that seems to contradict this observation: the emergence of large empires whose rulers have been content to use minimal armed force for the defense of their far-flung frontiers and have often preferred bribery to force in their dealings with neighboring barbarians. "Universal states" of this sort, to use a term Toynbee invented, arise through war and, in due season, perish through war. But for periods of several centuries, such states have been able to banish organized violence from large areas of the earth and reduce political catastrophe to comparatively trivial proportions.

For heirs of the European tradition, the Roman Empire is the obvious archetype of a universal state; but very exact parallels to the rise of Roman power over the ancient Mediterranean world are to be found in Mesopotamian, Indian, and Chinese antiquity and in the Amerindian history of both Peru and Mexico. The prominence and regularity of this political pattern inspired Toynbee to make it a key to all history—a burden it cannot really bear since there are parts of the world and eras of time in which local warfare and other forms of political struggle have been altered fundamentally by influences coming from somewhere outside the civilization concerned. The rise of Islam is one of the most remarkable examples of such a transforming force, and Spain's New World conquests of the early sixteenth century are another.

Many thoughtful observers of the recent history of the world have wondered whether the pattern of the rise of states to imperial hegemony may not reassert itself, this time on a truly worldwide scale. Ever since about 1500 in Europe, for instance, military and political history can be understood as a series of bids for imperial hegemony. All have failed, sometimes only narrowly, but the propensity remains inherent in the rivalries of the state system itself.

Short of world empire, and the bureaucratic management of both economic and military affairs on a global scale that such an empire would have to inaugurate, it is hard to see how new organizational inventions could resolve contemporary difficulties in a way analogous to that in which larger and larger states on the one hand, and larger and larger units of economic management on the other, have hitherto responded to recurrent catastrophe. But the future is always opaque, and some still unimagined change—catastrophic or not—may entirely alter human affairs—politically, economically, epidemiologically, environmentally, or even psychologically. For I need not remind you that economics and politics do not embrace all dimensions of human activity, even though I have chosen to illustrate the race between intelligence and catastrophe from that limited angle of vision.

*   *   *

Let me therefore draw back a bit and try to reflect in very general terms about the power of human beings to alter their lives and environment so as to banish catastrophe and about the limits of that power. It seems clear to me that the more successful a group of human beings is in avoiding catastrophe by using their powers of organization, foresight, and calculation, the greater become the catastrophes they invite by colliding with similarly organized and managed human groups. And if we imagine a world in which the entire human race were somehow organized so as to banish war and avert economic crisis, it seems likely that other kinds of catastrophe—perhaps greater than ever—might arise because of collisions between a newly organized humanity and the rest of the ecosystem of the planet.

Human affairs seem to proceed within a complex hierarchy of equilibria. We are parts of the physical and chemical world, after all; and atoms and molecules maintain a very reliable equilibrium in the neighborhood of our planet, at least for the time being. The law of entropy suggests that these equilibria will not last forever, but on a human and terrestrial time scale we can afford to treat them as stable and given. Far more volatile are the ecological and what I will call the semiotic equilibria within which human lives and societies exist, and it is at this level that public affairs arise and have their being.

The ecological equilibrium results from flows of matter and energy among living things. The food chain, whereby organisms feed on one another, is its central feature. The role of plants in using the energy of sunlight to synthesize organic compounds connects the ecological equilibrium firmly with the chemical and physical levels of organization. The body chemistry of animals is likewise rooted in what I like to think of as the same lower order of organization. The pyramid is then completed by a semiotic equilibrium perched precariously on top of the ecological equilibrium. It is constituted by the flow of symbolic messages that human beings rely on for regulating their everyday activity and collective behavior.

The interaction among these different levels of organization is very little understood. The recent advances in biochemistry have not resolved the question of how DNA molecules can propagate life in all its forms—remaining within chemical and physical limits, while attaining an extraordinary capacity to alter the way chemical and physical laws actually manifest themselves on the surface of our planet.

Higher up the ladder of equilibrium systems, the same mystery prevails. Ideas, conveyed in signs, symbols, and messages passing from person to person, certainly affect the ecological equilibrium around us by organizing and directing human intervention in myriad natural processes. Yet external realities also impinge on ideas, even though semiotic equilibria develop a dynamic of their own, which is only loosely connected to any of the lower equilibrium systems within which they operate.

Yet, in spite of the very loose connection between our semiotic systems and the material world, human successes have been truly extraordinary. We have transformed natural landscapes beyond recognition by exporting unexpected and undesired outcomes to some sort of boundary separating field from wasteland, us from them, the managed and predictable from the rest. The "rest" is of course where catastrophe continues to lurk. Indeed, the more perfect any particular patch of ordered activity may be, the more it alters older equilibria and the greater the resulting fragility. That, at least, seems a plausible summation of our entire endeavor to control ourselves and the world around us.

Modern societies, armed with contemporary levels of science and technology, are enormously powerful. No one doubts that. Yet they are no less vulnerable. Our reliance on flow-through production and consumption creates innumerable bottlenecks, where any obstruction becomes critical if prolonged. Think of what would happen if farmers failed to plant a crop next spring because gasoline and diesel fuel no longer flowed to their tractors. What would happen to a modern city if electric current were cut off for a few days? Or, to be really up to date, consider the consequences of the erasure of computer-stored data for our banks, the internal revenue service, and our society.

It certainly seems as though every gain in precision in the coordination of human activity and every heightening of efficiency in production were matched by a new vulnerability to breakdown. If this really is the case, then the conservation of catastrophe may indeed be a law of nature like the conservation of energy.

The big bang of atomic annihilation is, I suppose, the ultimate and now fully attainable human catastrophe, even though our warheads at their worst are only a puny, pathetic echo of the big bang with which our universe is thought to have begun. Nevertheless, I do not mean to imply that colossal human tragedy masquerading as cosmic comedy is the destined end of history. On the contrary, I tend to discount such eschatological views, probably more for temperamental than for intellectual reasons. As a historian who dwells cheerfully with the past, I am moved to say that in thinking ahead we ought to bear in mind how very many times human intelligence and ingenuity have prevailed, solving one sort of problem only to create new ones, of course, but nevertheless *surviving* and transforming the face of the earth far more rapidly and radically than any other species has ever done before. With such a record, we ought not to despair but rather to rejoice in how much we human beings can do in the way of capturing energy from the world around us and bending it to our purposes and wants, intensifying the risk of catastrophe with each new success.

Comments on William McNeill's Essay

CHARLES P. KINDLEBERGER: As an economist, I am aware that my subject is widely regarded as a dismal one, exceeded in gloom perhaps only by geology, which continuously comes up with the alarming news that the world is running out of something, or in the Club of Rome formulation, everything. The geologists have lately been joined by the ecologists and now, the philosopher-historian. McNeill makes economists look positively cheerful as he contemplates catastrophe after catastrophe, and the law of the conservation of catastrophe, emphasizing the unintended and often dire consequences of the efforts of those who try to control events.

Some years ago when I was working on financial crises, a theoretical economist with mathematical training tried to persuade me to model such crises in terms of catastrophe theory, the mathematics, as I dimly understood it, of falling off cliffs, or of moving around a curve generally concave to the origin until one came to a cusp where the curve reversed. Catastrophe theory had a brief run without help or hindrance from me and then, as I hear it, faded away. Today the action is in chaos theory, which says that anything can happen in given circumstances. It especially says to me that positive economics that would allow us to predict outcomes from simple models—as in what is called rational expectations—is frustrated by the enormous variety of mutations that may happen in nature—for example, in evolution—and in human affairs.

Catastrophe and its control in economic matters, especially financial crises, are more my line. In Britain, in the nineteenth century, for example, the financial crises of 1810, 1816, 1825, 1836, 1847, 1857, 1866, and 1890—the crisis of 1873 on the Continent having left Britain unaffected in the short run—have interest in themselves but should be considered from the point of view of catastrophe against a strong uptrend of growth. Moreover, the "catastrophes" were not alike: 1847, 1857, and 1866 were like summer storms, dramatic but ephemeral, as compared with the hurricanes or typhoons of 1873, 1890, and 1929. Control meant especially the provision of a lender of last resort, a device worked out in varied practice and articulated initially by Henry Thornton in 1802 and more fully in 1873 by Walter Bagehot. Lender-of-last-resort action—halting a panic run out of other assets into money by making money freely available—has unintended consequences, to be sure, in what is called by insurance companies moral hazard: units insured against untoward accidents lose incentive to act prudently and are sometimes wont to take undue risks.

In the economic realm I have difficulty too in regarding the so-called Great Depression from 1873 to 1896 as a catastrophe. Wage earners in Europe and the United States did well on the whole, as prices fell more than wages. The period is more properly regarded as profitless prosperity. Depression, as Schumpeter insisted, provides incentives for innovation to cut costs, an unintended, or more accurately, an unanticipated, consequence. The changes in business structures described by Alfred Chandler in the book that McNeill and the rest of us admire are hardly to be described as catastrophic.

In the *Pursuit of Power* and in his 1985 MIT seminar, McNeill notes that population pressure produces different outcomes in different settings—in consonance with chaos theory. The surge in births in the eighteenth century led to one catastrophe—the French Revolution, plus the French move to birth control—and to one windfall—the Industrial Revolution in Britain. The Industrial Revolution was not without its suffering in addition to disruption but again is hard to describe as catastrophic. Population pressure, McNeill asserts, produced World Wars I and II, and has now embroiled the Middle East in a race between Marxism and religious wars. War is not always an unmitigated disaster, to be sure. It speeds up economic processes of decline but also of growth, as the economic history of the United States demonstrates. Arthur Schlesinger, Jr., is fond of quoting Justice Oliver Wendell Holmes, who said that one who had no part in a war misses out on the great adventure of his generation. World War II is sometimes called the good war to distinguish it from World War I and especially the Vietnam war, although the adjective can hardly be approved by those who think of the dead, the maimed, and especially the victims of genocide.

I readily grant McNeill's contention that in contrast to the claims of rational-expectations theory and of positive economics, there are a great many attempts at control that produce unintended consequences. The Mississippi flooding example he cites is telling, although perhaps he should have taken into account the benefit of the years of absence of floods against the cost of levee building and raising. Another example close to my heart is land conservation in the town I live in, Lincoln, Massachusetts. Thirty years of preserving open land has produced the benefits of a lovely landscape and large capital gains for those who acquired houses early. The catastrophe is that the Lincoln of the early postwar era has been lost socially. When land is selling for more than $100,000 for a two-acre house site, it is necessary to build houses costing up to $1 million and more—what the *New Republic* writing about the advertisements for luxury houses in the *New York Times Magazine* calls real-estate porn. Assistant professors, young professionals, working-class natives, and old people who have lived there all their lives can no longer afford the place. Nature has been conserved at the cost of social catastrophe.

I find it difficult, however, to subscribe to the law of conservation of catastrophe, the notion that whatever goes up comes down, the bigger they come the harder they fall, what McNeill claims are bigger and more intractable catastrophes when control is attempted, or the matching of every gain in precision of coordination by a new vulnerability to breakdown. This may prove right, although McNeill's cheerful *l'envoi* suggests that he himself has doubts. I should have thought rather that unintended catastrophic consequences historically have left large parts of the globe better off than they or their ancestors were earlier and that catastrophes of late have been milder and more widely spaced.

As a Toynbee-esque alternative to the law of conservation of catastrophe, I suggest the pervasiveness of the Gompertz or "S-curve," what my MIT colleague Cyril Stanley Smith, the historical metallurgist, calls the phase transformation of materials. In *As You Like It,* Shakespeare describes the seven parts played by one man in his time, starting with the infant, mewling and puking in his nurse's arms, going through five stages of growth and maturity, to second childhood and mere oblivion, "sans teeth, sans eyes, sans taste, sans everything." Empires and nations wax and wane for reasons that many present-day commentators—among them Paul Kennedy, Mancur Olson, and Carlo Cipolla—seek to adduce. But Cyril Smith expresses it well in a long paragraph, from "Metallurgy as Human Experience," that partly complements, partly substitutes for the law of conservation of catastrophe:

> These and hundreds more materials and uses grew symbiotically through history, in a manner analogous to the S-curve of a phase transformation of the materials themselves. There was a stage, invisible except in retrospect, wherein fluctuations from the *status-quo,* involving only small localized distortion began to interact and consolidate into a new structure; this nucleus then grew in a more or less constant environment at an increasing rate because of the increasing interfacial opportunity, until finally its growth was slowed and stopped by depletion of material necessary for growth, or by the growing counter-pressure of other aspects of the environment. Any change in conditions (thermo-dynamic = social) may provide an opportunity for a new phase. We all know how the superposition of many small sequential S-curves themselves tend to add up to the giant S-curve of that new and larger structure we call civilization. . . . Because at any one time there are many overlapping competing sub-systems at different stages of maturity but each continually changing the environment of the others, it is often hard to see what is going on. Moreover, nucleation must in principle be invisible, for the germs of the future take their validity only from and in a larger system that has yet to exist. They are at first indistinguishable from mere foolish fluctuations destined to be erased. They begin in opposition to their environment, but on reaching maturity they form the new environment by the balance of their multiple interactions. This change of scale and interface with time, of radical misfit turning into conservative interlock, is the essence of history of anything whatever, material, intellectual or social.

I have a strong impression that the United States is an aging economy and an aging society running out of the material necessary for growth and meeting growing counterpressure from other aspects of its environment. Its ability to control by providing the international public goods of peace and economic stability is slipping. What McNeill calls the marcher states, Japan and the Federal Republic of Germany, have been strong supporters of American hegemony, but after their failed aggressions of the 1930s and 1940s, show no inclination to challenge this country to take over its hegemonic role. I, too, like Bill McNeill, have an optimistic, perhaps even Panglossian, disposition. I doubt a catastrophic big bang as U.S. leadership ultimately gets superseded, and I don't much mind if the process goes forward with a whimper.

D. Anthony Low

Development's Contexts: Asia, Africa

T HE WEST'S CONCERN with Third World development long
preceded its interest in the idea after World War II. In the late
eighteenth and early nineteenth centuries Britain, for instance,
initiated a number of development policies in India. They were
inspired by, among others, the physiocrats and the utilitarians, and
led to land settlements under major British administrators such as
Cornwallis and Munro, legal and educational innovations under
Bentinck and Macauley, and a good deal of infrastructural development, particularly under Dalhousie. In tropical Africa (not at the time
under direct British administration) the more informal capacities of
Christianity and commerce were looked to. In the second half of the
nineteenth century and well into the first half of the twentieth, British
development policies were overtaken by deep anxieties about the
fragility of societies. In India Britain chose to protect peasant societies
through legislation against landlords and moneylenders; in Africa
and elsewhere, "indirect rule" and the maintenance of traditional
authority became the order of the day. Later, the example of
Keynesian economics, Russian five-year plans, and the Tennessee
Valley Authority brought further change toward "development and
welfare."[1] Meanwhile, a clearer sequence ran through Dutch colonial
policy, with its "culture system" from 1830 to the 1860s, its "liberal
system" from then until 1900, and its "ethical policy" thereafter.[2]

Professional economists interested in development were Johnny-
come-latelies. In East Africa, until the mid-1950s, for example,
scarcely any could be recruited. Economic historians were appointed
instead. Only later were professional economists to dominate the

16

field. Characteristically, they gave little or no cognizance to issues of politics or government. Whether this was because they have little time for disciplines such as history and political science, which seem quite incapable of holding their variables steady, or because their government connections inhibit them from political inquiry is difficult to say. We know that it would have been inconceivable for any oil company interested in the Middle East in this century to undertake any kind of development there without paying considerable attention to political matters. Yet, in the otherwise splendid *World Development Report,* one looks in vain for anything that even verges on the consideration of political variables. In this respect, that is typical.

This is a curious matter, when one considers the importance of governments in the handling of (to take only a single example) the crisis created by famine. In the past century India has twice been grieviously afflicted by the specter of famine. Each time it has been dispelled by government action. First, by the opening decade of this century, the British imperial government had alleviated conditions through its development of railways, canal colonies, and famine code. More recently, following the protracted failure to notice that population growth had greatly outstripped food production, India's independent government acted under a remarkable minister, Subramaniam, who after 1964 masterminded the Green Revolution there. In Africa, it is no accident that the worst famines in the 1980s have been in those countries wracked by civil war—Ethiopia, Sudan, Chad, and Mozambique. India (and Kenya) by contrast, have managed to survive major droughts in the 1980s. Just two decades ago, India was expected to starve; Africa seemed less vulnerable. The turnaround in both places stems principally from different governmental histories, which in turn reflect differences in politics. It is high time that these were brought into account.

THE HISTORY OF EACH GLOBAL REGION

Many matters deserve discussion, but three issues stand out. The first is how important the large-scale historical dynamics of each global region are. Accumulating evidence shows that they are essential to understanding Third World polities. Thus, the development of the newly industrialized countries (NICs) of East Asia, the Southwest "Pacific way" (with its countless democratic changes of government in the past quarter century, until the recent Fiji coup), the trauma of the Islamic world following on the successive breakup of the Mughal, Safavid, and Ottoman empires, and the Central American story are all significantly different.

So, also, is that of "monsoonal Asia." It seems to have been driven since the beginning of the twentieth century by a dual concern to rid itself of Western imperial control and to create some kind of better social order. The first, particularly salient through the first decades of the century, issued in those *anni mirabiles,* the four short years from 1946 to 1949. In 1946, the Philippines secured political independence; in 1947, India and Pakistan followed; in 1948, it was Burma and Ceylon; in 1949, the Indonesian Republic finally won recognition from the Dutch, and on 1 October of that year Mao announced the People's Republic of China. Since then, these countries have passed through three rectifications, if they may be so termed.

The first, which I call the renovations, occurred within a few years of the great events of the 1940s. For there was soon discernible unease, exemplified in contradictory ways, in many of these countries because of the shortcomings and inadequacies of what had then been achieved. Magsaysay's land reforms from 1953 to 1957 in the Philippines—the only near serious ones to date—coming in the aftermath of the Huk rebellion, were a characteristic early example. Bandaranaike's electoral victory in 1956, on behalf of the Sinhalese and Buddhist majority against the elite who had negotiated Ceylon's independence in 1948, was clearly another one. Two years later, rather different renovations were attempted in Pakistan and Burma when the military finally brushed aside the quarreling politicians. In similar fashion, Sukarno and the army in Indonesia moved in 1958 toward his so-called Guided Democracy—a renovation indeed. By then, Mao had not only embarked on full-scale collectivization in China but had, following the Hundred Flowers campaign, launched his Great Leap Forward. While nothing quite so dramatic occurred in India, one can see certain of the same impulses at work in Nehru's push at Avadi in 1955 and at Nagpur in 1959 for a more "socialistic pattern of society," and in his attempted seventeenth amendment to the constitution in 1964, which would have established land ceilings.

By this time, however, what had simply been unease was turning, particularly in the more radical quarters, into open anxiety. Second starts were now sought. The earliest example was Ne Win's second coup in Burma in 1962 and his commitment to "the Burmese way to socialism." Had the Communists capped their third resurgence in Indonesia in 1965 (after their earlier disasters in 1926–1927 and 1948), there could well have been a Communist second start there; but following the fiasco of the thirtieth of September movement, Suharto instituted a second start of a very different kind. Capturing the rhetoric of the day, he proclaimed "a new order" for Indonesia. By then, China was embroiled in the most potent of all the second starts, Mao's Great Proletarian Cultural Revolution. Even this, however, did not stand on its own. Not only was there a rash of Maoist revolts elsewhere—by the Naxalites in India, by the Muhkti Bahini in Bangladesh, and to everyone's surprise in 1971 by the "JVP" in Sri Lanka—but also Bangladesh's liberation in 1971 and a return to civilian rule in Pakistan under Bhutto. In India, the national congress split in 1969 and Mrs. Gandhi's *Garibi hatao* (Abolish poverty) campaign in 1971 constituted a similar attempt there. Finally, the ever wily Marcos skillfully captured the spirit of the day when, on assuming dictatorial powers in the Philippines in 1972, he proclaimed "a new society."

Yet, before very long a third set of rectifications followed, though this time of a very different order. For over half a century, the most energetic leaders of these countries had constantly played on the necessity for a great new thrust toward a better future. There was a good deal of support for what they had originally promised. Still, once a country had passed through one great bouleversement, attempted a renovation, and then made a deliberate second start, the old thesis—that revolution will bring about a new order—began to pall. In due course, there ensued what we may call the conservative outcome, which in the late 1970s and through the 1980s spread widely in monsoonal Asia. (This may of course prove to be nothing more than a conservative interlude.)

Perhaps the first signs came with Mrs. Gandhi's "emergency" in 1975–1977, which seemed to spell the end of the apotheosis of second starts, Narayan's vapid campaign in India for "total revolution." The major events, however, occurred in China, where following first Chou En-lai's and then Mao's death in 1976 and the fall of the Gang of Four, Deng Xiao-ping was restored for the second time and China adopted the Four Modernizations. These developments were paralleled, however, by the persistence (against all odds) of

Suharto in Indonesia, Marcos in the Philippines, and Ne Win in Burma. They coincided too with successive military takeovers in Bangladesh, the return of the military under Zia in Pakistan in 1977, and the moves toward a Gaullist regime in Sri Lanka. The upshot has been the pragmatic, growth-oriented regimes that now extend across all of East and South and Southeast Asia.

The dynamics and propellants of tropical Africa's development have been very different. The largest has been perhaps the least noticed. A century ago one could count 1,000 (or was it 10,000?) autonomous political units. These are now reduced to a mere 50 or so nation-states—not a process of fragmentation so much as an astonishing and often painful process of aggregation. After independence, tropical Africa's three largest countries—Sudan, Zaire, and Nigeria—all suffered from traumatic civil war. While nineteenth-century Africa saw widespread and endemic though intensely localized violence, which persisted after the European advent into the twentieth century, European colonial rule then curbed open violence even if it did not obliterate its local causes. In many ways these quarrels intensified after independence. Africa's tropical agricultural products came to have a world market; they tended to dominate territorial market economies. Yet, in the three decades before 1960, the impact of the 1930s slump, the wartime shortages and controls, and the postwar inflation and accompanying colonial exploitation created many tensions. A short-lived euphoria during the Korean War boom quickly evaporated, and widespread downturn generated great frustration. Throughout these decades Africa was plagued with local strikes, riots, and holdups, all coming at a time of rapid development of African nationalism. In Africa more than in Asia, nationalism was a disaggregated force. It proved far more difficult for European imperialists to withstand, and for nationalist elites to command. (Nkrumah tried to do so with his brilliant slogan "Seek ye first the political kingdom, and all the rest will be added unto you," but in the end it backfired.)

At the time of independence, then, Africa's new prime ministers and presidents faced the enormous problem of fashioning single nations out of arbitrary miscellanies of peoples. Africa was a continent where traditions of violence were still very close to the surface. Popular appetites, first whetted and then frustrated by the new economic opportunities, became, in the absence of established elites, increasingly volatile. Not only was there a breathless struggle to enter and command newly created institutions, but in the absence of well-established tax regimes (for example, in land), control of the country's agricultural export returns, often channelled down a single railway line and through a single port, was not simply a significant source of wealth but a battleground.

The new states of the southwest Pacific suffered from these disabilities too, yet aside from the aberration of the Fiji coup, they did not lead to the coups and bloodshed so common in Africa.[3] It is just not the case that all impoverished new states have traveled the African road. How, then, is one to explain the African phenomenon?

From the beginning, when independence came, there was fear that many of its new states would fragment. Separatist movements abounded. But Biafra's defeat by 1969 put an end to this affair, and aside from the special case of Bangladesh, no subsequent movement anywhere has succeeded. Since many Third World countries have potential breakaways, they have effectively joined up internationally to ensure that no fateful precedent is set. While, however, this major danger has persisted, the concern about it was very real.

At the same time, in contrast with the southwest Pacific states, several major nationalist figures in Africa won electoral majorities immediately before independence. This achievement fueled their hubris; it made them treat subsequent opposition as sedition and dispelled any tendency toward compromise. With much stray Marxism around, one-party authoritarianism was soon generated (principally by African Francophone leaders following their experience of the collapse of the French Fourth Republic and the return of de Gaulle)[4] and was then compounded by military interventions. These were prompted from two different quarters. It is important to recall that in the late 1950s the anti-imperialist Middle East provided an enticing model for tropical Africa. Its anti-aristocratic, anti-imperialist military coups (for example, in Egypt in 1952 and Iraq in 1958) gave coup attempts elsewhere a certain legitimacy. Significantly, tropical Africa's first coup occurred in the Sudan in 1958. Soon after, Congolese "other ranks," marginalized in the Belgians' precipitate transfer of power in mid-1960, mutinied against their Belgian officers. Africa's sergeants as well as its colonels were thereby given their go-ahead. The countless coups from the 1960s to the early

1980s then ensued. Whether their rate is now slowing down is a matter that deserves to be watched.

These different sequences were far more salient to postwar changes in Asia and Africa than anything more directly related to development. The nexus, however, was important. Subramaniam's thrust, like that of the Berkeley mafia, was part of India's and Indonesia's second starts. The economic collapse of so many African states has at bottom had a political cause. The truth is that the development process in all these countries has had to fit in as best it could with these much larger changes over which it has had only limited control—as some development practitioners have still to appreciate.

STATE STRUCTURES IN DEVELOPING COUNTRIES

A second basic issue in the development story has to do with the nature of state structures and how they operate in developing countries. Certain governments have considerable authority and legitimacy; others do not. India, for instance, has a far more effective government than any African state; it enjoys more traditional authority and has a far longer habit of bureaucratic rule (Mughal in origin and not only British); and its ruling party has long possessed much charismatic authority.

At the same time, we should note that the world's two most populous countries—China and India—have been held together by powerfully led countrywide parties. That situation, however, is very unusual. Generally, elsewhere the political health of new states turns on how they manage to accommodate the powerful subnational communities that operate within them, some religious, some racial, many ethnic. There are various ways in which this has been done.

The core stability of some states has derived from their ability to mobilize their natural majorities: in Indonesia the Javanese, in Pakistan the Punjabis, in Sri Lanka the Sinhalese, in Burma the Burmese, in Malaysia the *bumiputras,* in Sudan the northerners, in Zimbabwe the Shona. The trouble is that while this system works well for the majority, it dangerously exposes the minority, as the Irianese, the Sindhis, Sri Lanka's Tamils, the Karens, Malaysia's Chinese, and the southern Sudanese know all too well. It is to Mugabe's and Nkomo's immense credit that they have lately taken this point in Zimbabwe.

Natural majorities, however, are not always at hand. Sometimes they have to be composed. Senghor composed his Wolof majority in Senegal; Banda centered his southern majority on his own Chewa; Kaunda managed constantly to reconstitute his majority in Zambia; Museveni may now have brought together the first successful majority in Uganda; Ratu Mara was able to form a coalition between his Fijians and Fiji's Indian Muslims and Gujaratis till some of his own Fijians ran out on him.

Where there is no natural majority and a composed one is difficult to create, all is not lost. A cohesive group can seize control of the center. The Punjabis did this in pre-Bangladesh Pakistan. In Africa the Sara clans have held just such a position in Chad, as Houphouet-Boigny's landed-commercial-administrative elite has in the Ivory Coast. Sekou Touré employed his own Manlinké in a similar position in Guinea; by all accounts, Mobutu's position in Zaire rests on core groups from his own Equateur province. Perhaps the most notable example were the Kikuyu in Kenya under Kenyatta. President Moi has clearly sought to widen his base there into a composed majority, with an alternative core in his own Kalenjin peoples.

Alternatively, as Mohammed showed at Medina long ago, political leaders can secure authority by holding the interstitial position between rival groups. Gowon held such a position in Nigeria; Ahidjo, a Christian as well as a northerner, had like advantages in Cameroon. Nyerere's provenance in a small community in Tanzania was crucially important to his holding the interstitial position between such large communities as the Chagga, the Nyakyusa, and others. Given the order he shaped, it is hardly surprising that his successor should be another interstitial figure—Mwinyi—from offshore Zanzibar.

When all these cohesive forces are lacking, a regime can still be successful if the government includes representatives from all parts of the country and the head of government is no more than first among equals. This system operated under Prime Ministers Somare and Chan in Papua New Guinea and Wingti, their successor. The most interesting example in Africa followed Siad Barre's coup in Somalia in 1969.

Fifty-fifty regimes are conceivable also—there is Belgium with its Flemings and Walloons, Lebanon once upon a time with its Christians and Muslims, and Fiji in the past with native Fijians having political power and Indians enjoying economic primacy. This system was also tried in Uganda in 1963–1965 and again in 1985. Surprisingly, such arrangements sometimes persist; but as each of these examples shows, the prognosis is never good. It is when none of these expedients operates that certain rulers descend to the last resort—terror. That is precisely what happened in Uganda under Amin and Obote. The moral here is that if development is to proceed, it is of first importance to understand the crucial underpinnings of a country's governmental structure.

DOMINANT PEASANTS

A third issue to note is the consequence of the steady destruction of large landlordism, or its nonexistence. Egypt provides a paradigm case. Before 1952, 5 percent of the population owned 35 percent of the land. The 1952 revolution abolished the pashas; an egalitarian land reform was announced. Yet, by the end of the 1950s, rich peasants held 60 percent of the cultivable land; 30 percent of the rural population remained landless. During the 1960s, the Arab Socialist Union sought to undermine the rich-peasant control of village affairs by establishing "leadership groups" for poorer peasants. By the late 1960s, however, because of a new compromise between the urban and rural elites with the established regime, little had happened. The nature of the new regime was dramatized in the person of President Sadat, scion of a rich peasant family.[5]

India provides the classic example. Dominant peasants of still powerful castes have existed there for many centuries. Indian village studies have endlessly described village dominance by dominant castes, even where their composition has changed or earlier dominant castes have moved away. From these studies, it is easy to ascribe class differences between those who live at the apex of village societies and those who exist at the bottom. Yet, several points require emphasis. The dominance, particularly within a nucleated village, of those with preponderant amounts of land is real; among other things, it gives them the time to conduct their own affairs while looking after the village's external relations. Class distinctions among those in a middle position, however, are more difficult to discern. Such people characteristically emulate those at the top and gravitate toward them. The poorest, as a consequence, are frequently in the minority; the village often stands foursquare against them.

Dominant castes, rich peasants, dominant peasants—call them what you will—were carefully succored by the British through the final century of their rule in India. From World War I, however, these groups increasingly joined up with the Congress party, which they had come to dominate by the time of independence. Many advocated *zamindari,* landlord abolition. Yet, as Charan Singh, the program's principal architect, put it, the purpose was not to create an egalitarian society but "by strengthening the principles of private property . . . at the base of the social pyramid" to create "a huge class of strong opponents of the class war ideology."[6] In the 1960s Gunnar Myrdal wrote that "perhaps the most conspicuous result of postwar policies in India . . . has been the strengthening of the upper strata in the villages . . . on which the present governments depend for critical support."[7] A large library of other studies contains nothing to refute this conclusion.

It is important to note that essentially the same thing happened in Africa, in Ghana, Nigeria, Uganda, Kenya, and Tanzania. Ugandan studies tell how leaders of work parties constitute the village's dominant peasant elites; how, over a midday banana beer, they make their crucial corporate decisions. Kenya's political history in the 1960s revolved largely around the conflict between the rich-peasant commitments of Kenyatta's Kenya African National Union and the more populist ideology reflected in the short-lived Kenya Peoples Union. Kenyatta's power base lay in the rich-peasant coffee cooperatives of his own Kikuyu, to whom he sometimes had to make major concessions.

Nyerere in Tanzania made a much-proclaimed attempt to erase peasant differentiation. The classic statement of the case—against that of Charan Singh, as it were—is to be found in Nyerere's *Socialism and Rural Development* of 1967 (published a few months after the better-known Arusha Declaration). His attempt, however, came to nothing—because of rich-peasant opposition, the absence of trained party cadres, and his own refusal to play the role of Stalin. Nyerere used force to produce "villagization," but as anyone who knows India can show, rich peasants welcome nuclearization—it makes control of their neighbors easier. What rich peasants will not abide is collectivization; they successfully forced Nyerere to abandon the idea.

The literature on the southwest Pacific (on Papua New Guinea, for instance) is likewise replete with accounts of how "big men" dominate rural society, and there are many parallels elsewhere, both in left-wing and right-wing regimes.

Early in this century, in Russia, Prime Minister Stolypin urged the tsarist regime "to place the wager not on the needy and the drunken but on the sturdy and the strong." This was code for giving the more energetic peasants their head, who could then be "called on to play a part in reconstructing our tsardom on strong monarchical foundations."[8] No one understood the threat better than Lenin, who in 1908 wrote:

> It would be empty and stupid phrasemongering to say the success of the Stolypin agrarian policy is impossible. It is possible! . . . If it succeeds, then the agrarian structure of Russia will become completely bourgeois . . . [and] conscientious Marxists must . . . abandon any kind of agrarian program.[9]

Twenty years later, Stalin mounted his massive forced collectivization program against Russia's *kulaks*. The resulting conflict, he later told Churchill, was worse than the Battle of Stalingrad. "I thought you would have found it bad," Churchill replied, making a highly perceptive comment, "because you were not dealing with a few score thousands of aristocrats or big landlords, but with millions of small men."[10]

The shah of Iran attempted to pursue a Stolypin-like program. After 1949, he began to distribute land from his own estates. Eventually, in the early 1960s, his government pressed ahead with the so-called White Revolution "to break the political and social influence of the landowning class . . . and bring about the emergence of an independent peasantry," by which, however, he meant only occupying peasants and "oxen owners" (i.e., rich peasants).[11] In 1963, a congress of 5,000 such proprietors swore to shed their last drop of blood in his cause. Yet he mishandled them appallingly—pressing many into state-run farm corporations, tightly controlling their rural cooperatives, handing out privileges to foreign-owned agribusinesses. When the ayatollah's revolution erupted, peasant hands were nowhere raised in the shah's defense.

Right-wing regimes have been much more adept in Southeast Asia, where village differentiation also prevails. The Suharto regime (like

the Dutch before it) allots a great deal of local power and corresponding economic privileges to village officials. They, not the army, are the
"Golkar legmen" (the ruling party's canvassers). So long as taxes are
paid, food is produced for the cities, and no radicalism appears, the
officials are left fully in control of their own bailiwicks. In Malaysia,
the corresponding connections operate through the governing
UMNO party, from dominant peasants at the village level to the
prime minister at the national level. Thailand's variant seems to be
not quite so formalized, but by all accounts the "big fish in the small
ponds" are encouraged to benefit in many ways from opportunities
the state superstructure offers, which few of their poorer countrymen
can emulate. Skillfully worked-out Stolypin policies are extraordinarily potent.

But what about left-wing regimes? Did they emulate Stalin, using
massive force? In 1975, the Marxist revolutionaries in Ethiopia,
having disposed of Haile Selassie (who had half-toyed with Stolypin
concepts), introduced a radical land reform under which everyone
was to have ten hectares of arable land. Producer cooperatives were
to be created. This task, handed over to some 28,500 peasant
associations, saw 60 percent of the land go to 24 percent of the
landholders. By 1979, however, the revolutionary government itself
was saying that "the leadership positions of peasant associations at
the present time are occupied by rich and middle peasants."[12] Do we
hear an echo here of rightist Indonesia?

Not surprisingly, the really interesting person in all this was Mao.
From the 1930s, he understood that rich-peasant dominance was a
singularly difficult nut to crack. Appreciating how serious a
dominant-peasant backlash would be, he proceeded with the utmost
caution. When, in the early 1950s, he finally inched toward collectivization, he shunned altogether the use of Stalinist force. Instead,
with consummate skill, he moved to marginalize the rich peasants,
making available through government and party hands the local
services that they had previously provided their fellow villagers, and
set out to build up new cadres of middle and poorer peasants who
would directly challenge the rich peasants' local dominance.[13] By the
mid-1950s, with his full collectivization program, he seemed to have
achieved an even greater success than he had anticipated. But the final
result of all this effort was that one dominant category—rich peasants—was superseded by another—new rural cadres. These were not

the committed socialists they were meant to be. So, in the early 1960s, the "socialist education movement" was launched, particularly in the rural areas, and in 1964 Liu Shaoqi carried out the largest purge of rural cadres that China has ever seen. Thereafter, while Mao was characteristically careful at first not to launch the Cultural Revolution against them, when it spread to the countryside, rural power holders often successfully resisted it. In the Deng years these groups have come into their own again.

The Communist story in Vietnam is very similar. Initially, in the 1950s, there was great fear lest there be a rich-peasant backlash. Thereafter, extensive transfers of land from individuals to rural cooperatives were made, and in the mid-1960s, Maoist notions of class struggle came to the fore. However, by the time of the Vietnamese Communist party's sixth plenum in 1979, they had been effectively replaced by commitments to "the dispersed economy of individual family households," a euphemism that now hardly needs translation.

The fact is that while the world—as the Philippines' elite will one day discover as well—knows how to destroy the predominant power of those who live in the big house at the end of the driveway, it has not discovered how to destroy the preeminence of those who live in the bigger houses within the village itself. Governments of all colors with overwhelmingly rural populations must come to terms with this basic fact if they are to enjoy a secure rural base. So must development specialists. Discerning how to assist the weakest in these circumstances is a major task. Since the issue has baffled the twentieth century's three major Communist figures—Lenin, Stalin, and Mao—it is not surprising that it baffles us as well.

ENDNOTES

[1]D. Anthony Low, "Empire and Social Engineering," chap. 2 in *Lion Rampant, Essays in the Study of British Imperialism* (London: Frank Cass, 1973).

[2]J. S. Furnivall, *Colonial Policy and Practice* (Cambridge: Cambridge University Press, 1944).

[3]Greg Fry, "Succession of Government in the Post-Colonial States of the South Pacific: New Support for Constitutionalism?" *Politics* 18 (1) (May 1983):48–60.

[4]Aristide R. Zolberg, *Creating Political Order, The Party States of West Africa* (Chicago: Rand McNally, 1966).

[5]Mahmoud Abdel-Fadil, *Development Income Distribution and Social Change in Rural Egypt (1952–1970)* (Cambridge: Cambridge University Press, 1975).

[6]Charan Singh, *Agrarian Revolution in Uttar Pradesh* (Delhi, 1958), 41.

[7]Gunnar Myrdal, *Asian Drama, An Inquiry into the Poverty of Nations,* vol. 2 (London: Allen Lane, 1968), 1367.

[8]G. T. Robinson, *Rural Russia under the Old Regime* (Berkeley: University of California Press, 1960), 56.

[9]Adam B. Ulam, *Lenin and the Bolsheviks* (London: Collins, 1969).

[10]Winston S. Churchill, *The Second World War: The Hinge of Fate* (London: Cassell, 1951), 447.

[11]A. K. S. Lambton, *The Persian Land Reform, 1962–66* (Oxford: Clarendon Press, 1969).

[12]Fred Halliday and Maxine Molyneux, *The Ethiopian Revolution* (London: Verso, 1981).

[13]Vivienne Shue, *Peasant China in Transition, The Dynamics of Development towards Socialism, 1949–1956* (Berkeley: University of California Press, 1980).

Comments on Anthony Low's Essay

PETER D. BELL: A major difference between Latin America and many of the African and some of the Asian countries that Mr. Low has been talking about is that the Latin American countries have been independent for more than a century and a half. I had some sense of frustration in reading the essay. In my days, I have done more than my share of bashing economists, but I assume that we have come here today to praise development economists. Even if we had not, I think that Mr. Low's characterization of at least some economists, including many development economists in the Latin American context, is unfair.

In saying this, I do not mean to whitewash economists. Certain international economists arriving fresh from the victories of the Marshall Plan tried indiscriminately to apply approaches to development in Latin America that had been successful in postwar European recovery. Also, some foreign-trained Latin American economists have tried to capitalize on the security apparatus of authoritarian regimes to pursue a sanitized version of development, practicing a brand of technocratic economics and wearing blinders to political and historical realities.

Still, Latin America has also had a rich tradition of economists and other social thinkers who have approached development as much in historical and political terms as in narrowly economic terms. That has been true of the "structuralists," whose theories have been built on the relationship between power structures and economics. It was also true of the "dependency theorists," who blamed Latin American underdevelopment on international asymmetries of power. Among foreign development economists, none is more properly acclaimed within Latin America than Albert Hirschman, precisely because of his capacity to look freshly at development issues within specific local situations while seeking local definitions for rationality.

Part of the problem with more complex and nuanced views of development is that they are often better at description than at prescription. Latin American postwar history has been characterized by one oversimplified model after another that seemed successful for awhile, then failed, and had to be corrected. Lately, there has been a kind of lurching, unbalanced, but forward movement in favor of more pragmatic and eclectic thinking about development in the region.

The drive toward development seems to me to have become so much a part of contemporary Latin American history as to be almost inseparable from it. There are exceptions, of course, as with the indigenous groups in the hinterlands of the Andean countries or in Brazil. Fundamentally, however, Latin Americans think of development as nation building and as increasing individual and collective choices, all underpinned by growth in per capita income.

In my view, it is not terribly rewarding to look at the "context" for development in Latin America. Much more important, I think, is the examination of the interaction of political, social, and economic institutions and processes. It does not much advance our understanding of development simply to describe the various social institutions and historical phenomena that exist. We must ask how these advance or impede—result from or contribute to—development.

Finally, on a somewhat related point, the fact that development has been the *leitmotif* of Latin American history in the postwar period is part of what makes the debt crisis so demoralizing and so dangerous in the region today. Prior to 1982, Latin America had experienced almost three decades of unparalleled economic growth. Development was the driving force behind every political regime, liberal or authoritarian. Now, for the first time, Latin Americans are beginning to think the unthinkable: the prospect of no growth for the foreseeable future. And beyond the reality of the immediate physical deterioration and human suffering, that thought is profoundly disorienting.

MICHAEL ROEMER: I think that if you take Mr. Low's complaint about economists and put the adjective *neoclassical* in front of the word *economist,* his complaint is probably justified. There has been an avoidance of politics. And yet, even there, as we look at questions of economic reform over the last ten years and ponder how it has and has not worked, even the most neoclassical and economic-minded have in fact begun to look at politics much more. We are obliged to; there is no way to avoid it.

Returning to Professor McNeill's comment about conservation, I would like to talk about the conservation of power, the competition between political power and economic development or growth. My observations come from my recent time in Kenya, where for two years I was deeply involved in policy advising. My experience may apply also to the socialist countries, now trying to liberalize, and the Philippines as well. On the one hand, we all know that stable government is a sine qua non for development; stable government is a prerequisite. On the other hand, the resources that some governments use to achieve stability may compete with economic development. There is some kind of a balance, an equilibrium, a trade-off, where you cannot develop without giving up certain things. It may be necessary to give up some of the possible potential of development in order to maintain political stability. The attempt to build coalitions in Kenya has, in my view, come at the expense of economic development. President Moi, in having to build constituencies in each of his forty districts, has probably spent money unwisely from the point of view of the development economist. He may be heading for a major economic crisis, no doubt exacerbated by rapid population growth. Still, had he not done this, it is hard to know how things would have come out, whether there would have been any possibility at all for economic development. Kenya's neighbors, particularly Uganda and Ethiopia, tell much about how political instability vitiates all possibility of economic development.

CHARLES WILLIAM MAYNES: I want to comment on what I understand is Anthony Low's suggestion that democratic forms of government might have survived in Africa had the Fourth Republic not fallen or had there not been political coups with very powerful symbolism, as in Egypt. It seems to me that the tradition the West handed over to the Africans was basically undemocratic, indeed authoritarian. Many of the African liberation leaders simply moved into the colonial governor's house and took over the country. Many of the institutions in Africa that we now find so economically retrograde were colonial institutions in the first instance, taken over and run along traditional colonial patterns, albeit not very well. But perhaps they never ran very well even under colonial rule; cost accounting at that time may have been more casual.

When you look at the role of economists in developing countries in terms of support for democratic forms of government, you ought to look also at another group that played a significant role, the political scientists. My memory of the late 1950s is that there was a growing body of literature that argued that democratic forms of government would be difficult to institute and that more authoritarian forms of government might be more successful in launching the development process. The whole debate of India versus China was very important at that time. It was argued that China was more efficient and that democracy itself was a barrier to development. So it does not seem to me that the tradition the West passed on was quite as benign as the suggestion that but for the fall of the Fourth Republic we would have had some sort of democratic model that the developing world might have followed.

Francis X. Sutton

Development Ideology: Its Emergence and Decline

FOR MORE THAN A GENERATION, we have heard the word *development* in the discourse of political leaders, bureaucrats, publicists, social scientists, philosophers, and ordinary citizens. They have used it as a label for nations, programs, international organizations, and bodies of doctrine but also as an expression of hope and aspiration. It has shaped the purposes and efforts of states, and of great public as well as modest private organizations. Development, in short, has been a major ideology of our times.

Like many other ideologies, development has been elaborated to rationalize policies and aspirations and to cope with competing doctrines. Serving diverse needs, both inspiring and frustrating those who have used the term, it has displayed vagueness, imprecision, utopian exaggeration, and the many contradictions that useful ideologies commonly show. Because it has been the focus of high aspiration and much organized effort, effective action in the name of development has mattered enormously. The theory and practice of development have become large and complex technical subjects; whole armies of professionals have devoted their careers to its study and implementation. The intellectual history of development is already a large subject; so, also, is the literature on development economics, modernization theory, and related specializations. In its international review of development policy and practice, the Brandt Commission estimated that 6,000 international meetings every year in New York and Geneva generated about a million pages of documentation annually.[1] This is one measure of the universe that could

33

be sampled in any serious scholarly look at development ideology. But the aim of this paper is not so much to retrace the intellectual history of development as to try to perceive how experience, political needs, and international rivalry brought into existence the idea of development in the years immediately following World War II.

The idea was hardly a novelty in the 1940s. In some ways the heir of the idea of progress—or perhaps more accurately, the rebirth of the idea after a period of weakened faith—development carried vestiges of many earlier theories. Reading again J. B. Bury's classic work, *The Idea of Progress,* one is reminded how much the idea of development, prepared and anticipated by the ideologists of progress, provided concepts suited to the needs of modern peoples, ambitious for improvement.[2] Divine Providence, inaccessible to human control, was replaced after Descartes by the idea of progress. In the eighteenth century, the enthusiasm of Helvetius made human nature seem infinitely malleable by education and the "science of legislation." As d'Holbach argued, there were no insurmountable barriers between the "advanced" and the "stationary" races of the earth. History (like cultural differences for some latter-day developers) did not matter. Indeed, d'Alembert imagined that history might be destroyed. Condorcet foresaw the "retrograde races" catching up with the advanced in a uniform civilization that would spread equality of the sexes throughout the world. This catching-up and leveling would be achieved through the application of science, through enlightened activity of governments. French theorists, then as now, were more hopeful about the latter than the English ever were.

The nineteenth century, less impressed with the potential of "universal reason," was more disposed to look for progress within national histories or cultures. This "developmental" theory became very important as new emphasis was given to what science and scholarship might bring. The impressive achievements of science and technology in the nineteenth century popularized the idea of progress, converting it into the dogma that Bury found it to be when he published his *Idea of Progress* in 1920. Bury thought progress might one day be replaced by another dogma, just as it had once displaced the idea of Providence. That prophecy has so far not been fulfilled.

The idea of progress grew in times when nations and societies were increasingly trying to control their destinies by organized rational effort. Governments in most places from the nineteenth century on became engaged in the sorts of activities we now call development. But it was not until the years after World War II that a coherent and widely accepted ideology of development appeared.

In those years the idea of progress was refurbished in an optimistic development theory that enjoyed remarkable success in both developed and underdeveloped countries, providing a common point of view to nations and governments starting from very different positions. The theory expressed itself in programs in which both developing and developed nations were expected to cooperate. At a distance of thirty or forty years, that theory now appears much battered by criticism. New generations may well wonder how it ever won the broad assent that it did. In this article, I seek to explain how and why this happened. To do so, it is important to start with a description of the ideology itself.

THE POSTWAR IDEOLOGY

The elements of the classical orthodox theory of development seem to me to have included the following ideas:

• Peoples everywhere in the world have basically equal capacities and rights—particularly, and most importantly, a right to political self-determination. Inequalities within and between nations are not to be accepted as natural. They were not ordained by Providence. They need to be viewed as challenges or problems to be removed or mitigated.

• All share responsibility for taking measures that will serve to surmount such imperfection and inequality. Long-suffering patience, resignation, and fatalism have been much esteemed in other times. They have no place in development ideology, which is resolutely activistic and optimistic about the results of effort.

• Development needs to be pursued with the use of modern, empirical knowledge; it is achievable through rationally organized effort.

• Command over the requisite knowledge for development is open to all peoples through education and training. The universal right to education, enshrined in the United Nations' Universal Declaration of Human Rights in 1948, was more than an individual right; it was an indispensable condition of development, a part of the moral responsibility to develop.

- Governments, faithfully representing their peoples' interests and aspirations, have central and primary roles in development.

- In the world's present state of inequality, the responsibilities of sovereign nations differ; nations that are underdeveloped have the responsibility to develop. They are not free to make use of their freedom and self-determination in any way they please. Their governments are not to confine themselves to being guardians of law, order, and national defense. They must see themselves as organizers and agents of development. The developed countries and their governments also have responsibilities; it is impermissible for them to treat developing countries as foreign entities, to be exploited or ignored as national interest may dictate. Their concern must be to help these countries develop successfully.

- Aid from developed countries needs to be politically and culturally neutral. It ought not to infringe on the sovereignty and cultural identity of developing countries.

- International relations must be consistent with national sovereignty under the principles of the United Nations Charter and conducive to development through the creation of appropriate conditions for trade and capital movement.

- Developing nations should strive to be democratic. They must respect the Universal Declaration of Human Rights of the United Nations and must apply it to all their citizens. While developing nations must be free to choose their own political systems, the developed nations may resist the spread of Communism and the adoption of Communism by developing countries.

This assemblage of ideas came from various sources in response to divergent interests and motivations. That it became an orthodoxy outside the Communist countries evidently depended on its generality and vagueness, which made public allegiance to it possible despite the sharpness of underlying differences. The right of self-determination, for example, had no rigid prescriptions, and nations could in good conscience resist movements that they regarded as illegitimately separatist and at other times support the rise of ministates. Nevertheless, this ideology has clear, distinctive characteristics:

- Development is fundamentally collective and therefore political. In the first instance it is about peoples, not individuals; its links with nationalism and the independence of former colonial dependencies stand out, and it is frankly statist in ways that have subsequently been challenged and criticized.

- Economic development is not as prominent in the ideology's tenets as it came to be in practice. Humanitarian concerns are implied in the mutual obligations of states, and the improved welfare of citizens in the developing countries is an obvious criterion of development. But in its fundamentals, development was primarily evident in concern for people as collectivities.

Much more than collective affairs underlay the social changes after World War II, and indeed the objectives of development, but strong emphases on individual welfare did not emerge till later. The United States, the ex-colonial powers, and the rest of the developed countries had to establish policies and practices vis-à-vis the developing countries. The developing countries were absorbed in the political process of nation building and of finding their place in an international setting they viewed warily.

ROOTS IN DEVELOPING COUNTRIES

Development is only one among many ideas that have taken shape amid the profound social changes that have affected people throughout the world in this century. Anthropologists remind us that new meanings and doctrines often envelop such changes. In a paper entitled "Religion, Development and African Christian Identity," Terence Ranger, for instance, argues that over much of Africa rural development was linked with the African Christian movement. He describes the intense efforts in healing, education, and economic development that the independent and mission churches made in southern Rhodesia and then in Zimbabwe from the beginning of the century on. The arrival of Europeans with their markets, roads, and ideas brought new opportunities and new questions. Was the influenza epidemic of 1919 a curse from the ancestral spirits or from the Christian converts? Was the book the missionaries and their African catechists taught from a key to a better life, here and now? The social change going on in this part of southern Africa in the early decades of this century had many forms and sources and did sometimes find organization around Christian churches:

> American Methodism providing in its combination of strong discipline, intense emotional experience, and "the gospel of the plough," an ideal mix for entreprenuerial pioneers; Anglicanism providing an explicit ideology of village communalism; and Catholicism offering both a sacralisation of place which brought back labour migrants from all over southern Africa on pilgrimages home and also a paternal discipline over resident female cultivators.[3]

Some of the hazards of change appeared with the collapse of the colonial economy in the depression. Then religious leaders arose to denounce mission education and call for withdrawal from the development process. Both the old colonial government and the new government of independent Zimbabwe went through much disquiet over the character and proper Africanness of these churches.

The momentous changes that the diffusion and intrusion of Western influences brought to the East and the South generated a mass of such ideological reactions, many religious in character, many broadly cultural, most political.

Western dominance was advanced by force and superior technology but sustained by the prestige and deference that followed from power. The treatment of non-Western peoples as inferiors was resisted and resented but also accepted as being in the natural order of things. The British control of 400 million Indians with perhaps 165,000 British residents in India (in the 1920s) could not depend on any widespread coercion. The feasibility of governing empires without making administrative and military costs prohibitive depended on the West's belief in its own superiority and imperial subjects' acceptance of such pretension. The rise of nationalism in Asia and Africa was a political expression of a growing refusal to accept inferior status.

In their ideologies the emerging nations had to respond to several motivations:

- The need to escape from subordination and humiliation. Nations claimed the fundamental equality of all humankind, analyzed backwardness as a result of historical conditions that were subject to change, or asserted some distinctive qualities that might prove superior to those of their Western competitors.

- The need to define the means of building a viable, defensible nation, whether maintaining independence or winning it from a colonial power.

- The need to respond to the internal social and cultural tensions provoked by the challenge of modern Western values and example, whether in assaulting the legitimacy of traditional authority and morality or in reconciling new standards with them.

The response to these needs was to accept, evade, or reject modern Western culture. Modern nationalism in Asia and Africa came with the emergence of sizable populations of people with Western education and the disposition to value Western knowledge, institutions, and accomplishments. Along with nationalism came the arousal of large groups that had previously been apolitical or apathetic and that gave new power to conservative indigenous symbols and attachments. As the great mobilizer of the Indian people, Gandhi brought a leadership fundamentally hostile to Western civilization and the ideas that became the development ideology. India, as elsewhere, had contending factions of Westernizers and "nativists," from the early followers of Gokhale and Tilak down to independence and beyond. At one time progressive Westernization seemed inevitable, but the ascendance of Khomeini's regime in Iran and the growth of religious fundamentalism worldwide has since shaken this conviction. (The *khilafat* movement in the years after World War I now appears as more than an incidental source of mobilization for the Muslims.)

Ambivalence toward Western civilization has of course been nearly universal in nationalist movements. Nations have had to reconcile their desire to acquire the powers of the West with their desire to maintain their identity. The struggles of Chinese leaders and intellectuals in this reconciliation brought formulations that anticipated the principle of the development ideology, in which purely technical knowledge can be introduced without violation of cultural identity. Dennis Duncanson in his writing on Vietnam has used the label "Tagorism" for the view Rabindranath Tagore inspired among Chinese intellectuals that the laws of history would ensure the ultimate triumph of the moral values and spiritual civilization of the East over the materialism of the overmechanized West.[4] Some such rationalization of the compatibility of acquiring Western knowledge with a dignified national or non-Western identity has been necessary everywhere, from Tagorism in Asia to negritude in Africa and perhaps Arielism in Latin America. The Marxist competitors to the development ideology have had to harmonize their espousal of modern scientific knowledge with the objective of saving cultural dignity.

The compelling necessity to defend themselves against Western military and economic power has been a prime motivation of modernization. Some of the earliest clear expressions of development aspirations came as what Walt Rostow has called reactive nationalism. In his recent book *Economic Development: The History of an Idea,* H. W. Arndt adopts Rostow's idea and writes that in Meiji Japan and after,

> National power was the dominant, but not the only, motive. Closely allied with it was an intense desire to stand on an equal psychological footing with the advanced nations of the West. The material and cultural achievements of Western countries made a profound impression on Japanese who travelled abroad. Just as the first great modernizer, Peter the Great, while wanting above all guns to fight wars, had also sought for Russia something of the civilized amenities and quality of life he experienced in his travels; so Japanese leaders were determined to bring "civilization" and "enlightenment" to Japan.[5]

Building the strength to cope with the West without losing its own cultural soul was more difficult for China. The struggles of Chinese intellectuals and political leaders to reconcile the adoption of Western ideas and techniques with the preservation of Chinese culture have been long and painful. Arndt claims that before World War I the Nationalist Sun Yat Sen pleaded for the economic development of China according to a plan that "more than anything else written before 1939, anticipated post-1945 thinking" and that his book *The International Development of China* (1922) "was almost certainly the first to advocate economic development in something like the modern sense and use of the term."[6] It became official Nationalist doctrine, however, that Western religion, institutions, social science theories, and almost every aspect of Western civilization was inapplicable to China; Chiang Kai-shek indeed published a study, *Chinese Economic Theory*, in which he argued that Western economic theory was applicable to Western economies but not to China.[7] The winning of the Chinese intelligentsia to Marxism in the 1930s was the triumph of an international ideology that had no place for the Nationalist emphasis on the uniqueness of China.

The great divide in ideological responses to the intrusion and dominance of the West has not been between indigenous and Western ideas but between branches of Western ideology. The classical development ideology has stood in a kind of dialectical relationship to Marxist-Leninist ideology and is hardly to be understood apart from this relationship. The attractions of Marxist-Leninist ideology in the non-Western countries have been evident. It combines hostility to the cultures of the capitalistic West with a turning toward the progressive ways that are needed to build a modern society. Mao wanted a "national, scientific, and popular culture" that could be "anti-imperialist" and "antifeudal," as Marxism-Leninism was.[8] In his autobiography *Toward Freedom*, Nehru says he was attracted to Marxism because its outlook is "scientific" and because Marxist analysis alone appeared to explain the Great Depression and point toward a solution for it. He had a discriminating but admiring eye for the Soviet Union, a country that "looked into the future and thought only of what was to be, while other countries lay under the dead hand of the past and spent their energy in preserving the useless relics of a bygone age."[9]

The historian of ideas Benjamin Schwartz has made particularly acute analyses of the way Marxism evolved, indeed "disintegrated," under its uses in the Soviet Union and Communist China.[10] Marxism had, Schwartz argues, the great appeal of combining faith in progress through cumulative and irreversible advances in technology and organization with the pathos of social drama in class struggle and revolution. Lenin and Mao used the pathos in building nationalist movements and organization but had to stand Marx on his head to claim that a socialist state was the way to technical and economic progress. Under Lenin and Stalin, socialism became not the product of industrialization but the way of creating it in backward nations and hence of strengthening them in inevitable struggles against imperialism. Under Mao, Chinese Communism moved still further away from anchoring possibilities of development in any historical stage; after at first accepting Soviet planning and organization for development, Mao then turned, in the Great Leap Forward and thereafter, to visions of transformation by the will of an unselfish and united people. The activism of the development ideology and its optimism about controlling humanity's future had formidable competitors in these Marxist ideologies.

The motivation to secure national independence through military and economic strength has led to the familiar socialistic dispositions in many developing countries. The relationship between industrialization and military capacity is responsible for another familiar disposition. In both respects, the model of the Soviet Union had evident attractions. Economic nationalism is little disposed to trust in internal and external market relations. Preoccupation with power and control makes submission to presumably impersonal market forces uncongenial and implausible. An unwillingness to view the international economy as dependent on general laws and conditions and thus as independent of the control of powerful national or private participants has been widespread. Lenin's doctrine of imperialism provides a vision of international relations congenial to these opinions and in its application has led to goals of isolation and autarchy. Lenin made international trade a state monopoly, and Stalin in his *Economic Problem of Socialism in the USSR* looked forward to a day when the Communist camp would have no need of imports from capitalist countries. Mao's China sought a similar autarchy and long provided an appealing model to non-Communist states yearning for "self reliance" in the greatest practicable measure.

Building nationalist movements has depended on mobilizing previously apolitical populations or in sustaining unity and morale in insurrectionary guerilla movements. As nationalist leaders became the ministers of independent governments, their ideas influenced the conception of development. China specialists talk of "the Yenan syndrome" in Mao's thought; it has had many parallels elsewhere. The enthusiasm of many national leaders for mass mobilization to attack development needs, whether in literacy campaigns, community development, or crop harvesting, was no doubt based on nostalgia for campaigns that had brought political freedom as much as or more than faith in the efficacy of such mobilizations. Such emphases on disciplined mass efforts have been no monopoly of Communist societies. On wider fronts, the attractiveness of solidarities has also contributed to the notion of a socialist camp or bloc and the division into First, Second, and Third Worlds.

In the 1940s and 1950s, orthodox views of development elaborated as responses to the concerns to protect national autonomy:

> The great hope, and the only hope, according to some, was for newly independent governments to plan change. They had to think big and operate in a big way. Planned investment in new physical capital was the main method, but mobilizing savings by increased taxation was a necessary complement and so was foreign aid. As much new investment as possible must flow into industry, which, in view of export pessimism, would be mainly import substituting. This investment, since it would be centrally planned to take account of interindustrial relations and trade inelasticities, would be more productive than market-directed investment. . . . Few doubted that the primary aim of LDC governments was to improve the standard of living of the mass of the people.[11]

This is an economist's formulation, and it neglects the social and political aspects of early development ideology. Japan, for instance, sought military security and an equal psychological footing with the West by building the institutions and competences of advanced nations, whether or not such efforts were optimal for economic development. Later and elsewhere, rulers of developing countries have shown similar desires for national airlines, steel mills, and great universities, which have more obviously served national prestige than the general welfare. Improved welfare had to be a measure of national achievement, but it was clearly not primary. As Edwin O. Reischauer said of Japan, the ruling group "was interested in developing a powerful nation rather than a prosperous people."[12]

On the other hand, the engagement of whole national populations was essential to valid development. The conception of a "free world" and the passionate concern to preserve democracy that characterized the 1940s and 1950s in this country were not purely defensive or political. We had faith that freedom and democracy would unleash energies that would promote development. The enthusiasm Nehru's community development program generated in Chester Bowles, Douglas Ensminger, and others was above all for its potential to build a modern, unified nation. Nehru's successive devotions to community development, the system of popular representation called *pan-chayati raj,* and universal education were ways to maintain popular mobilization in development, whatever their contributions to economic well-being. Nehru was of course a figure who brought together ideas from East and West in uncommon sophistication, and his leadership contributed greatly to the exceptional importance India won in the 1950s as a model developing country.

DEVELOPMENT IDEAS FROM THE WEST

Since development became a sort of common orthodoxy under the influence of the Western countries, the United States in particular, the historical events these countries experienced were bound to shape this ideology.

The Second World War was one crucible in which movements and forces long stirring were brought to flaring activity. The dominance of the West had been shaken by the new nationalism and the impetus that the First World War, Woodrow Wilson, and the League of Nations had given to self-determination. The legitimacy of colonial power was eroding in the West before the Second World War. The nature of that war as opposition to the imperialism of Nazi Germany and Japan and to racist ideology put "imperialism at bay," as William Roger Louis entitled a book on this period.[13] Sympathy in Europe and America for the new nations arose from the preoccupation with the distribution of wealth and income and with suffering during the Great Depression. The sense of unity inspired by common effort in a world war further stimulated concern for all the people at home, and thus particularly for the poor and disadvantaged; sympathy for the lowly and disadvantaged elsewhere was a natural by-product.

The readiness of the colonial powers to concede that in some distant future dependent peoples would justifiably exercise their right to self-determination was rudely prodded by American disapproval. The Atlantic Charter had espoused self-determination in 1941, Churchill with the victims of Nazi rule in mind, and Roosevelt the colonial peoples. Roosevelt's notorious anticolonialism was not idiosyncratic but widespread in American public opinion. *Life* magazine warned "the People of England" in October, 1942, that the American people were not fighting "to hold the British Empire together," and the State Department wanted to replace imperialism with "international trusteeship."[14] The British responded with alarm and sent their most persuasive spokesman for development under colonial rule, Lord Hailey, to temper American hostility through Washington talks and the pages of *Foreign Affairs*. In the aftermath of the war, the refusal of the Americans to back British trusteeship claims for Cyrenaica, the American antipathy to French colonialism in Southeast Asia, and pressures on the Dutch to terminate the colonial war in Indonesia (including the alarming suspension of Marshall Plan aid intended for the Dutch East Indies) brought concrete expression of the American disposition to see the end of empires.

The American vision of a peaceful postwar world rested on faith in the rule of international law and institutions, topped by the United Nations. The relations of states, new and old, were to be governed by general rules, not by special relationships or a gradual loosening of colonialism in a system of patron-client ties. The idealistic simplification of international relations in this vision included no anticipation of the profound changes the multiplication of new states would bring—certainly little appreciation that antipathies to the old colonial powers would spill over into a visceral anti-Americanism. The United States saw the main hazard to an equitable and peaceable international order quite differently—in the challenge of Communism. As the initial hope of embracing the Soviet Union in a new universal international order turned to alarm over Communist expansion and the "loss" of China, anti-Communism became a dominant force in American foreign policy. It tempered the anticolonial disposition with fears that a rapid dissolution of colonial control would bring chaos and opportunity for Communist seizure of power. Truman's Point IV as a way to ease misery and frustration in other parts of the world quickly followed the Marshall Plan in Europe. We sought alternatives to Communism through the building of stable new nations in freedom and democracy.

In its Charter the United Nations committed members to "employ international machinery for the promotion of the economic and social advancement of all peoples." While the commitment was general, its implication was that the stronger and richer were somehow committed to assist the weaker and poorer with whom they had formed a common organization. As international organizations came forth in the wake of the war, nations joined them with clearly different expectations and concerns. The negotiations for the ill-fated International Trade Organization showed these expectations perhaps most strikingly. The United States sought a universal ITO with common obligations for all, thus no special treatment for developing countries. Such a charter was quite unacceptable to the developing countries that went to the 1948 Havana conference. The U.S. drafts there faced a blizzard of amendments, aimed mostly at special and preferential treatment for countries that regarded themselves as weak and developing. The U.S. Congress did not ratify the ITO but gave the supposedly temporary General Agreement on Tariffs and Trade lasting life by conceding special treatment for developing countries because it was anxious to make GATT as nearly universal as possible.

The United States was willing to assume responsibility for the welfare of other peoples and nations in a variety of organizations that addressed relief and reconstruction needs after World War II. UN-RRA (the United Nations Relief and Rehabilitation Administration) and IRO (the International Refugee Organization) responded to urgent, immediate human distress. Charitable responses had long traditions and were readily aroused as long as they could be conceived as temporary. The initial steps toward indefinitely continued development obligations were restrained and tentative. The original conception of the International Bank for Reconstruction and Development was faithful to the order of purposes in its title. It was, as its historians have described it, a conservative institution, "an Anglo Saxon creation, with the United States very much the senior partner."[15] It was not conceived as a massive source of capital funds for developing countries, and during the first ten or twelve years of its existence, did not act as such.[16] Originally, the United States conceived of aid to developing countries as technical assistance, though by 1950, in the Gray Report on Foreign Economic Policies, the United States was arguing that it should undertake capital assistance as well. U.S. foreign aid grew to large proportions in the 1950s. During that decade it was overwhelmingly the largest source of development assistance, and in 1960 it was still the source of 64 percent of all grant aid and 58 percent of official flows of long-term financial resources.[17]

This movement in the United States to assume the obligations of a developed country in the pattern that became development orthodoxy was paralleled and anticipated by actions of the colonial powers. The old British pattern whereby colonies were supposed to pay for themselves had eroded under the rising conception of trusteeship and American pressure. The Colonial Development and Welfare Acts of 1940 and 1945 expanded resources, and the colonial services augmented technical assistance. In the years after 1945 the colonial powers had to make an effort to develop their dependencies and did not cut this effort off (except for notorious cases like Guinea) when independence came. It is rather curious that former colonial powers were more generous toward their ex-dependencies after their independence than before when they were "owned." Until 1960, most of the development assistance from sources other than the United States came from four European colonial powers. It was only then, as postwar prosperity grew, that they extended their development assistance responsibilities to all the non-Communist developing countries under the surveillance of the Development Assistance Committee of the Organization for Economic Cooperation and Development (OECD).

While the financial resources of the United Nations remained small in its first decade and a half and the developed countries resisted efforts to enlarge them through the embattled Special United Nations Fund for Economic Development (SUNFED), the United Nations early became an important advocate of development assistance. It produced the Expanded Program of Technical Assistance in the wake of Point IV, and its famous 1951 report, *Measures for the Economic Development of Underdeveloped Countries,* posed the challenge of increasing capital assistance from $1.5 billion to $10 billion per annum.

The United Nations and its regional and specialized agencies gave developing countries the opportunity to speak for themselves. Jagdish Bhagwati recalls the inspiration Raul Prebisch then brought to economists from the developing countries:

> To see that one's own can be innovative, ingenious and important is always, and was then especially, a matter of considerable psychological significance. For, among the colonial attitudes which afflicted our societies in those days was the belief that fundamental thinking required that one belong to the center, not the periphery, in Raul Prebisch's splendid terminology.[18]

But the shaping of development doctrines still depended critically on prevailing ideas in the Western world and in particular on the revived interest in economic growth.

That there should have been so little professional and ideological attention to economic growth from the late nineteenth century to the period after World War II now seems remarkable. The desire for economic growth came from many influences after the interwar preoccupation with stability, security, and distribution. Professional influences came through Keynesian economics, the rise of national income figures, and the comparisons they made possible. In *The Rise and Fall of Economic Growth*, H. W. Arndt is persuasive in making political concerns about full employment and poverty relief powerful stimulants.[19] By the 1950s, economic growth had become a central preoccupation in the Western countries, and development was identified with economic growth. It has often been remarked that Arthur Lewis's 1955 classic on development was called *The Theory of Economic Growth*.

Sympathies for deliberate national planning aimed at economic growth were very uneven in the Western countries, France and Britain being much more positive than Erhard's Germany or than the United States, which was bitterly divided over the Full Employment Act of 1946. But for the developing countries, national economic planning met little resistance. Planning was a natural complement to assistance programs and suited the disposition of developing nations' governments to take their countries' future in hand. The prestige of Soviet planning and the socialistic orientation of many developing countries further strengthened the idea of national planning.

THE FLOWERING AND FADING OF THE OLD ORTHODOXY

The circumstances that encouraged widespread allegiance to development as national economic growth persisted into the 1960s. The explosion of African independence at the beginning of the decade and the Latin American aspirations embraced in the Alliance for Progress kept the building and transformation of nations at the center of attention. Africa went through hot debate on readiness and the conditions of viability for new nation-states. The moral force of self-determination as a right overrode resistance, and challenges in education and institution building necessitated strong international assistance. The symbolic importance of Africans running their own governments made their effective functioning a prime objective of development. The attention given education and manpower planning and the theories of human capital formation that emerged at this time surely resulted in part from African independence. The Western countries tempered their concern that these new African countries emerge as democracies with an indulgent sympathy for the difficulties they faced, a reluctance to be patronizingly critical, and faith in the importance of economic growth. In the 1960s the Latin American countries emphasized modernizing old societies under the leadership of new, competent governments guided by national plans and benefited by international assistance.

The old doctrines of development flowered in the early 1960s and fell away with remarkable speed as the decade came to an end. Development orthodoxy, acceptable to both the First and the Third World, had always to be maintained despite the existence of underlying opposition. Leaders of developing countries had views very different from the tenets of the development ideology. Their voices grew stronger in the United Nations, the Nonaligned Movement, and regional organizations, and spokespersons in their own countries became increasingly articulate. They conveyed:

- A basic mistrust of developed countries and a conviction that international conditions affecting development were deliberately shaped to the less developed countries' disadvantage. The idea that terms of trade decline for the primary products of developing countries had long been a pillar of these views, but they came to be given a much more malevolent tone, as in the recent charge of the president of Senegal that "the present deterioration of the terms of trade in favour of the developed world is more than a swindle; it is tantamount to organized economic murder of our countries."[20]

- A related disposition to conceive international relations in terms of power and status and a corresponding reluctance to believe they are ruled by impersonal market forces, rules, or laws. We have noted the mistrust of dependence on the international economy that has stimulated the ambition for self-reliance or autarchy, in Marxist but other forms as well. The model of an insulated economy achieving development while protected from external dangers was an attraction of the classic development economics but hardly able to still fears of "the octopus stranglehold of international capitalism." The impulse to rationalize such fears in an ideology that made the international order not neutral or benevolent but hostile and confining had long been present. It gained expression in the early 1960s with the appearance of UNCTAD and went on through Latin American *dependencia* theories to the 1970s' demand for a new international economic order that is still with us.

• An interest in collective or national concerns that was stronger than the developed countries found congenial. The older development ideology had the merit of blurring choices between national development and individual welfare and rights. Rising income per head was taken as the prime measure of development but without critical assessment of distribution or the conditions under which it was achieved.

Changes in the developed and developing countries and in their relationships may have helped erode the old development orthodoxy. Concern about the state of their own countries arose in the citizenries of the West in the 1960s. The paroxysms of 1968 in Europe and America followed on increasing awareness of domestic imperfection and injustice; faith in the competence and benevolence of governments and the institutions of society such as universities declined. This period in the West had a cultural revolution, too, less official and violent than the Great Cultural Revolution in China but powerfully antinomian and anti-authoritarian. Governments questioned at home were thought to be particularly presumptuous and erring abroad. Mark Rudd, the tribune of Columbia's 1968 campus revolt, returning to celebrate the twentieth anniversary of this movement, denounced Columbia for "still doing defense research [and] still putting out personnel for foreign interventionist policies."[21]

Hostility to the U.S. intervention in Vietnam eroded faith in the competence and benevolence of Western governments participating in development. Moreover, the initial indulgence toward new governments stiffened into criticism of their competence and stability, of their abuse of human rights. The development ideology had depended on governments as the prime agents of development; questioning that faith took away the means of rationally controlling development. And doubting the character of developed countries deprived them of status as exemplars of what development might achieve. Writing as the European intellectual that he was, Pope Paul VI affirmed in the 1967 encyclical *Populorum progressio* that world-wide development was the necessary concern of the Church but warned of the temptations that come from wealthy nations. And this year, in *Sollicitudo rei socialis* John Paul II found "superdevelopment" equally "inadmissible" with underdevelopment.[22]

The tenet of development doctrine that developing countries can absorb modern techniques and scientific knowledge without betraying their cultural integrity was always an optimistic simplification of a profoundly complex and troubling process. The etiquette and courtesy of technical assistance were never without their failures, and as the self-confidence of the Western countries withered in the 1960s, they became less disposed to make assertive efforts. Development theory rested on propositions supposedly applicable anywhere, regardless of cultural differences. But these propositions had come mostly from the West and, as we have noted in the struggles of Chinese nationalism, were vulnerable to cultural resistances, to which the West grew more sensitive. By the early 1970s, when a conference at Ghent planned the European Association of Development Research and Training Institutes, the veteran development economist Dudley Seers reported views that it was "time that European Institutes phased out of the development business."[23] And this year in his encyclical, Pope John Paul II, in remarkable self-denial for the leader of an exclusive and proselytizing religion, declared, "Not even the need for development can be used as an excuse for imposing on others one's own way of life or religious belief."[24]

Such restraints and hesitancies have no doubt encouraged Third World leaders and intellectuals to make assaults on development and modernization. One of the shah of Iran's former ministers has called flatly for an end to development,[25] and an African analyst finds the cause of Africa's famine in "the rape of the peasantry, the rape of the environment, all in the name of development."[26] The principle that Third World countries should decide for themselves what kind of development to have has acquired a latitude that admits very radical questioning of Western science and technique. One United Nations author finds even the second law of thermodynamics to be "ethno-centric" and that "colonial science":

> has allowed the third world elites to legitimate a manner of handling the world that reduces to apparent worthlessness intellectual traditions of systematic inquiry everywhere except in the West, whether these concerned moral or physical worlds, and ridicules all life-styles unin-fected by Western science as infantile or uncivilized.[27]

Such views have gained support from the West's doubt about the general applicability of social science and its tendency toward cultural relativism.

The imperfect results from national planning and the classical development economics have had great professional attention as undermining forces in critiques of the "crises of planning," import substitution policies, and the priority given industrialization rather than agriculture. But the emergence of a variety of new development theories clearly had many sources other than the weakness of older doctrines. In retrospect, the old orthodoxy seems a fragile thing and its disintegration into the contending doctrines of the 1970s and 1980s hardly surprising.

THE FORMS OF DEVELOPMENT IDEOLOGY

In conclusion, some observations on the forms and uses of develop-ment theory can be ventured. In their magisterial history of the World Bank, for example, Edward Mason and Robert Asher observe that what the bank was distinctively equipped to do determined its conceptions of development:

> The Bank was set up to help complete specific productive projects rather than to make general purpose loans, to finance only the foreign exchange costs of those projects, to secure a guarantee of repayment from the government of the country in which the project was to be located, and to finance only activities for which other financing was believed to be unavailable. These requirements, along with the practical necessity of concerning itself only with projects large enough to justify review and appraisal by a global agency with headquarters in Wash-ington, D. C., practically assured a heavy concentration by the Bank on power plants, railroad lines, highway networks, and similar physical facilities.

The Bank became the leading proponent of the view that investment in transportation and communication facilities, port developments, power projects, and other public utilities was a precondition for the development of the rest of the economy.[28]

One can extend the Mason and Asher thesis to other organizations engaged in development programs. Conceptions of development in institutions devoted to its practice are shaped by that practice. The foundations engaged in education and research, for example, have extolled the building of human capacities and institutions as central to development.

General analysis of development has of course been attempted by social scientists but has had uneven and limited impacts on ideology and practice. The *International Encyclopedia of the Social Sciences,* published in 1968 in the heyday of interest in the subject, had no general article on development. It did list "Developing Countries" and refer the reader to "Economic Growth," "Industrialization," "Modernization," "Nationalism," "Power Transitions," "Stagnation," and "Technical Assistance." It had an article on development banks, but development planning was subsumed under "Planning, Economic." Still, despite the absence of a comprehensive theory, this encyclopedia did give quite abundant attention to development topics, reflecting the widespread interest of social scientists at the time.

The economists had a central position in a subject strongly identified with planning and economic growth, and technical assistance gave economists extensive opportunities to engage in planning and other development programs. Confidence in the possibilities of planning and controlling national development also encouraged the use of development theory by specialists in public and business management, education, and rural development. The policy of depending on university contracts in the U.S. foreign aid program further stimulated American social scientists' interest in developing countries. The concentration on area studies at the universities brought into existence large new cadres of specialists on particular countries and regions, and a great part of their work, as subsequent revisionists complain, was guided by the paradigm of development and modernization.

The rational and positivistic presumptions of development doctrine also made the training and deployment of social scientists a part of development practice. Modern governments were thought to need the competence of staffs trained in the social sciences and the guidance of social science research.

An enormous outpouring of professional and scholarly effort has come from this worldwide proliferation of social science and from Western scholars' turning away from their earlier focus on domestic and Western matters. Its significance may be seen at two levels, one technical and instrumental, the other broad and ideological. Policy-makers have used the social sciences to give a rational and empirical basis to development projects and programs. Arraying themselves with other technocrats on the side of rationality and modernity, many social scientists have seen development planning as a struggle against the irrational influences of politics and tradition. The demands of planning and managing development programs—and of the routine management of Third World economies—have indeed been formidable and the needs for applied social science and the contributions of economists and others in the refinement of development theory correspondingly great.

But development consists of more than technical problems. As I have argued, it embraces aspirations and visions of the future. Social scientists are hardly ever pure in their scientific detachment; they have had pressing invitations to contribute to the ideology of development and they have responded willingly. Such participation is often deplored, but it certainly need not be. The formation of enlightened public opinion in both developed and developing countries requires wide-ranging public discussion in which the voices of competent professionals would be muted if confined to facts and technical questions. Development as economic growth gave a powerful simplification of a complex social process and provided an agenda for action that could be pursued in the name of rationality. The edifice of economics as the theory of rational action could be put to use with good conscience.

Modernization has been a much more diffuse conception. Sociologists in the traditions of Weber and Parsons had a general idea of modern society that was arguably part of a neutral taxonomy of societies. But a world passionately engaged in questions of modernization and its relations to Westernization could hardly be perceived as neutral. During the years classical development ideology held sway, a vigorous growth of related concepts led to the writing of many textbooks on such subjects as comparative politics and political sociology. They have undoubtedly contributed to the common view that there is a theory beyond economics to be found in development and modernization. But the influence seems more in style, idiom, and methodology than in agreed conception, and social scientists of various persuasions have been prominent in the disintegration of the old doctrine. The reemergence of Marxist theories is only one aspect of the new diversification. Just as Western education gave voice to new nationalisms, the worldwide diffusion of social science may give voice to new forms of development ideology. Among them, a common idiom may yet arise.

ENDNOTES

[1]*North-South: A Program for Survival,* report of the Independent Commission on International Development Issues under the chairmanship of Willy Brandt (Cambridge: MIT Press, 1980), 268.

[2]J. B. Bury, *The Idea of Progress* (New York: Dover, 1987), 218.

[3]Terence Ranger, "Religion, Development and African Christian Identity," in Kirsten Holst Petersen, ed., *Religion, Development and African Identity* (Uppsala: Scandinavian Institute of African Studies, 1987), 29–58.

[4]Dennis Duncanson, *Government and Revolution in Vietnam* (New York and London: Oxford University Press for Royal Institute of International Affairs, 1968), 19–20.

[5]H. W. Arndt, *Economic Development: The History of an Idea* (Chicago: University of Chicago Press, 1987), 14.

[6]Ibid., 16.

[7]Robert F. Dernberger, "The Role of Nationalism in the Rise and Development of Communist China," in *Economic Nationalism in Old and New States,* ed. Harry G. Johnson (Chicago: University of Chicago Press, 1967), 54.

[8]From his New Democracy program as excerpted in Hans Kohn, *Nationalism: Its Meaning and History* (New York: Van Nostrand Reinhold, 1965), 182.

[9]Excerpted in Kohn, 177–78.

[10]See his essay "China and the West in the 'Thought of Mao Tse-Tung' " in *China's Heritage and the Communist Political System,* bk. 1, ed. Ping-ti Ho and Tang Tsou (Chicago: University of Chicago, 1968), 365–96.

[11]Ian M. D. Little, *Economic Development* (New York: Basic Books, 1982), 118–19.

[12]Cited in Arndt, 15.

[13]William Roger Louis, *Imperialism at Bay: The United States and the Decolonization of the British Empire, 1941–1945* (Oxford: Oxford University Press, 1976).

[14]This account draws on William Roger Louis and Ronald Robinson, "The U.S. and the End of British Empire in Tropical Africa" in *The Transfer of Power in Africa: Decolonization 1940–1960,* ed. Louis and Prosser Gifford (New Haven: Yale University Press, 1982), 27–55.

[15]Edward J. Mason and Robert E. Asher, *The World Since Bretton Woods* (Washington, D.C.: The Brookings Institution, 1973), 28.

[16]Ibid., 462.

[17]*Twenty-Five Years of Development Co-Operation, a Review* (Paris: OECD, 1985), 40–41.

[18]Jagdish Bhagwati in *Pioneers in Development,* ed. Gerald M. Meier and Dudley Seers (Oxford: World Bank, 1984), 197.

[19]H. W. Arndt, *The Rise and Fall of Economic Growth, A Study in Contemporary Thought* (Chicago: University of Chicago, 1978).

[20]Abdou Diouf, *U.N. Development Forum* 14 (9) (November-December 1986):10.

[21]*New York Times,* 22 April 1988, B4.

[22]An English text of *Populorum progressio* may be found in *The Gospel of Peace and Justice,* ed. Joseph Gremillion (Maryknoll, New York: Orbis, 1976), 387–416. *Sollicitudo rei socialis* is separately published in English as *On Social Concern* (Boston: Daughters of St. Paul, 1988).

[23]*Toward a European Association of Development Research and Training Institutes* (Ghent: European Association of Development Research and Training, 1974), 54.

[24]John Paul II, *Sollicitudo rei socialis,* 58.

[25]Majid Rahnema, "Under the Banner of Development," *Development: Seeds of Change* 112 (1986):37–46.

[26]Fantu Cheru, "Debt and Famine in Africa: The Year of Living Dangerously," in *Africa and the World* 1 (1) (October 1987):2.

[27]Claude Alvares, "Science, Imperialism and Colonialism," *UNU Work in Progress* 10 (3) (October 1987):11.

[28]Mason and Asher, 152.

Comments on Frank Sutton's Essay

TOM G. KESSINGER: Frank's paper has great sweep; it is particularly challenging to someone like myself, a social anthropologist by training and a South and Southeast Asian expert by experience. The question I would ask is why, when we think about development ideology or theory, despite its many early forms and tensions, it generally ends up being concerned primarily with economics, technology, or technology transfer. Also, why at this point in time, when we worry about its effectiveness and putative decline, do we choose to interpret the matter in these terms, ignoring the much broader range of questions that might be discussed, having to do with democracy, though even that may be a too narrow way to think about the problem. In my view, the more interesting way to think about it may be in terms of mobilization, participation, and issues of equity, not so much between nations as within nations.

While there is a good deal of concern with political questions at the ideological level and of big-power rivalry, of national politics as it relates to the legitimacy of governments and their particular political leaders, there is too little interest in mobilization and participation. Indeed, both are referred to rather pejoratively as indices of nostalgia on the part of a national leadership anxious to recreate the ethos of the original nationalist movement. When it comes to participation, it is viewed in statistical terms, in measurements of income distribution in various societies.

Similarly, culture and history do not receive sufficient mention, though Frank once again has mentioned them, suggesting the ways they have been thought about. I wish that we could be provoked into thinking about Uganda in this particular context. Development thinkers, to the extent that they have dealt with culture and history, have generally seen them as impediments, blocks on the road that positivist development interventionists seek to travel. They need to be seen as systems of meaning, factors that are actively and dynamically part of the process of change. Again, when it comes to technology, history, and culture, absent in much of the current discussion is any serious musing on what we have thought about the organizational setting in which technology is applied and played out in various developing countries.

Although Frank Sutton mentions the importance of nationalism and nation building as dynamic forces stimulating development over the last forty years, we have to reflect on why this proliferation of nations, still continuing, inhibits certain kinds of candid discussion. For someone who has spent time working in Southeast Asia, with Indonesia on the one hand and Brunei on the other, each occupying the same space, at least in the United Nations, and perhaps also in the OPEC oil cartel, it is a fact that they do not occupy the same space in any number of other respects. This is something that is too rarely thought about.

JAMES P. GRANT: I would go a step beyond your essay, Frank, and argue that something very important happened earlier in this century, captured by

Toynbee when he said that ours is the first generation in human history to have the capacity to bring civilization and progress to all mankind. If you go back a century, there was no expectation of such a possibility. Technology perhaps as much as anything has made such a dream seem reasonable.

With the advent of Marxism, specifically with the developments in the Soviet Union in the 1920s and 1930s, we witnessed a great additional push in a very short period of time toward universal health and education. I would argue that in many ways this was the first really organized approach to development. Then there was, as Frank has suggested, World War II, which mobilized whole populations. If it had not been for World War II, colonialism would probably not have ended before the end of the century.

Then came the Cold War; it became worthwhile for leaders to invoke a new moralism. New nation-states came into being when the imperial powers gave up power, in large part because of the moral pressures on them. Because of the Cold War, the West had to respond with a doctrine of development, to compete in some sense with the doctrine of development that initially came out of Marxist thought.

As democracy spread, this itself compelled developmental responses. Because more people vote, because more seek benefits, there is a push toward development. It is no accident that in the United States, for example, the highest infant mortality rate is in Washington, D.C., the place with a high per capita income but also with the least democratic processes in the United States. There is an obvious interface between the pressures of democracy and the pressures behind development.

GEORGE ZEIDENSTEIN: On the question of how development was presented to the electorates of the countries that were asked to appropriate money for it, I think that there is an interesting current change now going on that merits attention. In the Scandinavian countries, the Netherlands, and Canada, for example, the electorates support development assistance because they care about the well-being of individuals in the Third World. That is the way the situation is presented to them. Contrast that with the situation in the United States today. Collective improvement is no longer sufficiently compelling; protection against the Communist scourge is old hat; today we are being urged to support overseas development because it is economically advantageous for America; the Third World countries are important trading partners. In the United States today, overseas development is recommended from an almost strictly economic, self-interest point of view.

Panel Discussion

HOLLIS B. CHENERY: It may be useful to start our discussion by offering some examples of the relations among economic theory, development theory, and development policy. While it is possible to argue that economic theory does not have much to do with policies in many fields, that argument does not hold in the development field. I think the notions of what to do about development, how to classify it as an objective of national policy, if indeed you wish to pursue it, come from your perceptions of what development theory is, how it applies to developing countries, and why it is different for different countries.

Starting off, acknowledging that theory may modify existing economic tools, you have the Keynesian-type theory, which is demand oriented and inevitably leads to certain thoughts about development. Taking the neoclassical system, which assumes full employment and is therefore not Keynesian, you are necessarily led to look at problems on the supply side, to consider what we may expect to see in full employment. Sir Arthur Lewis correctly, I think, suggests that with developing countries today neither the Keynesian nor the neoclassical model is adequate.

The first synthesis of the 1950s, as described by Frank Sutton, certainly had its implications. If oversimplified in its diagnosis, it had many policy effects, not least in relations between the aid-giving countries and those who were recipients. Focused very much on capital as a source of growth, it assumed that growth was the universal interest. The question was how to achieve it. Many diagnoses were offered; higher savings rates were recommended, and we see this directly in the charter of the World Bank. Why is the World Bank commissioned to lend money? The answer, quite simply, is to increase investment and savings. How does it guarantee that countries use its funds properly? It looks at the creation of capital and capital stock— physical types of capital. When development theory went on from that perception, it was very hard for the World Bank to operate consistently. New perceptions of how development came about, with new emphases on human capital and international trade—which could hardly be described as development projects—required the bank, faithful to its charter, to talk about them as if they were projects, for that was supposed to be their business.

As Frank Sutton suggests, the profession did not long stay with the simplistic 1950s view of what caused growth. Most development economists can be identified as activists. Whatever else they believe in, they believe in doing something positive. Simon Kuznets argued that to understand the main phenomena of development, which comprise "modern economic growth," you must start off with the industrial countries, go on to the developing countries, organize all sorts of empirical perceptions, then theorize, and finally come to policy. If you are not certain of the facts, why theorize? How can you recommend policies when you are unsure of your diagnosis? This has proved to be a very durable research program.

What Kuznets, in retrospect, provided was a whole set of hypotheses that turned out to be fruitful. His work on income distribution, on the relation between growth and poverty—what is now called the Kuznets curve—is what many people spend their time defending or attacking. It remains a leading hypothesis; like all of Kuznets's hypotheses, there is a considerable element of truth in it. When you look at the conclusions he has derived from eight or ten countries, you can only conclude that his intuition was fantastic.

For those anxious to relate theory to formal approaches to policy, I think the closest thing to a theoretical framework was provided by another Harvard professor, Wassily Leontief. To this day, my guess is that his is the most widely used development model; the Indian five-year plan, now in its seventh version, is indebted to him. Each year, or every five years, an increasingly more sophisticated model is developed. This is of course the extreme case. Again, the model is being used for purposes that the author did not specifically intend. While Leontief was not a planner himself, most of the world's planners have used Leontief's system.

I would say that planning in the sense that we use the term—targets for the Indian steel industry, for example—has not been terribly successful either in the socialist countries or in most developing countries. But using planning models to understand what happens if you go through the typical sequence, starting off with the rural part—agriculture—then looking at the manufacturing sector, and so on, allows you to capture the main elements of the system. In its most modern version, you have computable general-equilibrium modeling, which is made possible by modern computers. As a tool of instruction, this can be very useful. If you believe in the neoclassical version of economics, you are able to insert all the neoclassical assumptions.

All the underlying development problems, to which these tools were applied in the 1950s through the early 1970s, saw development as a long-term process. If development policies were to focus on even longer consequences, on the relations among population growth, education, employment, and the like, the problems become even more complex. In 1973 the oil crisis, which wiped out the inflow of capital, more than offset the flow of capital from the developed countries, practically forcing all countries to put their long-term plans on the back burner and to focus instead on short-term problems emphasizing structural adjustment. What passes for development theorizing today has to do with how to redirect an economy so that it is again able to grow on a steady basis. That leaves out almost all the countries that Edmar Bacha knows about, starting with his own, Brazil. They are all concerned with debt problems. And the lending agencies, too, all are concerned with short-term adjustments. They have risked even more than their charters in order to help the World Bank work on structural adjustment.

JAMES P. GRANT: I'd like to be brief. As one who started out working on the Cold War front in the Far East in the late 1940s and 1950s, where the line between economic systems and development was blurred and where defense support seemed important, we saw in Taiwan and South Korea, not primarily for developmental reasons but for political reasons, land reform, promotion of universal education, and a whole series of programs oriented toward the poor majority that only subsequently did we learn also served to reinforce the development process. In Korea and Taiwan, there was a deep concern with full employment. When people became involved and productive, healthy and educated, and fully employed, it turned out not to be a welfare policy at all, but it was conceived in that way in the beginning. There is much to be learned from this.

So, also, in the 1960s and 1970s, when support for development cooperation assistance began to falter, we all may remember the demonstrations against World Bank president Robert McNamara in Copenhagen and in Cambridge. There were demonstrations by church groups in Washington, D.C. against the World Bank. Many held the view that the growth supported by the World Bank was just making the problems of the poor worse in countries like Brazil and Mexico. There was a desperate need for the aid community to build a new alliance structure; out of it came the basic human needs approach. Through the years, the concepts have changed in response to the requirements of political and geopolitical necessities.

We are now, in my view, in an era when feelings are growing stronger, so that the morality of the world must catch up with its capacity to bring about real change. This affects changing attitudes toward war. We see it also in the way we react to great disasters. At the time of the Ethiopian crisis, there was little enthusiasm in government circles in Washington for a large response. It took precisely two weeks after the dramatic TV footage from Ethiopia in October 1984 for public opinion to bring about a dramatic reversal of policies, not only in Washington but also in Moscow and Addis Ababa, an instance, in my view, of the power of world morality.

I would argue that the restructuring required to deal with the U.S. external debt situation requires the restoration of major economic growth in the South. In retrospect, I think we now see that the Marshall Plan in the late 1940s and the moves made to help Japan were vital to giving the United States the decades of prosperity it enjoyed in the 1950s and 1960s. Today, a new and comparable recycling of resources from the North toward, and adjustment in, the South is called for, and the resulting restoration of growth and increase in imports by the South would greatly facilitate the restructuring of Japanese and German surpluses and U.S. deficits.

SUSAN P. JOEKES: I would draw your attention to another aspect of the development story, concerning women. On the political front, it began with the suffragist movements in the West in the late nineteenth and early twentieth century, and continued with the feminist movement. The suffragist movement was strong in a number of places in the developing world, such as Egypt. Very active, composed overwhelmingly of middle- and upper-class women who had some Western education, they exerted a domestic influence on male members of ruling elites. The incorporation of women into the League of Nations' and the United Nations' charters—specific references to equal rights—were important early formal measures achieved through this route. The recognition of women's rights in the United Nations was maintained and expanded through the continuing work of several international organizations. The highly publicized United Nations Decade for Women—from 1975 to 1985—consolidated women's place in this international agenda.

In certain developing countries, especially in Latin America, but also in the Philippines, for example, women's presence is now felt politically in a different way. Grass-roots action now embraces women's movements that have become tremendously important. I suspect it has something to do with Roman Catholicism in these cases. The strongly male-oriented political systems in these countries clashes with the high symbolic value of women in Catholic doctrine. It has left a kind of space for women to step into the political arena as guardians of social welfare and morality.

In other parts of the world, women's groups and women's movements have also been increasingly active, the most successful of them geared towards income generation rather than social welfare. In Kenya, for example, there is a very strong tradition of self-help among women; in India, there have been successful groupings of women in cooperatives.

Still, the prevailing wisdom leaves only a small place in the process of development and modernization for women. In this view, women are relegated to economic activity of a traditional kind, essentially domestically based to accord with women's reproductive "duties." This view consolidates men's claim to newer resources, achieved mainly through education. Women are liable to be increasingly sidelined economically for this reason, denied the advantages of such material progress as is taking place through investments in, and application of, new technology.

The traditional terminology of economics formalized and helped perpetuate the view that women mostly operate outside the national economy. But this at least is changing. Ethnographic "time use" and other statistical studies concerned with refining and measuring employment have been leading to a redefinition and reassessment of the economic value of women's work in the household as well as in "informal" work outside. All the work of social reproduction is now viewed as part of the spectrum of economically valuable activity. This more sophisticated understanding of the integral importance of women's activities points to the growth potential of raising women's productivity.

The reassessment of women's activities also gives analysis of decision making and resource allocation within the household a new importance in economics, previously denied. The household is now acknowledged as the site of subordination of women, as a conflictual group where, on balance, women's interests are suppressed rather than promoted. There is much interest now in understanding how women as income generators and producers are constrained in this way from maximizing their potential.

The origin of women's subordination may lie in the household, but it is of course reinforced by prevailing institutional arrangements in product and financial markets, by civil legislation, and by social and cultural attitudes. The challenge now is for technicians of development to promote effective policies in these various dimensions, compatible with different cultural environments, policies that will match up with the vigorous demands of local women's movements and enhance economic development by advancing women's own economic position.

MIGUEL URRUTIA: My entry into development economics owes much to a course I took, jointly offered by David Bell and John Kenneth Galbraith. The thing I most remember about the course is that at one point it dealt with the Japanese experience. For a Latin American, that was a new and very interesting thing; it was precisely the comparative aspect of development studies that fascinated me.

I began by imagining that it would be interesting to explore how policymakers in my country, and also in other parts of Latin America, used development economics. I saw very early that in Latin America there are two different tendencies: some policymakers are very influenced by the example of other countries; others are very theoretical. In the 1960s, it became fashionable to talk in certain quarters about the state having to capture the commanding heights of the economy (the steel industry, oil); this was avidly discussed in certain political parties. I suspect that the interest reflected the debates in the United Kingdom. Until the 1960s, policymakers tended to look more at the industrialized world than at other developing countries.

Then came the late 1960s. In my own country, in part thanks to the Ford Foundation, quite a few of the young people who ended up working on development policy went to Hong Kong and Korea to see what was happening there. This was much before we received the interpretations of what was happening from professors at Stanford and Yale. These visits certainly had an influence on the way policy-making was pursued in some parts of Latin America. Normally, politicians and young businessmen were the ones who first visited East Asia. A group of businessmen who went to Korea and Taiwan and were much impressed did two interesting things. One was to start export businesses in manufacturing, in products where there was an obvious comparative advantage. The other was to finance nongovernmental institutions to think about these issues. One of the sources of the very limited private financing of some of the think tanks in Latin America came from businessmen who had been abroad, looking at these comparative experiences.

Vague oversimplifications were common, and such oversimplifications could be very dangerous. The idea that there is a rather simple model that you need to follow—that has produced incredible growth rates in Asia—has been peddled in Latin America. When one looks at the reality, of course, it is considerably more complex, not only in the economic sphere but also in the political and the institutional. Still, all this comparative economics has produced some very concrete and useful knowledge.

The other economic school in Latin America is more theoretical and less comparative. How do policymakers in Latin America use theory? The record there is much more mixed. When you have political change in many countries in the region, not only does the political party change, but the whole model of government is altered. This creates tremendous adjustment problems. While it is true that one cannot do any comparative analysis without theory—while I am not saying that there should be no theories—the fact is that in some cases the ideas come straight from the university to policy, and little thought is given to adapting the theory to the specific conditions and institutions of a country. These radical shifts in policy due to the adoption of different theoretical models have created too much uncertainty in many countries of Latin America and have therefore weakened private-sector investment.

Another feature of Latin American economics is its emphasis on the political determinants of economic policy decisions. One time when I was writing about planning, I tried to specify what the social welfare function of a Colombian head of state ought to be. When you think seriously about it, there is no question that the first priority is not economic development; in my view, it is national unity. The first priority of a head of state must be the survival of the system that elected him or that put him into power. While the second priority may indeed be economic development, if you are trying to create national unity, the important thing might be to create an efficient political machine and the improvement of the allocation of resources would take second place. Economic policy may therefore be validly directed toward the first objective and not the second.

Teaching about economic growth in Japan and my own country, I realized that one of the most interesting phenomena was the complete absence of internal violence in Japan after the first problems of industrial transformation had been resolved. In Japan, there is an almost total lack of crime and an absence of internal violence. The comparison with Columbia is instructive, where internal violence has been pervasive for almost 160 years but where there have been no international conflicts. There may be some relation between violence and political development that has not been adequately understood. Nationalism may minimize internal violence but lead to international conflict. A weak state, on the other hand, may not embark on international conflict but may be unable to control internal violence. In the case of Latin America recently, there has been a very peculiar phenomenon: as authoritarian governments abandon state violence, ordinary crime begins to grow. In Rio, there is much more crime today than there used to be. The issue of the pervasiveness of violence and what to do about it has implications for international relations that we do not understand. One of the ways to achieve democracy—some degree of decentralization—is to have a very weak central state, but where such weak states exist, there may be significant internal violence. There seems to be a trade-off between internal social cohesiveness, and decentralization and democracy. Latin American societies have chosen weak states, which create economic uncertainty but make possible less authoritarian forms of government. Even military regimes in Latin America tend to be weak and not very authoritarian. The recent exceptions of Argentinian and Chilean authoritarianism are very unusual.

John P. Lewis

Government and National Economic Development

I
T IS NO ACCIDENT that when David Bell led his team of
planning advisers to Pakistan in 1954 he had never had a course
in development economics. There were no such courses then. Not
even Arthur Lewis was yet teaching them. The field was just
beginning to take shape, in official circles more than in universities.
Nineteen fifty-four was the year Lewis published what still may be
the greatest development economics article of all,[1] an article anticipated in part in a 1951 United Nations report, the work of a group
of five experts that included D. R. Gadgil and Theodore Schultz.[2]
Lewis served on that body and may well have been its most
persuasive member. Raul Prebisch, similarly, has done his first major
writing on development under U.N. auspices a year or two earlier.[3]
Such literature, at that time, was a step ahead of anything being
produced in universities.

The reasons are not hard to find; Third World development was
seen at the beginning to be a predominantly prescriptive, policy-bent
subject. In my view, it still ought to be thus perceived so that it can be
differentiated from the older subdiscipline of economic history. The
latter, written in a positive, descriptive idiom, engaged economists
like Arthur Lewis, Simon Kuznets, Walt Rostow, and Hollis Chenery, who also went on to the more normative enterprise of development studies.

The universities were not hostile to policy analysis in 1950. Those
in this country and in Europe, with the Marshall Plan in full stride,
were much preoccupied with problems of national reconstruction.

66

Retrospective courses on wartime planning and controls, on regulation, and on international trade and financial policy were common. Substantial attention was being given to Marxist-Leninist economics and planning. In Western Europe and North America, academics were trying to evolve national economic policies capable of coping with unemployment, underproduction, and inflation.

What differentiated development as a policy field in 1950, causing it to start its life mainly under public-sector auspices, was the subject matter of its policy focus. That focus, concentrating on Third World development, had to do primarily with economic growth. Such growth acceleration did not figure very high on the agendas that engaged universities and governments in the West. Averill Harriman, in 1952, to whom Leon Keyserling was feeding arguments, may have been the first serious American presidential candidate to make the acceleration of U.S. economic growth a major campaign issue. While the Harrod-Domar model was well known in academic circles at the beginning of the 1950s, most viewed it as a hypothesis of limited interest, not as a policy guide for the United States or Western Europe.

Growth forecasting was becoming important, and provided a benchmark against which the successes and failures of certain stabilization policies could be measured. Still, the growth rate itself was not widely viewed as a target for policy. This situation changed rapidly in the United States during the 1950s, but in the interim when growth acceleration came forward insistently as a policy objective in the newly emerging and other developing countries, it was left to governments, together with their multinational creations and the consultants they were able to hire, to build up the subject as best they could.

In a conference on development held in 1950, no one would have been asked to write an essay on "government and national economic development." Such a topic would have been thought the subject of the whole conference. Development was a matter of policy; policy was the business of governments.

Since the early 1950s, attitudes about the centrality and the capacities of governments as promoters of development have changed dramatically. To go over some familiar ground, one needs, first, to explain why governments received such a central role as leaders and managers of development in Asia, Africa, and Latin

America after World War II. Then one needs to explain the reaction that set in, particularly in the 1960s (in part, a neoclassical response), that has continued down to this day. Reflections about the relative advantages of governmental and nongovernmental institutions and interventions are in order; it may be that we have overreacted as we have remarked the limits of governments.

Many of us remember—indeed, shared—the high hopes common in the early 1950s about the roles of government in promoting development. There were many reasons for such an opinion; some of them may still hold.

First, there was an acceptance of the de facto primacy of governments. In the modern era of nation-states, at least secular nation-states,* governments, if identified with the states they govern, appeared to be the dominant organizations. Within their respective terrains, they were the only ones to enjoy universal and compulsory membership. Whatever national constitutions might say, citizens expected governments to be able to deal with problems perceived to be serious and believed to be soluble.

Second, at least in the early 1950s, reliable, socially efficient markets were not thought to be primordial institutions; they were considered creatures of government. Efficient markets did not operate in a state of nature. Large societal systems are structures of hierarchical authority within which spaces for freely fluctuating, self-adjusting markets have to be carved out, just as do the spaces for individual rights. Governments contrive effective markets by supplying them with frames of operating rules and adjudication.

Third, there was a need to protect the economy's disadvantaged participants and to supply public goods. Undirected and unsupplemented, markets were thought to deal with the economic losers in society more harshly than the polity's sense of social justice allowed. Because private enterpreneurs failed to provide a variety of services demanded by the public—defense, police, and civil law but also support for the aged and certain transport, communications, education, and health services—governments were required to supplement as well as bound the market. Within any society, there were generally Left-Right differences over the appropriate scope of the needed transfers,

---

*The Islamic revival is presenting a growing set of exceptions to the assumption about secularism, a point not pursued in this article.

subsidies, and supports; between societies, variations in the levels of support generally reflected to some extent the availability of resources. Still, there is no country today where government has not preempted a substantial fraction of output for market-supplementing purposes.

Other reasons that government was thought central to the development problems of Latin America, Asia, and Africa had to do with the recent experiences of the developed countries themselves. Before the Second World War, the West had suffered the worst depression in the history of capitalism. The market's reputation was tattered, both for economists and other social scientists, but also for politicians. Microeconomics was mainly concerned with the imperfections of competition and the need to repair market failures with new, improved industrial and financial regulation. Only the Keynesian revolution provided the macroeconomic cover under which the virtues of microeconomic decentralization and flexibility could begin very gradually to reassert themselves.

Meanwhile, many, including those offended by Soviet politics, were impressed by the economic aggrandizement as well as the social restructuring that a command system had been able to achieve in the Soviet Union. In the West—particularly in the United States and the United Kingdom—wartime experience with extensive central planning and economic controls had been positive. Fear of "creeping socialism" had been allayed; many saw no reason to believe that a government occupying the economy's commanding heights could not remain democratic.

Finally, the progovernment school in the 1950s found support in the developing countries themselves. Many of their governments were descendants of independence movements; they were governments in a hurry. A good number felt the need to mediate between weakly joined factions and subregions; they sensed the appetites of their elites as well as their masses (insofar as the latter understood the situation) for rapid material advances. Because their institutions were weak, their private-sector entrepreneurial initiatives hesitant, their markets underdeveloped (and in former colonies suspect), and their traders in disrepute, the newly created states were seen as the only possible agency of large-scale development.

Many saw a need for more than the sorts of incremental changes one could hope to achieve from markets. The system needed to be shaken loose from rigidity, privilege, and inertia. The poor required a champion. Where structural transformation was called for, the pressures were almost irresistible on governments, never lacking hubris, to plan challenging economic futures, to create all manner of needed institutions, to fill financial and industrial deficiencies, to take charge.

The conventional view is that governments overreached. Their acceptance of responsibility far exceeded their capacity to perform. Experience has taught us a great deal about the limits of government. A common observation, worldwide during the past generation, that transcends ideologies is that official hierarchies—command systems—have a tendency to become cumbersome, clogged, and top-heavy. This is especially true of populous centralized countries, which have abundant bureaucratic layering. Governments have been using two stratagies to escape the clumsiness and overload of highly centralized structures. One involves the delegation of more decision making to lower levels of the official hierarchies. The other calls for passing such decision making on to nonofficial mechanisms.

It is this second strategy that I mainly consider here. Governments and official bodies since the 1950s have been renewing their long-standing appreciation of the *Wealth of Nations* proposition that the discharge of major and diverse responsibilities does not require governments to do everything themselves. There are what can be called servomechanisms—notably, self-adjusting markets—which, properly bounded, can serve as admirable labor-saving devices for bureaucrats. Without detailed governmental intervention, markets can generate many of the fine-textured economic decisions that a thoroughgoing command system would have to produce administratively. They can often do so in a more timely way and, in the process, accord enterprises and perhaps also workers, investors, and consumers greater measures of freedom.

From the viewpoint of governments, therefore, a market system offers managerial economy. A second point, widely appreciated in the context of developing countries during the past two or three decades, is that it is also ethically economical. Little altruism or public mindedness is demanded of most actors in the system. They are allowed, indeed encouraged, to do what comes naturally, that is, pursue their own interests. By the magic of the Invisible Hand, these self-seekers collectively advance the common good.

This reading of the market system's ethical economy reflects a different scaling of the comparative virtues of public and private motivations than prevailed shortly before Adam Smith, as Albert Hirschman has reminded us in *The Passions and the Interests*.[4] Hirschman notes that, in the eyes of Montesquieu, Sir James Steuart, and a number of their contemporaries, governments were apt to be dangerous, quixotic, beastly institutions driven by the passions of rapacious tyrants. In these circumstances, it was a blessing for such leadership to be superseded by the cooler "interests" of a Calvinistic countinghouse.

Steuart's type of sharp-penciled government, actuated by the calculus of entrepreneurial gain, rather reminds us of the imagery of the contemporary public-choice theorists. However, the governments of the neoclassical renaissance that overtook development policy, especially from the 1960s onward, were very differently motivated. Their intentions were supposed to be benign and lofty—but their capabilities were limited; hence, they were pleased that it did not require elevated private purposes to generate desirable social outcomes.

The decline in the reliance on governments can be put in more familiar terms: under the overweening interventionism of the 1950s, many developing economies were both overplanned and overcontrolled. Import-substitution strategies brought overvalued exchange rates; these led to self-augmenting and rigid controls, with distorted pricing and misallocated resources. As the unbroken criticism of Ian Little, Jagdish Bhagwati, T. N. Srinivasan, Anne Krueger, and Bela Balassa suggest, the cost of governments' overextensions has been pyramided inefficiency.

Misfeasance soon blurred into malfeasance. Excessive controls generated and entrenched institutionalized regimes of rent-seeking activities (Krueger) and unproductive profit-seeking activities (Bhagwati). Though usually legal, these activities were thoroughly wasteful. Also, it was only a short step from bare legality into proliferating corruption.

Such thinking has gathered strength since the 1960s. There have been other refrains of course—an expanded concern about equity and related matters in the 1970s and again, after a lapse, today; keener interest in human-resource development; revised and heightened attention to science and technology; a thrust of concern for the environment; and a resounding, now abating, North-South dialogue. But the theme of market-activating, efficiency-motivated, outward-oriented, get-the-prices-right reform has become the strongest strand of conventional West European and American development-policy thinking. It is the new orthodoxy.

As preached by the World Bank, for example, the new orthodoxy is a culmination of the neoclassical revival. It is not a doctrine of anarchy. The instruments of the orthodoxy—structural and sectoral adjustment loans, IMF standbys, and the rest—are all addressed to governments. The policy neoclassicals have no wish to banish governments from the development effort; they simply ask them to play more measured and more indirect roles.

Finally, in reaction to the progovernment excesses of the 1950s, there has developed in the recent Thatcher-Reagan years yet another tendency. Less concerned with government restraint than with government bashing, a new emphasis has been given to privatization.

The central tenet of the new orthodoxy is the rehabilitation of the market—not an unregulated one, but one that works. The theme antedates the elections of 1979 and 1980. In its present form, it was discernible in the early 1960s. It was one of the themes of the World Bank, though obviously not the only one, throughout the 1970s. It is not essentially an ideological theme; it is technocratic, and its rationale is efficiency. It has been gathering adherents in a great variety of places—in Yugoslavia, Hungary, China, and the Soviet Union as well as in Japan, Western Europe, the United States, the newly industrialized countries of East Asia, and many other developing countries.

Throughout the 1970s many of the technocratic market advocates, including those in the World Bank, were careful to draw a distinction between the market and the private sector. Technically, they argued, efficiency depended much more on competition, freedom of entry and of factor, product, and technological choices, flexibility of prices, access to finance, and the scales of operations and markets than it did on who, juridically, owned particular assets. Ownership, they said, was socially and politically sensitive; it was best left to local option. As between public, private, and cooperative ownership, the technocrats recognized that ownership was a mixed matter in many individual enterprises as well as in whole industries and a great number of countries. Economic performance did not seem to sort itself out in any very clear way along the ownership spectrum.

Technocrats schooled in the United States had learned from Berle and Means in 1932 of the important gap between ownership and control in the modern corporation.[5] Contrary to simple entrepreneurial incentive models, efficiency in a large private bureaucracy is in principle nurtured much as it is in a large public bureaucracy—especially if both are engaged in marketing products for profit. If their masters choose to do so, the award of merit badges and salaries to both public- and private-sector managers can be conditioned very heavily by their companies' performance at the bottom line.

The tendency until the end of the 1970s was to push the market, to soft-pedal the private sector. That has now radically changed. Part of the explanation is certainly ideological. The Reagan and Thatcher administrations have been marketing privatization evangelically. Still, part of the new pro-private-sector push stemming from the World Bank, is pragmatic; it is specific to Africa in origin. The team commissioned to produce what became the Elliot Berg report in 1981 found the condition of African parastatals* so outrageously bad that the only reasonable recommendation seemed to be to damn the whole class of such enterprises.

Whatever the reasons, the fragile but important fencing between the market and the private sector, preserved in 1970s policy thinking, was bulldozed away, as World Bank and other documentation will show. Privatization is now on a roll; false expectations are perhaps being raised. When a country's problem is a gross deficit in trained managerial and technical personnel, anointing one of its foundering public enterprises into a state of privacy will not advance matters very much. On the other hand, it will serve to remove at least one mess from the government's job description temporarily, and that may be worthwhile.

Many of our best contemporary economists, whose analyses one reads with awe, live in a kind of two-dimensional space. They find what they do so fascinating—so technically and conceptually exhilarating—that they begin to believe that their findings, in an ab-

---

*Parastatals are publicly owned output-marketing enterprises intended (but seldom managing) to become self-financing.

stracted slice of reality, provide adequate answers to most problems. While there is little point in enumerating the noneconomic roles that governments can and do play in the developing countries, there is one general distinction that needs to be drawn between certain economists (particularly the neoclassicals) and certain noneconomists. Neoclassical economists tend to have an atomistic, Newtonian, individualistic view of society—of a nation, for example—which is little more than the sum of the individuals or households composing it. People approaching from other directions, including from other social sciences and other kinds of economics, may have more organic concepts of society. The nation-state is far more than an accounting unit in the developing world (and elsewhere). It is an emotion-charged identity that in this era particularly dominates social decision making to an extraordinary degree.

The neoclassical paradigm does not cope very well with the phenomenon of contemporary nationalism. Applied development economists tend to say that goals of national economic development are three—not only growth and equity but also self-reliance. Yet we offer a pretty pallid, balance-of-payments version of self-reliance. The great Indian neoclassicals, Bhagwati and Srinivasan, for example, will tell you that the reason Nehru and Mahalanobis chose their import-substitution strategy was "export pessimism." If you read Nehru himself, you will find forecasts of sluggish exports not very important. Driven by history (the independence struggle) and to some extent by security concerns, in part by the size and pride of the country, there was a deep, intrinsic passion for nondependence.

We are on the verge today, in my view, of having an effective consensus in the development community that during the adjustment of the 1980s, redistributional transfers to the poor and to the vulnerable, as well as outlays on public goods in many of the social sectors, were squeezed too tightly. Some redress is in the cards. Adjustment, as James Grant's colleagues have put it, must be given more of a human face,[6] and is, I believe, going to get one—in the budgeting of many developing-country governments and in the programming of most development-cooperation agencies, almost without regard to the influence of privatization doctrine.

Pragmatic pressures during the next ten years or so are likely to force an increase in concessional transfers to developing countries. The needs for Overseas Development Assistance (ODA) are greater, not less, than they have been in recent years, and not only in Africa, but in South Asia as well. Also, there is a desperate need to patch over part of the debt crisis. Endless soul searching about the effectiveness of aid has recently been through a strenuous phase that has yielded a verdict that gives such programs, on balance, a clean bill of health.

Hence, the demand side of the aid picture is positive. To forecast that the supply side will respond sufficiently to allow a significant increase in real ODA during the next ten years will be regarded by some as wildly unrealistic, especially in the United States. For nearly twenty years, the aid outlook here has been bleaker than in the rest of the donor group. Yet, the conventional wisdom on this score needs to be resisted if only because it is based on pretense—the myth, constantly refashioned, that the United States and other donors cannot (because of the Gramm-Rudman Act or whatever) "afford" to increase their transfers. The argument fails on simple grounds of comparative magnitudes. The donors can afford to do more in the same way that a poor man can afford to buy more chewing gum. Even doubled, ODA in the United States, for example, would claim only a trivial slice of the federal budget, indeed of the defense budget. Its level is not constrained by lack of resources in any real sense; it is constrained wholly by political priorities.

Whether the feasibility of greater aid will allow the needs for such transfers to drive the totals upward through the medium term is unpredictable. The outcome will be determined less by public opinion than by how much of their political capital leaders in the donor group are prepared to spend on behalf of development assistance. The possibilities of increases in much of the donor community—in Japan, for example—are considerable. They reinforce what has been said about the developing countries' own outlays on public goods—the arithmetic of the governmental budgetary role in development seems again to be on the rise, even if the rhetoric has not as yet turned around.

Some of our stereotypes of governments and of private enterprises and other nongovernmental institutions tend to become too widely separated. The propensities of salary and wage earners in public and private organizations are not all that different. Both strive in ways that are wasteful and error prone. While one set is chastened by market tests much more than the other, the difference is by no means absolute. What drives enterprises to their performance frontiers neoclassically, of course, is supposed to be the discipline of competition. Yet the private market contains a variety of monopolistic, protectionist, information-scarce havens for inefficiency. Governmental institutions that market their products often benefit from the same kind of competitive discipline as their private counterparts. Many governmental institutions—in fields such as education, research, and health, and even in the military sector and general administration—often exhibit energy that derives from constructive rivalries.

The alleged difference between governments and nongovernments that is particularly suspect is the claim (or assumption) that the former have a particular propensity to become corrupt. In some sense, this is true. But the counterargument is not only that it usually requires someone in the private sector to offer a bribe to someone in government; in addition, it is that norms for the two sectors are very different. Certain actions that are corrupt if taken by public officials are classified as crimes if in the private sector; but most of them are simply normal business practice if done privately. Behavioral norms vary greatly between governments and over time. The unholy alliances between governments and entrenched interests—not to say between governments and organized crime—make it difficult to allocate blame. Yet, if one had a single yardstick for probity that could be laid across all governments and nongovernments, I would be fairly confident that the first would outpoint the second, though, of the two, government misbehavior is much the more widely reported.

But then, on the other hand, some government-nongovernment differences are more noteworthy than contemporary comment might suggest. In the classic Adam Smith paradigm of laissez-faire, governments and businesses march to different drummers. The former seek the public interest, with a limited reach, often clumsily. Governments are lucky that, when the market is unleashed within appropriate boundaries, self-seeking private actions collectively can work to serve the public interest. Motivations at the public center and at the private periphery of the system are very different.

In all the writings of organization theorists accumulated during the past generation, there has been a tendency to lose sight of this distinction. Instead, there has been a focus on the commonalities that private and public bureaucracies share. It must be emphasized that a complex of motives is at work in all large organizations. When

Chester Barnard, on leave from New Jersey Bell, wrote *Functions of the Executive,*[7] he tried to establish new meanings for the terms *effective* and *efficient*. (Fortunately for the language, he failed.) An organization is effective, he said, to the extent that it accomplishes its announced purposes, efficient to the extent that it serves the personal interest of its participants—staff, workers, officers, executives, whatever. At about the same time, Robert Merton was drawing a similar distinction between organizations' "manifest" and "latent" purposes. Other branches of the large body of organizational and administrative literature have dwelled on the politicking and bargaining that must go on among groups internal to the organization but also on the external pressures that come to bear on organizational choices.[8]

These are concepts that play across the private and the public sectors jointly without, however, challenging the motivational differences between the two arenas. More recently, and one can date the public-choice literature from the latter 1950s, a splinter group of neoclassical economists, together with some look-alike political scientists, have done a remarkable thing—they have simplified the model of government motivations into a single-track form, supplying the public sector with a brain transplant straight out of the marketplace.[9] It is no longer pretended that government actors operate on a different ethical or motivational plane than private actors. The whole issue of Barnardian effectiveness is washed out; Barnardian efficiency is all that counts. People who run governments make no attempt to achieve public goals, except as this may serve their own interests.

While there is nothing new about the proposition that self-serving transactions of many kinds—patronage, pork barreling, lobbying, other quid-pro-quo exchanges—enter heavily into the political and bureaucratic process, what is ethnocentric on the part of the public-choice splinter group is the proposition that, in terms of motivations and purposes, nothing else is going on. I cannot imagine a class of behavior that it would be easier to document than instances of government decision and action that appear to have been driven neither by class nor by self-seeking but by the actors' notions of the public interest. It would be easy to cite individuals, agencies, or whole governments at particular periods. Such public-interest behavior tends to be episodic, but this does not mean that it never happens.

Government *is* different, motivationally; it also differs in another respect. The public interest is hydra headed; government grapples—has to grapple—simultaneously with a whole set of manifest and not only latent purposes. Some of these are incompatible; they conflict. Almost no government in recent memory has been a monolith; the branches and factions are inclined to grind different axes—not simply because of personality differences or lack of coherence but because the missions of government are various; they span the spectrum of social concerns. In this respect, governments are not unique; they are simply at the pole of a continuum. They have many more major purposes than does Harvard University or the Ford Foundation, and vastly more than General Motors.

What all this comes down to is the irreducible complexity, even ambiguity, of policy issues—as they bear, for example, on national economic development. The public-choice cartoons are a superb example of the confusion and distractions that oversimplified models can inject into practical discourse. Governments, as development promoters, are in some ways, like other agencies, in other ways different. In addition to all of the latent-purpose-serving static that intrudes into their behavior, they are obliged to pursue a number of quasi-conflicting manifest goals simultaneously.

Moreover, governments, like nearly all other institutions, function inconstantly, intermittently, episodically. Operating on different tracks at different times, they tend to work nine to five, taking off holidays and weekends, going on vacations. Much of what they do is spasmodic, crablike; they ratchet matters along. Still, every Monday, Wednesday, and Friday they probably have a better handle on the public interest than others do.

This essay will be read as a progovernment piece. The downswing in the fashion cycle, in my view, has gone too far and is due now for redress. However, nearly all this discussion has implied a focus on national Third World governments or on external agencies that deal with national governments.

It is a safe guess that in the years ahead there will be increased attention also to the role of local government in the development process. Partly, as I have suggested, this will be the result of the growing awareness of the need for decentralization. More often than not, as is now widely acknowledged, unrelieved top-down management works rather badly. There is a need for passing significant official decision making on to lower levels, for encouraging greater grass-roots, bottom-up participation in the process.

A second reason for focusing on local self-government has to do with its virtual absence in many Third World provincial jurisdictions. The grass-roots sentiment now in vogue among development promoters, in their effort to break loose from the limits and infirmities of both indigenous central regimes and official aid agencies, is on NGOs—nongovernmental organizations, domestic and expatriate. In many places, networks of NGOs are proliferating. Local popular-suffrage self-governments, by comparison, are frequently weak or missing altogether. They will need to be developed, particularly if the concern is to build institutions in these countries to which the poor and the disadvantaged can have entitled access.

A final discordant note: the nation-state is our dominant institution. Yet, for all the good things I have been saying about it, it may be a roadblock to much global development, particularly to Third World development. Nationalism in Africa, for example, promises to delay or abort the evolution of needed patterns of transnational education, research, finance, and natural-resource development. In Western Europe, the United States, and Japan, it promises to keep major governments from investing seriously in United Nations institutions and programs so long as they are governed on the one-flag, one-vote rule. Generally, nationalism continues to trivialize investment in serious development and in the maintenance of global systems.

National sovereignty, in short, may be development's ultimate catch-22. Short of major disasters, the only hope, it would seem, is in gradual, incremental, grudging, sometimes almost surreptitious shifts in functions and scales of activities to the advantage of multilateral bodies. The latter will need to continue to build and sustain cadres of professionals who will operate at least every Monday, Wednesday, and Friday in the global public interest. The governance of these multilaterals will need to be jockeyed slowly toward some sort of accountability to constituencies weighted less by their national flags or national wealth than by the size of their populations. One can almost imagine a gradual hollowing out of the nation-state so that it progressively relaxes the ultimate development roadblock. But that, plainly, is fanciful. Under peaceful conditions it will be a long time before the diminished autonomy of either Tanzania or the United States begins to match that of the Commonwealth of Massachusetts.

ENDNOTES

[1] W. Arthur Lewis, "Economic Development with Unlimited Supplies of Labour," *The Manchester School* 22 (May, 1954):139–91.

[2] *Measures for the Economic Development of Under-Developed Countries* (New York: United Nations, May 1951).

[3] Raul Prebisch, *The Economic Development of Latin America and its Principal Problems* (New York: United Nations, 1950).

[4] Albert O. Hirschman, *The Passions and the Interests: Political Arguments for Capitalism before Its Triumph* (Princeton: Princeton University Press, 1977).

[5] Adolph A. Berle, Jr. and Gardiner C. Means, *The Modern Corporation and Private Property* (New York: The Commerce Clearing House, 1932).

[6] Giovani A. Cornia, Richard Jolly, and Frances Stewart, *Protecting the Vulnerable and Promoting Growth,* vol. 1, and *Ten Country Case Studies,* vol. 2, of *Adjustment with a Human Face* (Oxford: Oxford University Press, 1988).

[7] Chester I. Barnard, *Functions of the Executive* (Cambridge: Harvard University Press, 1938).

[8] See Graham T. Allison, *The Essence of Decision: Explaining the Cuban Missile Crisis* (Boston: Little, Brown, 1971).

[9] See, for example, Anthony Downs, *An Economic Analysis of Democracy* (New York: Harper & Row, 1957); James M. Buchanan and Gordon Tullock, *The Calculus of Consent: Logical Foundations of Constitutional Democracy* (Ann Arbor: University of Michigan Press, 1962); and William Niskanen, *Bureaucracy and Representative Government* (Chicago: Aldine-Atherton, 1971).

Comments on John Lewis's Essay

CRANFORD PRATT: In recent years, I have been much concerned with the North component of North-South relations. Fred Hirsch argued brilliantly, I think, that Western democratic capitalist societies are living off an inherited, but diminishing, moral capital. His central point was that capitalism, to be socially tolerable and morally adequate, requires the state to prescribe its limits, correct its abuses. An ethically tolerable capitalism requires the widespread presence of values and attitudes which the possessive and materialist individualism of capitalism persistently undermines. A binding sense of community, trust, acceptance of responsibility for the welfare of others, and high evaluation of public goods—these are examples of attitudes that tend to erode under the impact of a popular capitalist culture. Therefore, Hirsch believed, we must anticipate that our political institutions will become less able to constrain acquisitive individualism in the interest of collective values. A closely parallel argument may be made that our governments may well become less able over time to respond to cosmopolitan values or to pursue humane internationalist policies.

To summarize what I have extracted from Hirsch, advocates of liberal, socially responsible policies may be of declining interest, not because of any short-term swing of the pendulum but because of a rather long-term secular trend within our popular culture. I do not mean to suggest that Hirsch had the last word on the health of cosmopolitan values in our culture, but I must remind you of his pessimism.

John Lewis's argument that governments continue to play an important role in the promotion of development is powerfully reinforced by the substantial literature in recent years on the economic development of Europe in the nineteenth century and of the newly industrialized countries more recently. That literature, to use the title of one of its outstanding books, is engaged in bringing the state back in. The literature is rich and rewarding, very much in the tradition of Karl Polanyi and Barrington Moore. It is, in its central assumptions, statist. Governments are the key actors, powerful social institutions pursuing their own interests. If a state has the appropriate capabilities and the requisite autonomy from dominant social forces—two key concepts in this modern political-economy literature—its interests will invariably include the health and development of the national economy. Thus, to use John Lewis's phrase, at least on Mondays, Wednesdays, and Fridays, it will see economic development as being in its own interest.

Many of us involved in development work of one sort or another in Africa, in the last several decades or in the decades immediately following independence, were either openly affirming or "closet" statists in our perspectives on the issue. We sought to influence development by helping governments to improve their planning, by recruiting skilled people to implement policies, and by securing the finances that made it possible to pursue these policies vigorously. We assumed that nationalism would be deployed by the political leadership to maintain stability, with the public service providing the major driving force for development. Our understanding today, as Anthony Low underlined, suggests that we were far too apolitical. We downplayed such factors as inadequate resources, low capability levels, misconceived policies. More importantly, we ignored the frequent absence of any real political will to promote equitable and self-reliant patterns of growth. It took us far too long to recognize that many governments, not even on Mondays, Wednesdays, and Fridays, were much interested in promoting such a pattern of development.

What did we rely on to contain the ambitions and to direct the energies of both politicians and senior bureaucrats? In different national settings and in varying combinations that primarily reflected our own ideological presuppositions, we relied on four factors—the nationalism of populist leaders, the modern national dimensions of an indigenous bourgeois class, the professionalism of bureaucracies and armies, and the socialist commitment of the more radical leadership. There is now a growing realization, particularly in the Third World, that none of these factors was sufficient to limit ambition and greed. We remain ill equipped, both intellectually and conceptually, to discuss the dynamics of socially responsible governments in Third World societies. We are similiarly ill equipped to consider the strategies by which the West could facilitate the emergence of such governments. A recent book by Achebe, the Nigerian novelist, may provide an insight on which to build. Achebe writes of the self-indulgence, insecurity, and moral insensitivity of the Nigerian political elite; he believes the key reason for this to be the total absence of any sense of common identity, joint destiny, shared life, and integrating values between the elite and ordinary Nigerians. The leadership is seen to view ordinary people in purely instrumental fashion; ordinary people feel themselves to be totally apart from and ignored by those in power.

While we struggle to integrate this kind of insight into our study of Third World politics, we are still only at the beginning. Still, there are recurrent themes in contemporary discussions of Third World politics which suggest a greater importance is today being given to the achievement of socially responsible governments. There is a greater emphasis on human rights by those writing about development assistance. There is new stress on the importance of activities that empower popular groups to be more self-reliant economically and more assertive politically. There is greater skepticism within the Third World of authoritarian shortcuts, be they of the Left or the Right. And there is new reaffirmation in the Third World, both on the Left and the Right, of the importance of somehow increasing genuine popular participation while protecting basic political liberties. We are only at the beginning of this, but it seems to me that the challenge to the political science wing of the development community is to combine John Lewis's continued recognition of the important role that governments must play in the development process with a greater sensitivity to the importance of those relationships and structures likely to increase meaningful linkages between leadership and people.

ABIOLA IRELE: There is a distrust of government as an agency of development in most African countries, certainly in Nigeria. The reasons are not far to seek. Government has been used in Africa essentially as an instrument of power, giving some people access to certain material benefits while excluding others. Yet, the whole idea of independence was to guarantee freedom for all, to make life more abundant. Since there were no other structures, the whole task of development fell squarely on government. This is the problem. While government must clearly be given some kind of responsibility, how do we induce responsibility, how do we make those in positions of authority sensitive to certain issues? It is a human problem much more than an abstract economic problem.

I think, for instance, that the role of government in Nigeria has been counter development, counterproductive. There has been a tremendous bureaucratization of all government processes. You cannot start a small business in Nigeria now—you cannot do anything—without running up against some kind of bureaucratic barrier linked to the rule of corruption. There is a real question of what scope can be given to government institutions in respect to development, particularly now when the army is involved in most African countries. That complicates the problem enormously. How much can be safely given to private initiative, which will always drift in the absence of clear direction. I find unpersuasive the neoclassical idea that private interests will always translate into public interest. I have no solution to offer, but there is a very real difficulty here that ought not to be skirted.

FRANCIS X. SUTTON: In my mind, the decline of confidence in governments in the development process was part of a wider decline of confidence and respect for governments, characteristic of the whole Western world since the mid-1960s. It shows itself in public opinion polls, but in other respects as well. In considerable part, it must be seen as hostility to large organizations. It showed itself in the parallel decline in confidence in large business, which came just a little later. And it showed also in its effects on the approach to development. The popularity of private voluntary organizations today, and the increased popularity and legitimacy of private institutions in the developing world—which was not common twenty years ago—has come because of this hostility and loss of confidence, not only in government but in large organizations generally. If this were a room full of Africans—to take a group I know fairly well—they would almost all be hostile to all large organizations doing anything in Africa. Not just the World Bank, but any large organization. It is a shift of popular mood that has to do with more than just performance. It is not only that governments overreached themselves; some certainly did. We are in the sway of a movement, and what turn that movement takes will be related to other major cultural dispositions.

CHARLES WILLIAM MAYNES: I think one of the reasons for discontent in this country and in other democratic countries with multilateral institutions relates to the inherent conflict between democratic practice and multilateralism. The more power one gives to multilateral institutions, the more difficulty one has in reconciling that power with democratic practice. A technocratic group acquires power that is not democratically accountable. I was the assistant secretary for United Nations affairs in the Carter administration and was stunned to see that the most unpopular multilateral institution in Congress was the World Bank, not UNESCO. This was because the World Bank had real power in the form of major resources. We ought to be concerned with changing the contours of the debate. The Congress ought to work out new approaches to the problem of accountability in an organization like the World Bank.

This problem comes up in other ways with other countries. France elected Mitterand to reduce unemployment, and he found he could not do it because France was a member of the European Economic Community. The British and the Germans refused to go along with his plans for reflation; so he faced a choice—either leaving the EEC or abandoning promises he made to win office. Not surprisingly, he did the latter. In other words, the more power we give multilateral institutions, the more likely it is that they will create sensitive and difficult problems.

MICHAEL ROEMER: I want to raise a question about government as a generic term or subject. When we talk about government and development, we really have to introduce regional differences. If you take the question of whether we want, need, or could use more or less intervention in economies to promote development—which I define as structural change, industrialization—the answer depends wholly on what you are looking at. In East Asia, the answer has clearly been more government; this has worked. Japan and Korea are examples of statist intervention, in market directions to be sure, but statist interventions to achieve development. If you ask the question in South Asia, you will get the opposite answer. In Africa, the answer is clearly less government. So, you cannot avoid the question of what institutions you are talking about and which cultures you are addressing.

But even in Africa, if you accept the idea of less government, you are talking neither about less discipline nor less power. It probably takes greater discipline and greater power for government to step out of the market than to become more intimately involved. The natural tendency is for government to involve itself in the market as a way of supporting itself, politically and economically. To step away from that role, to allow the market to function, is something that governments do not want to do. If they try to do it, their own constituents will stop them, so it is not a matter of giving up power. It is a matter of taking on more power in a way, but with the object of ultimately giving it up.

Nancy Birdsall

Thoughts on Good Health and Good Government

S HOULD THE DEVELOPMENT COMMUNITY rethink the role of
the state in improving health in the developing world? The role
of the state in other areas of development has been the subject
of considerable concern since 1982. The external debt crisis of the
1980s, combined with internal fiscal deficits in many developing
countries, has exposed the apparent disadvantages of a large public
sector with substantial involvement, often through state-owned public enterprises, in industry, agriculture, and finance. The same period
has seen much the same question raised in the industrial world, which
has also been plagued by fiscal deficits. Such politically successful
national leaders as Mr. Reagan and Mrs. Thatcher have espoused an
approach to government that says, simply, less is better. In the same
period, some highly planned socialist economies, including Hungary,
China, and the Soviet Union, have sought ways to imitate, if not
duplicate, the apparent advantages of so-called market-led economies, in which the planning functions of government are limited.

The role of the state in the social areas, including not only health
but also education and social insurance (for old age and disability),

The views and interpretations in this article are those of the author and not of the World Bank.

*The author gratefully acknowledges the comments made on an earlier draft by Philip
Musgrove, Davidson Gwatkin, T. Paul Schultz, and Jere R. Behrman as well as the comments
of a large number of World Bank staff members, especially those of Anthony Measham, Willy
de Geyndt, and Vicente Paqueo. None of these, of course, is responsible for remaining errors
of fact or interpretation.*

has, however, hardly been questioned and has in the modern era been much greater in these areas.

THE ROLE OF THE STATE IN PAST ACHIEVEMENTS IN HEALTH

The economic growth of western Europe in the eighteenth and nineteenth centuries was accompanied by the first sustained increase of population the world had ever known. Until then, population increases were irregular and vulnerable to fluctuations in mortality; life expectancy was probably little higher at the beginning of the eighteenth century than it was 2,000 years earlier.* The increases in population growth resulted almost entirely from declines in death rates—from about thirty-five per thousand at the end of the eighteenth century to perhaps twenty-five per thousand at the end of the nineteenth century for all developed countries; birthrates rose slightly during this period because of declines in age at marriage but had probably fallen overall by the end of the period. The combination of sustained population growth with increases in per capita income was unprecedented; it put to rest forever, at least for modern industrial economies, Malthus's fear that increases in population would absorb increases in total income, thus preventing growth in per capita income and in living standards.† In fact, the unprecedented combination of population growth with per capita income growth provided, in the view of economist Simon Kuznets, the very basis for the definition of modern economic growth.[1]

By Kuznets's definition, the developing countries have without question enjoyed modern economic growth throughout the whole of the postwar period. In fact, postwar population growth in the developing countries has been far more rapid than it was in industrializing Europe; rates have averaged between 2 and 3 percent in most developing countries throughout the entire period (China since

---

*Small population increases probably began during the fifteenth century in China, South Asia, and Europe (see John D. Durand, "Historical Estimates of World Population: An Evaluation," *Population and Development Review* 3 [3] [1977]:253–96).

†Malthus actually modified his bleak view in his second essay on population, as explained in Nancy Birdsall, John Fei, Simon Kuznets, Gustav Ranis, and T. Paul Schultz, "Development and Demography in the 1980s," in *World Population and Development: Challenges and Prospects,* ed. Philip M. Hauser (Syracuse: Syracuse University Press, 1980), 211–95.

TABLE 1. Rates of Natural Increase of Population, 1950–1985

	1950	1965	1980	1985–1990
Developing countries				
Sub-Saharan Africa	2.1%	2.7%	3.1%	3.2%
Middle East and North Africa	2.5	2.8	2.7	2.7
South Asia	1.7	2.5	2.2	2.2
East Asia (excluding China)	1.5	2.6	2.3	2.1
China	1.7	2.7	1.1	1.4
Latin America and the Caribbean	2.6	2.8	2.5	2.1
Industrialized countries	1.1	0.9	0.5	0.4

Source: World Bank projections for 1985–1990.

the mid-1970s being a notable exception—see Table 1), whereas in nineteenth-century Europe population growth averaged between 1 and 1.5 percent. During most of the postwar period, with the exception of the years since 1982 in parts of Africa and Latin America, per capita incomes have also grown.

As in the developed world, rapid postwar population growth has been fundamentally the result of declines in death rates—from something on the order of thirty per thousand per year in 1945 to about ten per thousand in 1988. Increases in birthrates may have occurred in some regions for certain periods and contributed to population growth. The main contribution to population growth, however, has been the decline in death rates, if anything gradually offset (especially since 1965) by the decline in birthrates.[2]

Future historians are almost certain to view the extraordinary decline in death rates (and the accompanying increase in population growth, worldwide but especially in developing countries) as a critical, if not the critical, event of the second half of the twentieth century. The decline in death rates has been shared across all parts of

TABLE 2. Crude Death Rate and Life Expectancy at Birth, by
Region, 1950–1985

	Crude Death Rate (deaths per 1,000 persons per year)				Life Expectancy at Birth (years)	
	1950	1965	1980	1985–1990	1950–1955	1985–1990
Sub-Saharan Africa	29.3	22.8	17.7	15.3		51.5
Middle East and North Africa	24.0	18.1	12.6	10.9		59.0
South Asia	28.8	20.6	14.5	12.2	38.9	55.8
East Asia (excluding China)	27.1	16.3	10.5	7.3		67.9
China	27.3	16.0	7.9	6.7	40.8	69.0
Latin America and the Caribbean	16.6	11.7	8.5	7.2		66.6
Developing countries					41.1	59.1
Industrialized countries	10.5	9.6	9.1	9.3	65.8	73.1

Sources: World Bank, *World Bank Development Report* (New York: Oxford University Press, 1984), 5;
World Bank projections, 1985–1990 (for death rates); and United Nations, *World Population Prospects:
Estimates and Projections as Assessed in 1984* (New York: United Nations, 1986) (for life expectancies).

the developing world and can be translated into an increase in life
expectancy at birth from about forty in 1945 to over sixty today (see
Table 2). Historians of economic development are bound to mark the
period through 1980 as one of extraordinary success, even for the
poorest of the developing countries. Throughout the developing
world, more people are enjoying higher average incomes, and the
increase in population has resulted from an extraordinary improvement in at least one measure of human well-being—the likelihood of
living and of living longer than earlier generations.

There is little doubt that governments have played a major role in
bringing about this mortality decline and the accompanying improvements in health in developing countries. Governments have played a
role most obviously through direct interventions such as immuniza-

tions and malaria control, but also through more general public investments in education and sanitation, as well as in improved communications and transportation, which have reduced the mortality toll once taken by periodic famine.

The case for the importance of public intervention is most clear with respect to the use of health technologies such as immunization, antibiotics, and pest control, particularly in the first two decades of the postwar period (though the relative importance of, for example, antimalarial spraying is still disputed). Also important was the introduction of environmental health actions such as safe water and solid-waste disposal. Most of these measures became possible only in the 1930s and were widely introduced in developing countries in the 1960s and 1970s. The introduction of these technologies (with the possible exception of antibiotics) was largely planned, organized, and implemented with direct government sponsorship, if not directly by government itself. These new technologies have had the advantage of requiring limited behavioral change on the part of beneficiaries in order to be effective (with the possible exception of antibiotics, which at the least required that patients seek health care).

The introduction of these newly available technologies almost surely helps to explain why mortality in developing countries has fallen more rapidly and at average income levels lower than those associated with mortality decline in the West. For example, life expectancy in India in 1980 exceeded life expectancy in France in 1930, despite incomes and educational levels much lower in India than in France at that time.[3] In 1965, crude death rates in Bangladesh and much of Africa, where per capita incomes were below $200 per year, were between twenty and twenty-five per thousand, similar to rates in England and Sweden at the turn of the century, where income levels were probably above $1,000 per capita (in 1982 dollars).[4]

The small role of income growth in comparison with government-sponsored intervention is suggested also by various cross-country analyses. The decline in death rates between 1930 and 1960 indicates that on a worldwide basis income gains alone explain only an estimated 20 percent of that decline.[5] Analysis of trends in the causes of mortality between 1938 and 1963 suggests that improvements in income alone over the twenty-five years accounted for only two years of the total increase in life expectancy of over twelve years worldwide.[6] Though such factors as improvement in the distribution of income within countries, decrease in the cost of using personal health services or of other health-enhancing goods (such as food), and increase in educational attainment probably explain some part of the remaining improvement in life expectancy, it is unlikely that any of these were particularly important from 1938 to 1963, with the possible exception of decline in the price of food.* Indeed, for the immediate postwar period, it is more likely that improvements in transportation and communication, largely through government-sponsored investments (often with international financial assistance) were more critical than food price declines or other nongovernment factors.

The availability of new technologies and the ability of governments in developing countries to exploit them partly explain the drop in mortality in the first two decades of the postwar period. Beginning in the early 1960s, and in the period since then, the effect of increased educational attainment, particularly of women, and the indirect role of government via support for increased educational opportunities need also to be considered. There is increasing evidence that education, particularly of mothers, is the critical determinant of infant and child mortality probabilities.[7] Comparisons of developed countries as they were at the turn of the century with developing countries in the 1980s show much higher levels of educational attainment in the latter, despite lower incomes, suggesting that some of the higher life expectancies in developing countries are due to widespread education. In several of today's poorest developing countries, including India, China, Indonesia, and Kenya, primary school enrollment rates, at close to 100 percent, are well above the enrollment rates of 40 to 60 percent in England, Sweden, and Japan around 1900.[8] In cross-country analyses, increases in education have been estimated to explain at least one-half of the decline in mortality in developing countries between 1965–1969 and 1975–1979.[†]

Moreover, increases in educational attainment in developing countries, mostly in the postwar period, have clearly been the result of

---

*In a few countries, such as Sri Lanka and Costa Rica, widespread access to social services as early as the 1950s was important.

†Samuel Preston's "Mortality and Development Revisited," in *Quantitative Studies of Mortality Decline in the Developing World*, World Bank staff working paper no. 683 (Washington, D.C.: World Bank, 1985) shows that income, education and nutrition together explain about two-thirds of the mortality decline of the period and that the effect of education is at least ten times as great as the effect of income.

TABLE 3. The Role of the Public Sector in Educational Enrollment in Developing Countries, by Region

Region	Percentage of public school students in total enrollment, 1980	
	Primary	Secondary
Sub-Saharan Africa	84%	80%
Francophone	90	83
Anglophone and others	78	78
Asia	87	78
Latin America and the Caribbean	84	75
Middle East and North Africa	92	91

Note: Unweighted averages are used for each country group.
Source: World Bank, *World Development Report* (New York: Oxford University Press, 1988), 13–15.

government efforts to expand access to education. That effort has been most obvious in Africa, where since 1960 alone, the primary school enrollment ratio has risen from 36 to 75 percent, and the adult literacy rate from 9 to 42 percent, and where between 1970 and 1980, public domestic expenditure on education almost tripled.[9] The effort has been made elsewhere in the developing world as well, however. In Asia and Latin America, primary school enrollment ratios rose from 50 percent or below in most countries in 1950 to over 90 percent in the mid-1980s.[10] Though private schooling has played a role, particularly in some countries of Asia and Latin America at the higher level, governments have without doubt been the major actors at the primary and secondary levels; in 1980 more than three-quarters of primary and secondary students in most developing countries were enrolled in public schools directly supported by government (see Table 3).

Finally, in a few countries and regions—including China, Costa Rica, Cuba, Sri Lanka, and the state of Kerala in India—government has taken an active role in improving the delivery of personal health services, including maternal and child health care, family planning, basic nutrition, and, perhaps most important, basic curative care, especially through the use of drugs. (Basic curative care has also been provided by the private sector, particularly in Sri Lanka, and also in China, where the barefoot doctors have acted at least partly as private providers of services.) Delivery of these personal health services at low cost has clearly contributed to the high levels of life expectancy in these places, despite their low income.[11] In these countries, governments have also been effective in employing new technologies and have provided access to education, and these factors have obviously mattered as well. But the case of China suggests strongly that the delivery of basic health services (including access to food) to individuals have contributed over and above education. The female literacy rate was still relatively low in China in the 1960s (probably 50 to 60 percent for all women, somewhat higher for women in their twenties and thirties). By 1970, much of the country's spectacular improvement in life expectancy had already been achieved.

The apparent success of governments in the developing world in bringing about major declines in mortality* is a strong argument for what might be called the public-interest view of government.[12] This is the assumption that government acts in a benign way† (though mistakes and failure are not ruled out, they are not inevitable or irreversible) and that governments need to intervene directly to foster

---

*The fertility decline that has occurred in most of the developing world is also probably due, at least in part, to the effects of government interventions. Though controversy persists about the contribution of the most obvious form of government intervention—support for family planning programs—cross-country analyses and case studies demonstrate that access to family planning of reasonably good quality has contributed to the rate of fertility decline over and above what would be expected solely on the basis of increases in education and urbanization (see Bryan L. Boulier, "Family Planning Programs and Contraceptive Availability: Their Effects on Contraceptive Use and Fertility," in *The Effects of Family Planning Programs on Fertility in the Developing World*, ed. Nancy Birdsall, World Bank staff working paper no. 677, 1985). Governments have played an important role in accelerating access to family planning, especially in Asia since 1975, partly in response to a perception that fertility could be reduced more rapidly through government sponsorship of family planning programs (see David Wheeler, "Female Education, Family Planning, Income, and Population: A Long-Run Econometric Simulation Model," in *The Effects of Family Planning Programs on Fertility in the Developing World*). Fertility decline is also clearly associated with increases in women's education (World Bank, 1984), which, as noted above, have resulted from government interventions to expand education.

†Of course, government may do good things even in response to pressures from self-interested groups. For example, self-interested groups might pressure government to reallocate resources from hospital care to control of a widespread communicable disease that seriously threatened both the elite and the masses. The elite might create pressure for primary schooling that would instill discipline and national values in the masses. Thus, despite use of the word *benign*, what matters is the outcome, not the motivation behind government actions. Past success in malaria control and primary education, though not complete in reaching the poor, may have led to a breakdown of the coalition of the overlapping vested interests, including the rich and the middle class, which once supported these programs, shifting pressure to support for programs that benefit primarily the rich. Thus, governments have not gone from "benign" to "bad"; rather, political conditions have changed. I am grateful to Vicente Paques for pointing this out to me.

development. Given poor capital markets and entrenched economic and political interest groups, private agents alone are unlikely to address the huge unmet needs for physical and social investments in developing countries. Among development economists, the public-interest view has prevailed in much of the postwar period. The case for government involvement in health is particularly strong in this view because free markets are so unlikely to provide the public goods and services, including many basic health services, that bring benefits beyond those accruing to the consumer or the producer. Also, private markets are unlikely to reach the poor with what is viewed as a "merit good," freedom from avoidable illness and death. Moreover, private markets are likely to overproduce goods and services inimical to health, such as pollution and unsafe traffic conditions.

In the last two decades, however, particularly in the 1980s, an alternative view, the private-interest school,* has come to influence views of development economists regarding the role of government in developing countries, particularly in industry, finance, and agriculture.[13] In the private-interest view, the interests of those who control government are confined to advancing their personal goals, not to advancing the welfare of the commonweal. In this view, even the involvement of government in the provision or financing of public goods needs to be questioned and is warranted only if it is clear that government will do less harm than unbridled private markets would. (Thus, for example, society should only with great caution endorse government provision of health services for the poor, since most resources are likely to go to support bureaucratic interests and to reach the poor at higher cost to society than private, voluntary efforts would.)

Though the private-interest view of government is generally not held by members of the international health and development community (indeed, a premise of the primary health care movement is the need for increased government involvement), it has affected attitudes. It has increased discussion of such policies as decentralization of government programs and user charges (to increase the likelihood that government programs will share some of the advan-

---

*Although the term is confusing, among economists this school is known as the public-choice school.

tages of market-led systems) and of the use of private, especially nongovernmental, organizations for delivery of health services.

EXTENDING THE CURRENT ROLE OF THE STATE

Obviously, declines in mortality cannot continue at the same pace indefinitely, because there is a biological limit on human life expectancy. The question is whether the past success of governments in reducing mortality can be maintained along some reasonable expected path of mortality decline and whether the high direct contribution of government-sponsored investments will continue.* There are at least three reasons for doubt about the future contribution of government, short of some change in government's role.

The Diminishing Returns of Successful Programs

The most obvious success of the state in reducing mortality in developing countries has come via programs based on new technologies, programs to immunize people and to control malaria and other endemic diseases, for example. These have not relied on changes in behavior at the individual or household level to be effective. But there are several reasons to believe that the major reductions of mortality through these programs were largely reaped a decade ago and that further mortality declines depend much more than in the past on changes in individual behavior, particularly among the poor.†

What are the reasons for doubt? First is a difference between the developing and the developed countries at a similar stage of mortality decline in the diseases that kill. For example, mortality from diarrhea in the developing world is two to three times as high as it was in the West when overall mortality levels were similar, in large part because prevalence of other diseases has been reduced by technological interventions (see the figure on the next page).[14] Diarrhea is a disease of the poor; it is found along with, and contributes to, malnutrition

---

*See Davidson Gwatkin, *The End of an Era? Recent Evidence Indicates Unexpected Changes in the Pace and Pattern of Third World Mortality Declines* (Washington, D.C.: Overseas Development Council, May 1980) for the argument that mortality decline has slowed too soon in developing countries.

†Some changes in behavior such as better diet, reduced smoking, and use of seatbelts in cars could bring health improvements independent of poverty reduction—but alone would not reduce high mortality, especially of infants, among the poor.

Figure. Schematic Representation of
Changing Causes of Mortality

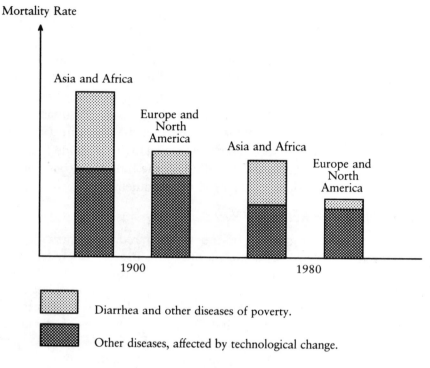

Mortality Rate

Asia and Africa

Europe and
North
America

Asia and Africa

Europe and
North
America

1900   1980

Diarrhea and other diseases of poverty.

Other diseases, affected by technological change.

Source: personal correspondence from John Briscoe.

and is caused by lack of access to clear water, simple health services, and basic education. To date, diarrhea has been relatively impervious to the programs and technologies that have reduced other causes of mortality. There is some hope that the "new technology" of oral rehydration therapy (ORT) can reduce mortality due to diarrhea, but use of ORT itself requires change in the behavior of mothers and other caretakers. Moreover, it is not clear that repeated handling of diarrhea through ORT actually reduces mortality in environments in which infants are likely to die from other diseases of poverty.*[15]

Second, within developing countries, the differentials in mortality associated with income and other measures of socioeconomic status

---

*This means that even if diarrhea were vaccine preventable, effects on mortality reduction independent of other changes in the environment of the poor might not be great.

have persisted, even where overall mortality has fallen substantially. In Brazil, infant mortality rates among the rural poor in the northeast are two to three times higher than rates in the urban south, though deaths due to infectious and parasitic diseases accounted for only 8 percent of all deaths in 1980, whereas they accounted for 80 percent of them in 1940.[16] These continuing differences suggest that progress in reducing mortality among the very poor and uneducated may require something other than more of the same programs that succeeded in reducing aggregate mortality in the past.

Third, countries such as Sri Lanka, China, and Korea, which have unusually high life expectancy given average income,[17] are where other factors and other programs have clearly mattered. In those countries, the barrier that intractable poverty and lack of behavioral change poses to mortality decline is less important because income is relatively well distributed, illiteracy is low, and basic health services are widespread.

In short, further mortality declines (at least among infants and children, where the bulk of deaths occur) are likely to stem from behavioral changes in relatively poor populations; though there may be some hope that new technologies (e.g., vaccines against diarrhea and respiratory infections) will emerge, at least some degree of technological pessimism is warranted.

What are the likely future sources of behavioral change and thus reductions in mortality, especially among the high-mortality poor? The most obvious is further increases in educational opportunities for women. Such increases will continue to contribute, especially in Africa and South Asia, where female enrollment ratios are still low. But there are two causes for concern about the continuing potential of higher female education. Much of the positive effect of increasing education may well be behind us, particularly given the evidence that the major effect of education in reducing mortality occurs among people who attain only a primary level of education. Most women in many countries have already reached this level.* Further increases in women's education are likely to come more slowly than those in the past, however. It is low in the predominantly Moslem countries of

---

*Cochrane, O'Hara, and Leslie report on seven micro-level studies, in most of which the variable used was mothers' literacy, or mothers' education (with the mean below completed primary), with the dependent variable either proportion surviving to some age or number of child deaths. Most studies occurred in low-income, low-education countries. The effects of mothers' education were always statistically significant and, in absolute terms, large.

Pakistan, Bangladesh, and those in the Arab world, where there are religious and cultural barriers to educating girls. Expansion of enrollment there is bound to occur, but probably not at the rapid rates achieved by other developing countries in the last several decades. Female education is also low in Africa. Ethiopia, Burkina Faso, and Sierra Leone all have primary school enrollment ratios below 50 percent.[18] Continuing economic difficulties there will probably preclude the rate of expansion of educational opportunities enjoyed by much of the rest of Africa in the 1960s and 1970s.

Further increases in income also hold some potential for bringing further mortality declines, since increases in household income encourage good nutrition, sanitation, and housing, (and ultimately eliminate "the poor" as a group). But the contribution of income gains at the national level has, as noted above, not been very important in the past (as the countries that have attained good health at low cost amply demonstrate), and even the minor gains attributable to income may be hard to duplicate. It is not clear that income increases will come at the same pace in many developing countries as they did in the past. The income gains of the 1960s and 1970s have already slowed down or reversed in the 1980s; the 1980s may or may not be an exception. Also, further income gains will have little effect on mortality unless they occur in groups that are poor; given diminishing returns to income gains in terms of mortality decline, and given current levels of average absolute income higher than in the past, the same income gains, shared among income groups in the same proportions as in the past, will matter less to mortality decline than they did. (Of course income gains that favored the poor more than did those of the past could have dramatic effects.)

A remaining potential source of further mortality declines and improvements in health will derive from increases in the demand for and delivery of simple but good-quality personal health services, including nutritional supplementation, particularly to the poor, who have limited access today in most countries. For such services to be effective, they must be in demand; they must be sought and understood by their clientele and held accountable by their clientele. Of critical importance are the correct use of effective drugs (against respiratory infections, tuberculosis, malaria), family planning, nutritional supplementation for children under three, and prenatal and obstetrical care; all these require behavioral change on the part of consumers. The difficulty is that with the exception of those countries and regions discussed above, most governments have not succeeded in bringing these simple services at reasonable quality to poor and vulnerable groups.

The critical question for the future is therefore whether more governments will succeed where most have to date not done well: in strengthening basic health services for the poor. Table 4 summarizes the past success and future potential of government and public-sector programs in bringing mortality reduction and health improvement to developing countries.

Fiscal Pressures and New Demands

The expenditure of central governments in developing countries rose dramatically from about 5 percent of the gross national product (GNP) in 1945 to almost 20 percent in the early 1970s. It has continued to rise since then, though more slowly, and in 1985 it was about 22 percent of GNP.[19] Excluding expenditures on social security, which are generally higher in industrial countries, the share of the public sector in GNP in developing countries now exceeds that in industrial countries and is more heavily dominated by direct investments and expenditures of state-owned enterprises. In general, expenditures of the public sector have risen faster than revenues, so that annual deficits have increased from less than 3 percent to over 4 percent since the early 1970s.[20]

The growing deficits do not bode well for spending on health or education (which as discussed above has potentially positive effects on health in addition to its other benefits). Between the early 1970s and 1985, the share of central government budgets in all developing countries going to health fell from 7 to 4 percent; the share going to education fell from 14 to 10 percent.[21] In some countries, particularly in Africa, the falling shares translated into real overall declines and even larger declines on a per capita basis. In seventeen out of twenty-five countries in Africa, real spending per potential pupil declined between 1972 and 1985.[22] The same is probably true for health expenditures. Though state and local governments may have taken up some of the slack in some countries, the dominance of central government spending in most of the developing world means that expenditures of other governments are not likely to have compensated.

TABLE 4. The Public Sector and Mortality Decline:
Past Success and Future Potential

Factors Associated with Mortality Reduction	Impact on Mortality in Developing Countries	Degree of Public-Sector Involvement	Future Potential
1. New technologies: Immunizations Pest control Antibiotics	All high, especially 1940–1965	High High Low	All low, without behavioral change
2. Education	High, especially 1960 to present	High	High, at least in principle
3. Other government programs (transport and communications, sanitation and waste disposal)	Low to moderate	High	Low to moderate
4. Basic personal health services, including nutritional supplementation	Low, except in a few settings (China, Kerala)	Low, except in a few settings, but potentially high	Moderate to high
5. Income (and thus higher private demand for nutrition, sanitation, and personal health services)	Low to moderate	Low	Moderate

In health, these fiscal pressures come at a time of rising demand for health care on the part of populations, particularly for costly and technology-intensive personal care, generally at the hospital. Demand for hospital care is high in relation to demand for "primary," or basic, services because people procrastinate, or have poor information about the benefits of prevention, or both. Demand for curative care will probably continue to rise for at least three reasons. One is higher average income: the income elasticity of demand for health care exceeds one (that is, a 1 percent increase in income leads to a greater than 1 percent increase in spending on health care). Higher income is also associated with higher number of trained physicians;

more physicians may create so-called supply-induced demand for more services. Also important, however, are changing demographic and epidemiological factors.

The aging of the population in developing countries, a result of fertility declines over the last two decades and the falling death rates, means that the prevalence of such chronic "adult" diseases as cancer, hypertension, and heart disease in comparison with parasitic diseases and the childhood infectious and diarrheal diseases is increasing. The number of people over age 65 in developing countries is expected to double between 1980 and 2000. By the year 2020, this elderly group will exceed 10 percent of the population in many developing countries, a proportion comparable to that of the United States today.

Brazil provides a telling example of the effects of changing demographic structure on the pattern of disease. In 1950 heart disease, stroke, cancer, and accidents accounted for 20 percent of deaths there; in 1980 they accounted for about 50 percent. Though there has been little change in the prevalence of these diseases to date (the increase in their relative contribution is due largely to a decline in the proportion of deaths caused by infectious and parasitic disease), changing age structure means that from now on their prevalence is likely to rise as the proportion of the elderly in the population increases. Age structure changes alone imply a 60 percent increase in deaths due to these diseases from 1980 to 2020.[23]

In addition, there are likely to be changes in epidemiological patterns as a result of increases in age-specific death rates from some of these chronic diseases. Age-specific rates are likely to rise because of increasing exposure to such risks as smoking, poor diet, and urban pollution. For example, increases in tobacco consumption in the developing world over the last forty years are likely to cause increases in the incidence of lung cancer comparable to the large increases experienced in Great Britain in the 1960s and 1970s and in the United States more recently (in both places the peak has already been passed).

These changing demographic and epidemiological patterns will put tremendous financial pressure on health systems in developing countries, even in the poorest countries where the "old" pattern of disease continues. By 1980 in Brazil, the treatment of patients with heart disease accounted for an estimated 25 percent of all in-patient costs and the allocation of public health resources for curative care had increased to about 85 precent of all spending (from 36 percent in 1965). Per capita health expenditures on persons over 60 were 3.5 times greater than the average for the population.*

Unfortunately, continuing increases in spending on hospital services for care of chronic disease will have little impact on the still high death rates in developing countries, particularly among the poor.† The estimated cost per life saved through preventive services (including maternal and child health care, immunization, promotion of good nutrition) and pest control programs ranges from $100 to $500; the estimated cost per life saved through curative treatment and care in private and public facilities ranges from $500 to $5,000.[24] Combined public and private spending on curative care in virtually all developing countries is already high in comparison with spending on preventive medicine and simple curative care (including drugs). The percentage of total health expenditure for curative care is between 70 and 85 percent, leaving only 15 to 30 percent for spending on preventive care and community services.[†25] Still further increases in spending on curative care will of course improve the welfare of some groups, particularly of urban adults.§ However, the cost will be high, particularly if the pressure of demand for such

---

*The cost burden could also rise because of the spread of AIDS, especially in Africa. The cost of treating AIDS patients in a typical African country could be as high as 10 percent of its current spending on health, even using what are modest estimates of current spending per patient on care (compared, for example, with spending in the United States). See Mead Over, *Testimony to the United States Presidential Commission on the Human Immunodeficiency Virus Epidemic* (Washington, D.C.: World Bank, 1988).

†It is worth clarifying at this point that not all hospital care need be costly, and even when costly, is not necessarily cost-ineffective. Small hospitals (say, of fifty beds or fewer) can be a critical part of an effective overall health system in which consumers can count on referral to higher levels of the system if their medical problems warrant referral. In general in this text, the term *hospital care* can be assumed to refer to hospitals at the tertiary level, facilities offering specialized and relatively high-cost services; even these may be a necessary part of an overall system that is cost-effective, in the sense of providing the full range of services society desires at minimum costs.

‡There is no correct allocation of total health expenditures, as Philip Musgrove points out in "E Quanto Mas Vale Prevenir que Curar?" *Economia*, Pontifica Universidad Catolica del Peru, 1987. He notes that it may be appropriate for the bulk of resources to go to dealing with the small proportion of the population with the most severe health problems, particularly if the cost of fully addressing the more common needs of the majority of the population is really very low.

§Indeed, it can be said that the health community has focused so heavily on reducing mortality through control of childhood diseases that the welfare gains associated with reducing adult mortality and morbidity have been almost completely overlooked.

services further reduces the already limited public spending on the more basic services.

Costs, moreover, could rise even more because of sophisticated medical technologies. Limiting the bill for curative care requires limiting the use of innumerable little-ticket items such as laboratory tests and X-rays and of a few big-ticket items such as organ transplants and kidney dialysis.[26] In Brazil, the use of X-rays has increased in the last two decades twice as fast as medical consultation.

In short, an accurate description of the current role of the state in improving health in developing countries must take into account the substantial financial commitment (either through direct provision by the state of services or through the financing of services through state insurance systems) to services that have limited benefits, at least in terms of reducing mortality. Moreover, given the trend over the last several decades and probable future pressures, it seems likely that whatever public resources are available for health may well go increasingly into costly curative hospital care unless the current role of the state in the health sector can be reoriented.

The Advent of "Bad" Government

Bad government comes in the form of bloated public sectors with substantial internal and external debt. Though its presence may well be overstated today (at least among members of the private-interest school of thought), there is increasing concern, at least among health and education professionals, that the public sector is less effective today than it was in the initial two or three decades of the postwar period.

The deteriorating performance of government in these sectors may have as much to do with changing patterns of demand as with inherent deterioration in government per se. In health, the aging of the population and the increase of chronic disease costs have made it difficult politically for governments to allocate public resources effectively. The success of governments in expanding coverage of national health insurance systems, especially in Latin America, has made control of costs in the system more difficult, especially where the mechanism is automatic reimbursement by the public insurer of charges to private providers; this coverage has probably fueled the rapid growth of spending on curative care. Similarly in education, past success has fueled demand for an increase in the already high proportion of public education resources that go to costly higher education; the argument that lower levels of education yield higher social returns is not politically important in face of the demand of the middle class that its children have the opportunity to get free university education.

Fiscal pressures in the 1980s have also probably contributed to a reduction in the efficiency of government spending on health. Though in the long run, the public sector may react to reduced resources for health by altering the use of its resources (by increasing spending on cost-effective basic health care), the reaction in the short run has been to protect spending on personnel. People are not easily laid off from public-service jobs. Another reaction has been to cut spending on nonpersonnel operating costs, including drugs, fuel for vehicles, and maintenance of physical plant and equipment.[27] These reactions have been exacerbated by shortages of foreign exchange, which is critical in most countries to the purchase of drugs, fuel, and equipment but not to the payment of wages. Because the nonpersonnel inputs are usually a small portion of total costs (less than 20 percent), they must be cut drastically to reduce total spending significantly. The price of a small financial saving is a large drop in the effectiveness of the system as a whole.

It may be no coincidence that the current pattern of government spending in health and education benefits the rich and middle class more than the poor. The concentration of public resources on hospital care and university systems results in part from the political pressure of the urban middle classes. Even where the rich rely heavily on private health services, the current pattern still provides valuable benefits to government officials and their middle-class colleagues. Moreover, making changes in systems that are now reasonably well developed is more difficult today, in this period of restricted growth, than they might have been when the system was growing more rapidly. Many of the groups that benefit from the current system (including doctors in the private as well as public sectors in many countries) are accustomed to the current arrangements.

Put another way, it is not necessary to regard the private-interest view of government as fundamentally "bad" to believe that today's pressures require that government be unusually "good," at least in the area of health, if it is to continue to be as effective as it was in improving health in the initial three decades of the postwar period.

The task is inherently more difficult, and the flexibility of the public sector is more restricted.

A MORE PRAGMATIC VIEW OF THE STATE'S ROLE IN HEALTH CARE

Though the state has played a critical and positive role in reducing mortality and improving health in developing countries in the postwar development period, there are reasons to doubt that the success can continue without a change in government's focus. The challenge now is to improve health among the poor. Three points merit discussion.

Public versus Private Goods

The generally accepted notion that health, including all health services and programs, is a public good needs to be reconsidered. The conventional definition of public goods covers goods and services that are subject to externalities (that is, not all benefits are internalized by producers or consumers, so that too little is consumed or produced); and to nonexclusivity (it is difficult to exclude beneficiaries, so that charges for the good cannot be levied). (Among public goods may also be included "merit goods," that is goods to which all citizens have a basic right, which should not be denied them for lack of income. How much of health should be included under merit goods is a critical question. Are heart bypass operations merit goods?)

Some health programs are almost pure public goods, for example spraying to protect all residents from a vector-borne disease, to which the nonexclusivity principle applies. Others are almost completely private goods (aspirin taken for a headache, for example). Most health programs and services are neither wholly public nor wholly private goods, however, but are of a mixed type: the consumer captures some purely private benefits, yet others also benefit from that person's consumption of the service. The person who is vaccinated receives a private benefit of protection, but others benefit as well because they are less likely to be exposed to the illness. The person who receives treatment for tuberculosis captures large private benefits; but because the disease is contagious, the public or community benefits as well.

The distinction between public and private goods is not synonymous with the distinction between preventive and curative care, as the tuberculosis example above indicates. Similarly, many prenatal care, hypertension screening, and family planning services are preventive but bring benefits that are primarily captured by those who receive them.

The distinction between private and largely public goods is useful, however, in terms of the likelihood that consumers will be willing to pay; in fact, this distinction is likely to be more useful than the conventional assumption that consumers will pay for curative services (which is generally true) but not for preventive services (which is generally not true when preventive services bring private benefits). There is, for example, ample evidence that people will pay for such preventive services as immunizations and "well baby" care (particularly when they are well-informed about the benefits), for family planning and prenatal care.

The need for a strong role for the state in the financing or direct provision of what are purely or largely public goods is most obvious. Thus, the logic of government financing (or as it happens, direct provision) of immunizations and of antimalarial spraying is clear. The logic of government financing of simple curative health services in poor rural areas, where the market for private provision of costly modern medical care may be poor because income is low, relies on the less tidy, but still compelling, merit-good argument. However, the logic of government financing of physician and hospital care in urban areas, where the private market for provision of such care is likely to be adequate (as generally demonstrated in many countries, including some in Africa, by the presence of physicians in private practice), is not clear. In urban areas, government may want to finance provision of such care to the poor because of the merit-good argument. But they need not finance such care to those able and willing to pay; indeed, resources spent this way almost surely compete with resources spent on basic services for the poor.

This last category of care, of physician and hospital care in urban areas, is the very category that generally absorbs the bulk of current government expenditures on health. Though some members of poor households undoubtedly benefit from government financing of curative care in hospitals, scattered evidence indicates that most benefits of these government subsidies go to the nonpoor. For example, even in referral systems that function well, in which many hospital patients come from rural areas, hospitals end up serving primarily urban residents, who are, on average, better off than rural residents. In developing countries, 70 to 90 percent of hospital clients live within ten kilometers of the facilities they use. As a result, in China, Colombia, Indonesia, and Malaysia the average health sector subsidy captured by urban households is five times larger than that captured by rural households.[28]

Note that the term *financing* was used in referring to public-sector involvement in health care services. The distinction between financing and provision is an important one, particularly given the current wave of interest in the privatization of government activities, outside if not inside the health sector. The public-good criterion for determining whether government should be involved in a particular health service applies to financing the service; it is irrelevant (with respect to this point) whether the service is provided by the state or by private providers. The potential harm of substantial public involvement in costly private services occurs as long as government (or the public through taxes) is financing the service, even if it is not providing. The public provision of such services, if they are privately financed (for example, through user charges for those able to pay), need not do harm.

The Search for "Market" Solutions

Governments will almost certainly continue to be involved in financing costly private health services and, in most developing countries, where such services are still rare, in their direct provision. Indeed, the likelihood is that there will be increasing state involvement in the provision of such care,[29] despite the counterexamples of Chile after the 1973 coup and the recent attempt of the conservative governments in Great Britain and the United States to increase the role of the private sector in health. Some researchers attribute this likelihood to the emergence of a "medical world economy" based on scientific medicine and the high-technology practice that derives from it. In this medical economy,

> hospitals have become the central organizations for the provision of care, and physicians with equivalent training the dominant practitioners. . . . the state has been called upon to take the lead as the only actor

with enough resources to be an effective buyer, or with sufficient power to control the other powerful actors in the international private sector.[30]

In addition, industrialization creates a need for protecting the working population against the risks of sickness and disability, and a "world ideology of modernization," they say, calls for a strong role for the state as the legitimate agency of rational progress in an area like health.[31] This view of the state's role is certainly implicit in the approach of the World Health Organization, for example, and other international bodies, including the World Bank, which in their efforts to introduce reforms of health systems that would emphasize primary health care have assumed that leadership in this area must come from government.[32]

There are other reasons to expect the involvement of governments in the provision of health services to grow—reasons intrinsic to the nature of the health sector. First, since the critical gap at the moment is in the provision of simple curative and preventive personal health services to the poor, it is difficult to imagine these organized and provided by private agents. (Though the traditional practice of medicine flourishes in many poor rural areas, few private physicians operate for profit in those areas; the only real private market is for prescription drugs.) Second, it is not easy to separate essentially private, usually curative, services, for which the nonpoor would and could pay, from preventive and curative services directed to the poor. This difficulty is most obvious in tertiary hospital care that is provided in the context of a large referral system, including publicly provided outlying health posts.

In this context, what mechanisms could encourage a reorientation of government's role toward "public" goods, especially more public spending on basic care for the poor? At least three approaches are under discussion: the use of selective user charges—particularly charges to the nonpoor for private curative services; decentralization of government provision of health care; and greater use by governments of private-sector providers, including nonprofit, nongovernmental organizations (NGOs) and the private sector. These are three of the four policy reforms suggested for consideration in a recent World Bank policy study.[33] Each of these represents a market-oriented approach, in the sense that each brings some advantages of a competitive market to public services.

Selective user fees are based on the idea that even though the state is providing a private service (in part because it is so difficult to separate the provision of private and public services), individual consumers can in principle finance those private services, since they are both willing and able to pay. The problem of distinguishing poor and nonpoor is discussed below.

Decentralization is based on the idea that the public provision of service will be more responsive and accountable to the needs of local clients the closer it is geographically and bureaucratically to those clients. The problems of making regional branches of centralized bureaucracies responsive or of finding ways to make true local governments self-sufficient are discussed below.

The privatization of service is based on the idea that even when government is financing some part of a service, it need not provide the entire package of services directly. Governments can subsidize some part of the costs of NGOs in providing services (subsidizing, for example, the cost of services to the indigent) and even some costs of private practitioners. Canada and the United States use this model by paying private providers to care for the indigent (in the United States through the Medicaid system). The problems of adequate regulation of the private sector, and of controlling costs, are discussed below.

Information and Education

The third point in considering a more pragmatic approach to the role of the state in health care is the need for enhanced dissemination of knowledge about health. Information and education about health are largely public goods. They deserve mention because in terms of resources they have received little attention from government health agencies. In developing countries it is rarely possible to glean from information about public health expenditures the proportion they devote to information and education programs. It would be useful to confirm my suspicion that the proportion falls below that of the developed countries, even though the level of general understanding on the part of populations in developing countries is probably not nearly as good. Information about drugs and their appropriate use is one example; information about family planning is another. Even where the private sector provides drugs and contraceptives in response to consumer demand, government cannot abdicate the role of providing information that would advise and help protect people. In

Brazil, most women using the pill for contraception obtain it at pharmacies virtually without attention to medical contraindications. Throughout the developing world, a tendency to multiple prescriptions and overuse of antibiotics hurts consumers' pocketbooks and possibly their health.

PROBLEMS AND CAVEATS

Each of these points raises new issues—issues rarely and only recently treated in the literature on health and development, most of which has focused on the need for increased resources for primary health care and the relative effectiveness of various aspects of primary health care. These can only be briefly noted here.

Means Testing

The use of selective user charges in public facilities requires that the poor be distinguished from the nonpoor. There is ample evidence that differential or sliding-scale fees, which allow the poor to pay less or even nothing for services, are commonly used by private physicians and traditional practitioners, and by nongovernmental (for example, missionary-provided) services. Some scope for means tests also exists in the middle-income developing countries with reasonably well-developed tax systems and high levels of literacy (for instance, Jamaica and Cuba). Emerging evidence also suggests the possibility of means testing at the community level in rural Africa and Asia.[34] Since selective user charges are ideally applied at the tertiary level in urban hospitals, the simple solution of geographical targeting is not usually applicable. On the other hand, in the context of a good referral system, the use of "bypass" fees (under which only those who bypass the first level of the system and come directly to hospitals for nonemergency cases are charged a fee) provides a kind of means test. Other approaches need to be tested, and a great deal more study of the effects of fees on households' use of services and on health outcomes needs to be made.[35]

Meaningful Decentralization

In most parts of the developing world, local government with real power to tax and allocate resources hardly exists. Even in countries like Nigeria and Brazil with federal systems, the revenue-raising capacity of municipal-level governments is extremely limited, and in the case of Brazil it is actually deteriorating. The use of transfer mechanisms that are relatively automatic and transparent to transfer resources from the center to local areas would increase the accountability of local government to local populations for the use of funds, but in fact such transfers are relatively rare; in general, it is difficult for central governments to resist the temptations of political favoritism that transfers invite. In turn, central governments may fear that funds provided to local governments without oversight will be used for local political purposes rather than for long-term social investments. Mechanisms must thus be sought that combine some automaticity in transfers with some use of incentives related to performance and coverage of services; incentives are especially useful in a context in which competition is allowed among public providers as well as between public and private providers.

Complete reliance on local revenues, even were it possible, might not be desirable in any case since it would not ensure adequate redistribution of public funds in countries with marked differences in the regional distribution of assets and income.

In short, it is difficult to separate the problem of improving health services through decentralization from larger questions about local governance and revenue-raising capacity in developing countries, as well as questions of earmarking of public tax revenues to sectors and regions. In Africa and parts of the Indian subcontinent, the problem may be particularly intractable because of the reluctance of central or state governments to yield power to secessionist regional and local groups.

Regulation and Cost Controls

Greater reliance on the private sector, including nongovernmental organizations, is only possible if governments can exercise reasonably well a regulatory and quality-control function. The same is true where the central government devolves provision of services to local governments. Reliance on consumers is inadequate in an area like health, where information is poor and people are often required to make rapid decisions under stress. The entire issue of regulation in developing-country health systems has received little attention in the international health-policy community. It is, of course, closely tied to the limited role of government in developing countries in the provision of health-specific information and education.

Cost controls are an even more difficult issue, especially where the government finances some provision of health services by the private sector. The acceleration of costs in Brazil and other countries of Latin America as coverage of health care through national insurance systems expanded is one example. The recent difficulties in the United States with controlling costs are another. The issue has hardly been explored in developing-country contexts.

The Insurance Problem

The World Bank has suggested that governments make an effort to expand health insurance coverage by making such coverage (provided by the state or privately) compulsory for those with regular salaried employment in government and large firms. In the short run, such an approach is bound to reduce the high subsidies currently received by the middle class through access to free public services in urban specialized hospitals. In the long run, universal insurance (publicly or privately provided) in the context of a progressive tax system, may be a reasonable approach, particularly with the use of deductibles and copayments to discourage excessive use. However, as the experience in Latin America indicates, widespread access to insurance can exacerbate the problem of cost control (in a world of ever more costly technologies and in the presence of other distortions such as free medical education). In industrial countries with universal insurance such as England and Canada, cost control is the dominant issue. Again, it can be fairly said that there has been little systematic attention in the international health community to treatment of this issue in a developing-country context.

ENDNOTES

[1] Simon Kuznets, *Modern Economic Growth* (New Haven: Yale University Press, 1966), 200.

[2] World Bank, *World Development Report* (New York: Oxford University, 1984), 64.

[3] Frederick Golladay and Bernhard Liese, "Health Problems and Policies in the Developing Countries," World Bank staff working paper no. 412 (Washington, D.C.: World Bank, 1980), 22.

[4]See World Bank, *World Development Report* (1984), 5, where the following sources are cited: Carl Mosk, *Patriarchy and Fertility: Japan and Sweden, 1880–1960* (New York: Academic Press, 1983); N. Keyfitz and W. Flieger, *World Population: An Analysis of Data* (Chicago:University of Chicago Press, 1968); L. J. Zimmerman, *Poor Lands, Rich Lands: The Widening Gap* (New York: Random House, 1965).

[5]Alberto Palloni, "Mortality Decline in Latin America," paper presented at the annual meeting of the Population Association of America, April, 1979, p. 28 and Table 10.

[6]Samuel Preston, "Causes and Consequences of Mortality Declines in Less Developed Countries During the Twentieth Century," in *Population and Economic Change in Developing Countries,* ed. Richard A. Easterlin (Chicago: Chicago University Press, 1980).

[7]Susan H. Cochrane, Donald O'Hara, and Joanne Leslie, "The Effects of Education on Health," World Bank staff working paper no. 405 (Washington, D.C.: World Bank, 1980). See also John C. Caldwell, "Routes to Low Mortality in Poor Countries," *Population and Development Review* 12 (2) (June 1986):171–220.

[8]World Bank, *World Development Report* (New York: Oxford University Press, 1987); and Jee-Peng (Tan) and Michael Haines, "Schooling and Demand for Children: Historical Perspectives," World Bank staff working paper no. 677 (Washington, D.C.: World Bank, 1985).

[9]World Bank, *World Development Report* (New York: Oxford University Press, 1988), 13–15.

[10]UNESCO, *World Illiteracy at Mid-Century: A Statistical Study* (Paris: UNESCO, 1957), and World Bank, *World Development Report* (1988).

[11]Scott B. Halstead, Julia A. Walsh, and Kenneth S. Warren, eds., *Good Health at Low Cost* (New York: The Rockefeller Foundation, 1985).

[12]World Bank, *World Development Report* (1988).

[13]For example, see James M. Buchanan, *Liberty, Market and the State: Political Economy in the 1980s* (Brighton, England: Wheatsheaf Books, 1985).

[14]Davidson Gwatkin, *The End of an Era? Recent Evidence Indicates Unexpected Changes in the Pace and Pattern of Third World Mortality Declines* (Washington, D.C.: Overseas Development Council, May 1980).

[15]See W. Henry Moseley and Lincoln C. Chen, "An Analytical Framework for the Study of Child Survival in Developing Countries," *Population and Development Review* (supplement to vol. 10) (1984):25–48.

[16]John Briscoe, "Brazil: Chronic Diseases and AIDS Sector Study: Issues Paper," a World Bank memorandum (13 May 1988).

[17]Nancy Birdsall, "Population Growth and Poverty in the Developing World," *Population Bulletin* 35 (5) (Washington, D.C.: Population Reference Bureau, Inc., 1980).

[18]World Bank, *World Development Report* (1987).

[19]World Bank, *World Development Report* (1988).

[20]Ibid.

[21]Ibid.

[22]Ibid.

[23]Briscoe.

[24]John S. Akin, Nancy Birdsall, and David de Ferranti, *Financing Health Services in Developing Countries* (Washington, D.C.: World Bank, 1987).

[25]Ibid., 19.

[26]Briscoe.

[27]Akin, Birdsall, and de Ferranti.

[28]For other examples of urban bias, see Akin, Birdsall, and de Ferranti, 22. Regarding the urban bias of public spending on health in China, see Nicholas Prescott and Dean T. Jamison, "The Distribution and Impact of Health Resource Availability in China," *International Journal of Health Planning and Management* 1 (1984):45–56; and Nicholas Prescott and Dean T. Jamison, "Health Sector Finance and Expenditures in China," *PHN Technical Note* GEN-14 (Washington, D.C.: Population, Health, and Nutrition Department, World Bank, May 1983).

[29]Julio Frenk and Avedis Donabedian, "State Intervention in Medical Care: Types, Trends and Variables," *Health Policy and Planning* 2 (1) (1987):17–31.

[30]Ibid., 26.

[31]Ibid., 25–26.

[32]See "Health," sector policy paper (Washington, D.C.: World Bank, 1980); and the preamble to the constitution of the World Health Organization, cited in Frenk and Donabedian.

[33]Akin, Birdsall, and de Ferranti.

[34]Ibid. See also Charles Griffin, "The Main Themes of a Paper on Means Testing in Developing Countries," draft paper for Rockefeller Foundation, September 1988, and Ronald T. Vogel, *Cost Recovery in the Health Care Sector,* technical paper no. 82 (Washington, D.C.: World Bank, 1988).

[35]For a recent study, see Paul Gertler and Jacques van der Gaag, "The Willingness to—Pay—for Medical Care; Evidence from Two Developing Countries," draft manuscript, Washington, D.C., World Bank, 1980.

Comments on Nancy Birdsall's Essay

JAMES P. GRANT: On Nancy Birdsall's central question, should the development community rethink the corporate role of the state in improving health in the developing world, the answer is clearly yes. There may have been an advantage in my telling the group at a conference two months ago at Talloires, where the heads of the major development agencies met, under the sponsorship of WHO, UNICEF, UNDP, the World Bank, and the Rockefeller Foundation, with many health ministers. Of the fifteen health ministers there, ten were from the principal countries of the world, including ministers from China, India, Nigeria, and Mexico. The Talloires conclusion is worth quoting:

> Remarkable health progress has been achieved during the past decade. Global recognition that healthy children and healthy parents are central to human and national development is steadily increasing. Consensus has been reached on the strategy for providing central community primary health programs. The international community has become engaged in partnership with national governments in the creation of successful global programs, ensuring that they will have financial support and the appropriate technology.

In their conclusion, they spoke about certain targets for the year 2000, which would include the global eradication of polio. More importantly, they believed that it would be possible to achieve the reduction of infant and under-five mortality rates in all countries by half between 1980 and the year 2000, thereby saving the lives and preventing the crippling of more than 100 million small children. How is one to explain this optimism?

First, we have today in the child mortality area—and I would argue that the same is true in the adult mortality area—two-thirds to three-quarters of the knowledge of what is needed to substantially improve nutritional status and health at a low financial and political cost. Consider, for example, the biggest single killer of children in the world today—dehydration—the consequence of diarrhea. The simplest way to prevent it is to empower families with knowledge about the washing of hands, the boiling of water, sanitary practices, and the like. And, if dehydration from constant diarrhea occurs, there is a low-cost (less than 10 U.S. cents) technological response that can be administered in the home. Half of all mothers are still not aware of this, and of those that are only half are applying it.

On immunization, where we have seen spectacular progress in the recent years, it now costs only 50 cents to buy all the vaccines necessary to immunize a child for life against the six leading child-killing diseases in developing countries. Yet, these diseases are still taking 10,000 children a day.

Second, in the last twenty years we have experienced an incredible revolution in the capacity to communicate with the poor majority within the developing world. There has been a communications revolution that has brought radio, schools, roads, and retail outlets everywhere. Technology has brought television into even the most remote villages of Nepal. There is generally a video room in the villages. Even where there is no electricity or light, the television runs on a storage battery. There is an incredible capacity to communicate to the poor majority today where there is the political will to do so at this time.

Our problem five years ago in the health field was that its role, its relative status, was being downplayed. It was not considered politically important. What we have been able to do in an increasing number of countries recently is change the political climate in respect to the kinds of health care that are thought to be necessary. There is a move away from hospitals. In Indonesia, hospital construction costs have been reduced by some 80 percent, while expansion of maternal and child health facilities at the community level has taken place at a greatly accelerated rate. We have seen a parallel problem in Nigeria.

In Africa last September, the health ministers came together and proposed to press forward with the expansion of adult and child health care for the entire population of sub-Saharan Africa over the next six or seven years. They proposed a compact. They, on their side, will pursue decentralization of health services in a major way; they will reverse their long-standing policy of free drugs, to be replaced with a cost recovery and local financing program. The compact would be with the outside world, which would be asked to provide essential drugs, required to make the system work. What makes the program more workable than most people would think is that systems for quick and efficient distribution of drugs have been developed. In Tanzania, 35 essential drugs are being provided on a continuous supply basis for a total cost of about 50 cents a person per year. This may seem incredible, but it relates to procurement practices that WHO and UNICEF have been able to introduce. Vaccines that cost $18 in New York City to buy, we are able to obtain for 50 cents. Similarly, we are able to get 1,000 tetracycline tablets for only $12.

A major problem with drugs is that they are so numerous. If you can limit them to 35, or even better, some would argue, to 20, you can train all medical personnel in their use, in their merits. When there are 200 or 300 drugs, you cannot, particularly when they are available on a very intermittent basis, as in the existing supply system. Thinking on these matters is moving faster than we realize, particularly in the face of crisis pressures that compel governments to pull back in their services. Given the fiscal situation, there is a willingness to look for new measures that are politically attractive, that produce significant results.

Some 2.5 million children have not died, and a comparable number have avoided life-long disability in the past twelve months because of these accelerated programs since the early 1980s.

ARTHUR KLEINMAN: I am an anthropologist and a physician at Harvard. I heard this morning a kind of pathos and poignancy about where development has gone. In the last minutes, we have been hearing an answer to it; in health, it appears that the reformist tendencies that got us going in the first instance are about to pay off. With all due respect to Mr. Grant, whose work I greatly appreciate and whose message I would affirm in terms of desirability, I would like to side with Nancy Birdsall's analysis. I may be even more pessimistic than she is. I think there is great uncertainty and tremendous scholarly controversy over what the terms of the unprecedented decline in mortality are. Clearly, as Lincoln Chen knows better than I, there have been a number of transitions. The transition from epidemic disease as a substantial source of mortality has something to do with the organization of nation-states, the organization of local subpopulations, the social order. With endemic diseases like tuberculosis, control has something to do with housing, nutrition, sewage, water control, and the like. Immunization, together with some of the other public health kinds of intervention that we have heard about, has great importance. These changes have less to do with health services than with social change.

The China case is very uncertain, and I strongly doubt, Nancy, the significance for improved health you attach to the barefoot doctors. As David Mechanic and I show in a paper in 1978, for 50 percent of the medicines in the bags of these barefoot doctors—we interviewed a large number at a few sites—they had no idea what they were and certainly were not able to prescribe them. More than that, many of the other medicines they carried were nonspecific for curing disorders. It is hard to know what biomedically effective services they gave.

I do not think that all that people want is necessarily proven efficacy of health services. What they want has to do with their perception of illness as suffering, their perception of services being potentially effective or at least responsive in some way to the human burden of distressing complaints. Perception, I think, is particularly important. It is both the good news and the bad news—the good news because it is the basis for rationalizing help seeking, the bad news because when we look in our own society, all the things mentioned as desirable and achievable in the Third World are confounded. Ours is a society in which there is an immense amount of health education for the public, much of it misinformation but a substantial amount that is correct information. Yet there is underuse and misuse of services, wide misperception of the efficacy of biomedicine for every kind of problem, and widespread misuse of all the kinds of drugs that have been mentioned. That is not just carried out by the public; it is carried out by the profession as well.

You say that there has not been much debate about the relationship of health and government; in fact, there have been tremendous debates. If you think about the relationship of government and health services, of debate over the creation of national health services or over the organization and delivery of health services, all well documented, there is abundant discussion.

The last point I would make is the most pessimistic. Side by side with what Lincoln Chen often calls the unprecedented decline in mortality is another development that asks what direction health is really going in, what indices we ought to use to measure health. The costs of social development and of ill health going on simultaneously with health gains need to be considered. Many phenomena, including suicide, alcohol, alcohol-related violence, drug abuse, family breakdown, child abuse, clinical psychiatric conditions from depression to anxiety disorders, behavior problems in the youth and the elderly, are increasing. This increase is not simply an artifact of better statistical research. In the last decade, there has been significant evidence of such increases occurring in all the major cultural areas of the world. This represents an interesting and ominous set of experiences that, quite possibly, is the cost of development or some parallel process which development is unresponsive to. Moreover, this is not just a phenomenon among the poor; it crosses all classes.

In addition to that, there is a process that is equally as ominous that has to do with chronic disorders and child survival; it is the process of disability, which we hear very little about. The country that I do my principal research in, the People's Republic of China, has 45 million physically and mentally disabled individuals. Again, this creates an agenda of problems for which the health services and government policy have not developed effective answers. With the increase of the aged in the developing world, this is going to be a large burden for the future. When you think of the fact that the frail elderly average somewhere between three and four chronic diseases per person for those over seventy-five, the prospect for the future, I would say, is not clear-cut. If we are going to treat health as a major dimension of measuring the effects, consequences, and significance of development, we would do well to be prepared for the possibility of ambiguity, even for the possibility that, when behavioral and mental health indices are included, the outcomes may get worse.

LINCOLN C. CHEN: Nancy Birdsall's diagnosis is penetrating, but her hypotheses regarding new factors and emerging constraints may have mixed validity. Some caution should be exercised regarding her implicit proscription for the withdrawal of government and increased privatization of some aspects of health care for the sake of efficiency and effectiveness. As Jim Grant noted, the global health revolution of this century, which has accelerated in the past several decades, is one of the fundamental human achievements of our times. Many people in both industrialized and developing societies, however, have been "left behind." Health progress has been enjoyed very unevenly, both between countries as well as within countries. Improved longevity will lead by the next century, moreover, to a world population of more than 6 billion, nearly fourfold the number at the beginning of this century.

What about Nancy's proposition concerning diminishing returns to health knowledge and technologies? This conclusion may be premature. I cite here two examples, one in developing and a second in an industrialized society. UNICEF, for example, has been striving for the mass dissemination of simple, effective, low-cost health technologies, such as immunizations and oral rehydration therapy. In India, more than 50 percent of children remain unimmunized from the six basic infections of childhood, however. What a remarkable difference broader coverage of immunization could make on child survival! And there appears to be considerable space for improvements in our own country as well. In the past 15 years, we have witnessed remarkable gains in longevity among white adult men. The rate of increase, in fact, has been so significant that if current rates were to continue, American men would live an average of 150 years by the end of the next century! So, it is not at all clear that we should be pessimistic over the possibilities for future advances.

Historical lessons with regard to government intervention also cast doubt upon Nancy's proposition. Health successes in developing countries have been precisely in those societies that have adopted strong government policies and public-sector investments in health services. Countries that are "health successes" (in the sense that their health status is substantially better than what would be predicted by their gross national products) are Sri Lanka, China, Costa Rica, Cuba, Chile, and Jamaica. Most of the investment has not necessarily been targeted at preventive or promotive health services. Rather, there has been substantial investment in curative and hospital-based services. It is often puzzling to draw direct paths between longevity improvements and these medical investments. In industrialized countries, Great Britain enjoyed great improvement in health during World War II, when government intervention in health (food rationing, health care, etc.) was most active. So, it is not clear that government's role in health necessarily declined or ended during a particular era.

We are at a point where we are uncertain about the optimal mix of government and private engagement in health; indeed, the uncertainty extends to many aspects of social development. The debate ultimately may not focus on generic issues of government versus private. The debate, I suspect, may take on a more culture-, time-, and location-specific character. What's good in one society at a particular time may not be good for another. In any case, I agree with Jim Grant's conclusion that, whether from the Left or the Right, support for improving health is becoming increasingly popular with the political leadership. "Good health" can be an important slogan for any populist-oriented regime.

KAMLA CHOWDHRY: I was very interested in the comments that Jim Grant made about boiling water. He also mentioned the washing of hands. I wanted to bring to the notice of this group that there are many areas, at least in India, where you do not have enough fuel to cook even two meals a day. Therefore, the whole problem of health care, which depends on sufficient water for cleaning hands or for boiling, is a serious one. Planning commission documents say that our need for fuelwood alone is 133 million tons. We produce 36. We are today short of 97 million tons. If we want health to be based on good cleanliness—boiling water, washing hands, and the like—health issues will have to be related to environmental issues.

Abiola Irele

Education and Access to Modern Knowledge

THE MOST DISTINCTIVE MARKER of development in the current use of the term is the degree of technological capacity a society or a nation can bring to bear on the management of its environment for productive purposes. In this understanding of the term we see a correlation between the growth of science and its application to technology and economic development.

Our world today has a wide spectrum of societies and cultures coexisting at various levels of technological development, making for a tremendous disparity in material conditions. At one end of the spectrum, we still have *primitive societies*—in the strict academic sense, having nothing to do with the essential human quality of their members, which finds full expression in ways other than technological inventiveness—and at the other end, *industrial societies,* some of which are being transformed under our very eyes into postindustrial societies.

The relationship between models of civilization in the contemporary world is not only vertical—exemplified by relations between the developed industrial world of the "North" and the underdeveloped, premodern world of the "South"—but also horizontal: a complicated mosaic of life-styles and aspirations as well as of values exist in the underdeveloped countries. The division between classes, between the elite and the rest of the population, between urban and rural areas—these quite often follow cultural lines in terms of the mix between the indigenous and the imported. Everywhere the Western

121

model serves as a paradigm, and it helps to create the divergence in modes of thought and social organization.

Modes of communication employed by these various societies range from pure orality at one end, through writing and large-scale literacy at the other, which is evolving at the moment into a predominantly electronic mode. One of the enabling conditions for the development of technology has been the degree to which oral communication can be extended by writing, so that information is passed on both over space and over time. The fund of knowledge on which society depends for its survival and continued development is not only progressively built up but is consolidated. The technology of communication has played a much more important role in this than the preservation of facts and the recollection of experience; it has also determined a mode of perception that has influenced the development of modern science as a valid representation of the world. From this point of view, Western science can be considered an *inscription* of the world. The comprehensive frame that it seeks to project has included a representation of non-Western peoples and cultures in a "discourse," elaborated and explained by the discipline of anthropology, which serves as a means of establishing and enforcing a hegemony at the ideological level. This is a reflection of the relations of power on the ground between the West and the rest of the world. At the present moment, the technology of communication has advanced so far that the processing of information has become in itself a reinforcing element in the expansion of modern technology in the developed world. What is more, the development of new technologies, of communication and information, has created practically an entirely new sphere of knowledge on which the developed world has a virtual monopoly.

These two factors in the cultural composition of our universe at present—the technological stratification of peoples and cultures across the world as well as within contemporary societies and the communication modes available to them—have political significance. It seems to me, however, that discussions of their significance have not focused sufficiently on the correlation between a high level of technology, on the one hand, and economic and political power on the other. In the elaboration of the so-called dependency theory by Third World scholars such as Samir Amin, Claude Aké, Archie Mafeje, and others, for example, there has been a tendency to give priority to purely economic and ideological factors in the vision of the modern world. They divide it into a "center" located in the developed world and a "periphery" represented by the rest of humanity. The facts are much simpler than they have made out: the technologically developed societies enjoy an economic and political advantage in the world as a direct consequence of their technological capacity. Moreover, they have tended to dominate the less technologically oriented part of humanity, their own development being to a great extent dependent on the exploitation of resources (both human and material) and of markets beyond their borders. These technologically developed societies still feel required to command the resources of the rest of the world to sustain their internal economic and social processes and to maintain the momentum of their own development. In other words, what is now called neocolonialism is as much a function of economic need and technological power as was classic colonialism. This combination of economic need and technological power has been largely responsible for the peculiar nature of international relations in the modern period. In the ethic that has resulted, there is an opposition between dominant and dependent economies, and this has contributed to the continuing imbalance of power and material prosperity between the developed and the underdeveloped world.

The present ordering of the world derives in great part from the role that science and technology play on a global scale. To simplify, the historical ascendancy of the West in modern times has been due largely to the development of the scientific spirit and its intense cultivation, especially since the eighteenth century, over a wide area of human activity. This has led to an increasingly adequate explanation of the natural world and to the steady development of material conditions that have favored the emergence of an industrial and technological capacity unprecedented in human history. This is admittedly a very simplified view of history, but it provides an explanation for the prevailing attitudes in the non-Western world. They have crystallized around an association of technology with Western imperialism and thus produced an unfortunate ambivalence toward the Western model of economic development.

This underlines the essential contradiction of the intellectual expression of modern nationalism in the non-Western world, which can be seen as a form of cultural reaction to the historical trauma of colonial domination. In Africa, especially, this intellectual response was predicated on the affirmation of a fundamental cultural difference involving a nonscientific and often antirationalist posture, as, for example, in the concept of negritude. At the same time, with the recognition of the necessity for modernization, especially as an immediate and integral function in the process of nation building with which all African countries have been preoccupied in the postcolonial period, there has been a growing awareness of the importance of science and technology as a determining factor in development. It is beginning to be apparent that the contradiction between these two positions and the ambivalence it involves is at the heart of the failure and frustration that have marked development efforts in Africa over the past thirty years or so. The effects of this contradiction have been most marked in education.

While there has been nominal acceptance of the importance of science and technology for development, the functional goal of education to secure the basis for the initiation and maintenance of the development process has not been properly perceived, much less pursued with a sense of commitment. The connection between education and development seems at first sight direct. It has been taken to consist in the application of the training received by individuals at every stage and level of the educational system to the practical requirements of modern life. In this limited view, education is represented simply as the acquisition of skills appropriate to certain specialized tasks that are peculiar to a technically oriented mode of life. This view has the merit of going beyond education as a general socialization of the members of the community according to standard norms. But I think we need a broader conception.

We must see education as the acquisition of a new kind of mental equipment, appropriate for a new context for life. This amplification has long-term implications. It suggests that modern education is intended to increase the capacity of the community to undertake the profound transformations that development, in the modern sense, calls for. This implies the enhancement of the capacity of the community itself so to manage its environment as to effect significant improvements in the quality of life. This wider meaning of education offers a special challenge for us in the underdeveloped world, for, in the Third World countries, education has the additional function of

fashioning minds for the reception of modern technological civilization, which, I hardly need to add, is now accepted worldwide as the
defining context of contemporary life.

Education in the modern context, for us in the underdeveloped
world, especially in Africa, means nothing less than the development
of a new mental universe. It is not only a question of acquiring new
skills but also of orienting our conceptual disposition to the model of
modern science. This implies the systematic investigation of the
natural world and, ideally, objective reflection on the problems of the
social world—the fundamental principle of modern science. The need
to understand the world and human experience that takes place
within it thus underlies all scientific culture. This underlying spirit
finds its clearest expression today in the activity of research. It is
important to note in this regard that the significance of scientific
research goes far beyond the practical value of the applications of its
findings.

The real significance of scientific research as carried on today,
particularly in the Western academies, is that it serves first as a form
of discipline, prescribing procedures in matters such as observation,
measurement, and verification of results. These lead to habits of
thought and standards of performance in relation to an ideal of
objective truth. In this way, scientific research fulfills a wide social
function. It serves as an institutional support for the total educational
system, which is conceived both as the transmission of existing
knowledge and the creation and dissemination of new knowledge, all
made available to the general culture. Thus, modern science becomes
a cultural mode that permeates the whole of society.

Against this background of science as a mode of cultural expression in the context of modern civilization, I would now like to
examine the problems we have encountered in Africa with regard to
education and its bearing on development. This examination will be
largely intuitive and will therefore focus very much on the Nigerian
experience, which may, however, be taken as representative of the
general African situation.

The effort that has gone into this expansion of education over all
of Africa seems admirable, except that it has produced disappointing
results. After over thirty years of effort and expenditure, education in
Africa is yielding progressively fewer results today in terms of

contribution to economic development. Although the premium placed on education by African governments is justified in principle, the basis of policy has been falsified from the very beginning by superficial considerations. It is, I think, fair to say that education in Africa has generally been oriented to social goals, with implications for individual expectations, rather than to those of general economic and scientific development, having as a primary objective a fundamental transformation of the culture. The explanation for this orientation seems to me to reside in the fact that, because of its role in the creation of a new elite during the colonial period (as documented by the Nigerian historian Ade Ajayi in the case of Nigeria and with special reference to the action of the Christian missions) education has been valued in Africa primarily as a means of social promotion. Precisely for this reason the question of providing educational facilities has presented itself almost everywhere on the continent as a political issue.

These social and political pressures account for the hasty expansion of education undertaken by African governments in the years after independence, and for the lack of proper planning and the poor organization with which almost everywhere the program was carried out. What we have had in effect has been more an appearance of educational planning than the real substance. In many cases, it has meant bureaucratic management of education rather than a meaningful direction of education toward properly conceived goals of development. (One can cite the lack of a coordinated policy of curriculum reform and a concerted effort in teacher training as support for this observation.)

The word *disaster* is, in my opinion, not too strong to describe the result of this superficial orientation of educational policy. The indications can be seen in the output from the primary and secondary levels, in the mass production of semiliterates who are useful neither to themselves nor to the society. They have received training neither for specific skills nor for the kind of independent development of their mental faculties that would enable them to function in society, least of all in the modern society evolving out of the old structures of the traditional world.

The effects of this failure of educational policy at the primary and secondary levels are even more apparent at the tertiary level, where the same policy of hasty, uncoordinated expansion has been pursued.

The example of Nigeria is particularly instructive. Between 1970 and 1982 (the years of the so-called oil boom) the number of university-level institutions increased from six to twenty-five, this as a matter of deliberate policy by both the federal and the state governments. The need to train manpower for development programs was constantly invoked as a convenient rationale for an indiscriminate course of action. This expansion was inspired much more by political considerations than by any genuine appraisal of needs and possibilities. The creation of new universities in particular areas was seen as part of the national sharing of benefits from the apparent prosperity the country enjoyed at the time, and the policy was initiated and pursued largely as a method of scoring political points. Indeed, the political complexion this policy of expansion took on became increasingly evident in the direct intervention by governments in the Nigerian federation in university affairs.

Instead of consolidating the handful of existing universities for effective use of resources in teaching and research, it was decided to create more universities, in the confident expectation of a steady level of economic prosperity from oil revenues to keep them going. The oil boom years in Nigeria have been followed by a serious recession, developing into the present economic crisis. The policy of uncontrolled university expansion is one of the signs of improvidence, compounded by widespread corruption and inefficiency, which characterized the management of the Nigerian economy in those years and which has led to today's situation. In the universities there was much evidence of poor judgment and inefficient management of resources induced by the same mood of euphoria and the same careless approach to national affairs as was shown in official and government circles.

The effect of this situation on the university system in Nigeria has been shattering. The quality of university education in Nigeria—and almost certainly in other African universities—has sharply declined as a result of expansion. The emphasis on numbers at the lower levels of the educational system, combined with the inadequate preparation for the higher level that this has brought about, as well as the pressures on the universities for what was insisted upon as a democratic policy of admission, has meant that the average standard of the students entering the universities in the past fifteen years or so has been, to say the least, inappropriate. The science departments, for instance, generally complain that students admitted for science courses do not have a sufficient foundation in mathematics to follow their courses properly. And in the humanities, students have little competence in organizing or expressing their thoughts. (A universal problem, perhaps, but the scale in our context cannot be compared to what obtains in the developed world, especially as our situation is complicated by the use of second languages, the European languages.) The majority of students we receive are practically unteachable, at least to what we used to regard as acceptable standards. To this difficult problem must be added the ambitious proliferation of academic courses and programs in all the universities, which has put an unbearable strain on teaching and administrative facilities as well as on resources. All this effort would have been worth making if it had been guided by a discernible sense of direction. University education was expanded, however, for no more than a demonstration effect. The bankruptcy of our educational policy at the university level has been amply demonstrated by the overproduction of graduates, who can find employment neither in the diminished job market we now have nor on their own.

The greatest damage has been to the university as an institution. Because resources have had to be stretched, all the universities in Nigeria now suffer from an acute shortage of facilities. So severe indeed has been the rundown of the infrastructure in some of the older universities that routine teaching is difficult and research often impossible. At the University of Ibadan, for example, which is my alma mater and now the university where I teach, we have been battling for the past ten years with supplying water and electricity. Scientific instruments, not the most sophisticated, have broken down and cannot be repaired for lack of spare parts or expertise. The purchase and installation of serviceable equipment is out of the question because of foreign-exchange problems; even the most common chemicals and reagents are in such short supply that science teaching at the university has to do without the standard discipline of experiments. In these conditions, no serious research effort is possible. The university is supposed to be a point of reference for an advanced culture in a context of underdevelopment but is itself reduced to primitive conditions.

This deplorable state of affairs would perhaps have been tolerable if there had been books and journals available both to sustain the teaching program and to keep abreast of the scholarship that was going on elsewhere. But because of the economic crisis, we have found ourselves in the past five years trying to keep the idea of the university going without the elements of a literate culture on which this idea depends—books and publications. The university library at Ibadan is, for instance, at least five years behind in its subscriptions to scientific journals. Nigerian scholars cannot attend conferences abroad, cannot keep in touch through personal interaction with colleagues about the latest ideas in their disciplines. Not only does this isolation put them out of touch with the currents of modern knowledge, but a process of atrophy begins to set in, compromising what was acquired in earlier training. The process at the individual level leads to a general situation of intellectual sclerosis.

The steady decline over the past fifteen years of the University of Ibadan as a center of learning and research illustrates the problem. From 1948, when it was founded, until the mid-1960s, it developed into a national university, even when the newer universities at Lagos and Zaria were founded. As a result of the quality of scholarship at Ibadan, the university began to enjoy an enviable international reputation. In the humanities, for example, the Ibadan history series, composed of monographs and dissertations coming out of the history department and published by Longmans under the editorship of the distinguished historian Kenneth Dike, pioneered the emergence of African history as a discipline and thus gave direction to African historiography. Extremely useful work was also being done in the social sciences, particularly in economics and demographic studies. The same steady development of scholarship was taking place in the natural sciences. In the late 1960s and early 1970s, the University of Ibadan was engaged in some of the most important scientific research ever undertaken in Africa, analysis of hemoglobin chemistry. I understand that very encouraging work had in fact been achieved on the characterization of the thermodynamic properties of aberrant hemoglobin, so that the research project was in a position to contribute to research on sickle cell anemia, which as everyone knows is an eminently African medical problem. Indeed, the analytical chemistry laboratory at Ibadan had achieved such a respectable standing by the early 1970s that it became the principal African center of postgraduate training in this field. Similarly, the University College Hospital served as an important referral center for the West

African subregion and had developed a special interest in the area of community medicine. (Professor Lambo's work in psychiatry was in some ways an extension of this interest).

This is a tragic tale, because Ibadan had a unique opportunity to validate the idea of the university in Nigeria as a bridgehead of modern knowledge. It had a chance to set the pace in higher education, especially in postgraduate training, and in the kind of high-level academic work that promised well for the maintenance of the valuable tradition of scholarship that it had inherited. Above all, it was moving decisively in a direction toward the development of scientific research adapted to local needs and conditions.

As for the universities that were set up in the 1970s at federal and state levels, the less said about them, the better. They have for the most part never been able to aspire to being anything more than glorified high schools.

The tale of woe that I've narrated applies not only to Nigeria but also to other African countries. In English-speaking Africa, Makerere University in Kampala, Uganda, ravaged by the adversities of the recent political history of that unfortunate country, has been reduced to a pale shadow of its former glory; both the University of Ghana at Legon, and Fourah Bay College in Freetown, Sierra Leone, have seen their fortunes sink. A similar situation prevails in French-speaking Africa. In Zaire, the University of Lovanium is no longer a serious center of learning because of political interference and inefficient management. The possible exception to this catalogue of decline in university education in Africa is the University of Dakar, though it has a constant history of student unrest, which seems to be the sign of deep-seated malaise. The university system, which ought to be an agent for modernization, is on the verge of collapse all over Africa.

The demoralization in African academic circles is especially acute among the younger academics, who cannot get a fair start on their careers or look forward to any fulfillment in scholarship. For many African scholars with either experience or ambition, the only solution is expatriation, either to the West or to other Third World countries with better conditions. Saudi Arabia and the gulf countries at present offer the new alternate receiving area. (According to the latest report I have, the University of Ibadan has lost so far over forty teachers of its College of Medicine to institutions in the Middle East.) It must not be thought that this brain drain is due simply to the attraction of better remuneration and living conditions; exile for many African academics quite simply results from despair about ever being able to operate at an acceptable level in their native environment.

These problems in education are the scattered symptoms of a profound disorder. No doubt external factors have weighed in the balance, but they would not have had the force they have had but for our own poor judgment and lack of resolution. In the area of education as in other areas of development planning, in the whole effort for modernization in Africa as it has been carried on since independence, there has been a failure of will. It can be traced to an undeveloped awareness of the challenges we face. This lack of awareness is most manifest at official levels where policy decisions are taken. As I have tried to show, such decisions have been based on narrow considerations and have been nothing less than devastating in their effects. They stem from the misunderstanding that education is a commodity to be spread as widely as possible. The spreading has been so indiscriminate that it has led to a pitiable thinness. One of the most durable of the fallacies guiding educational policy in Africa is the idea that the mere expansion of facilities represents an input to development. The quantitative expansion we have had, we now realize, is entirely different from the qualitative growth we need. Neither the rhetoric of cultural nationalism nor that of our radical social scientists has helped matters very much. For the development effort to succeed, education must be rethought so that it cultivates a frame of mind that is attuned to the scientific model.

The insensitiveness shown by governments almost everywhere on the African continent to the fate of the universities is ultimately self-defeating. (The "flip side" to this attitude is the ingrained anti-intellectualism that often expresses itself as an active hostility to the university as an institution). Moreover, the facile conception of the university as a kind of factory for the production of manpower must now be abandoned for a more fruitful, more fundamental, idea. Certainly the assumption that a mass of trained personnel directly affects the pace of development has some truth, but the trouble is that this equation has been translated in Africa to mean simply mass literacy. This in turn has been extended upward, so that the higher levels of education have been seen as merely a kind of open end to the educational system, without a consideration of the necessary differentiations that have to be applied. (It is often forgotten that general education became a reality in the West only after the Industrial Revolution had run a substantial part of its course; it was a consequence rather than a cause of economic development.) Through this distortion of economic theory, expansion of education at all levels has been taken practically to mean a sufficient condition for the requirements of development, without attention to the strategic role of the university.

The university remains the main platform for moving us into the center of modern civilization. That is why I cannot subscribe to the idea that seems to be rapidly gaining ground that higher education is a luxury in Africa and should be deemphasized. On the contrary, I believe that the focus of formal education in Africa should be the university level, with the rest of the system restructured in such a way as to reflect the preeminence of the university as the apex of the mental and intellectual training that modern education implies. (One would like to think that the new national policy on education adopted a few years ago in Nigeria suggests a step in this direction, although the habitual muddle with which it is being implemented gives no cause for encouragement that it will be carried through adequately.) I cannot pretend to make proposals here in any kind of detail for the lines along which such a reform should go. Certainly, I believe there ought to be greater emphasis on quality, as much as regards the training of minds as of hands. I believe too that teacher training needs to be given far greater attention than it has at present. The poor esteem in which teachers are held by our governments is well demonstrated by the low salaries they are offered. Any effective reorientation of educational policy for development must include plans to promote awareness of science and technology, beginning with the lower levels of the educational system. I would suggest the introduction into the curriculum as soon as possible—certainly at the secondary level—of the history of science and technology as a subject, such history to take in developments in every part of the world. (The notable achievements of China in the past, and of Japan more recently, as well as advances in other parts of the Third World need to be brought to the attention of the African child; moreover, the positive record of the African continent itself should be emphasized, not as an alibi but as an inspiration.)

We must begin to limit ourselves to what can be handled within the limitations of the resources available to us. Not only should the number of universities be reduced, but many programs should be abandoned. Above all, we need to promote and enforce a new sense of the significance of the university as an institution. On the part of those involved with university education there has to be a sense of commitment to laying down the conceptual foundation for the development effort. Such education would bring a new order of life to the African continent.

The relationship between education and development also has an international dimension. I would like to make two points in this respect. First, what Africa needs most of all at the moment is intellectual aid, not the ad hoc economic aid that has become standard between the developed countries and the underdeveloped world. The benefits of economic aid have been at best ambiguous. The effects of intellectual aid, based on a new understanding of knowledge as a common heritage of mankind, will be more enduring.

The second point brings me to my conclusion. Development is not merely an economic concept but essentially a moral idea. It has its basis and justification in a humane conception of life, in a deep concern for the quality with which it is lived. Such a concern must imply a universal standard of evaluation, or it is meaningless. The ethics that govern international relations at present do not lead to the establishment of such a standard. This is where the principle of rationality that underlies the scientific model could be of assistance. I want to think that international cooperation in the pursuit of knowledge, based on a disinterested pursuit of a common ideal of the scientific understanding of the universe we all inhabit, is possible. I hope that this understanding will give the world a framework for the emergence of a new ethics in the relations between its peoples.

Comments on Abiola Irele's Essay

F. CHAMPION WARD: Professor Irele's paper reminded me of an odd exchange of paradigms at twenty paces that I once had with Sir Eric Ashby in the first years of Nigerian independence some twenty-five years ago. He had been chairman of a national commission on the future of the Nigerian universities, and in the course of Sir Eric's travels and reflections, he had been impressed with the plans to have a practically oriented university at Enugu in the eastern region. He called on me in New York to press upon me the promise of this institution and the importance of the Ford Foundation's attention being called to it. I was so alarmed by the prospect that I put *his* hat on and warned him of the grave danger that standards at the British-founded college at Ibadan would be lowered. Then we realized that he was behaving like an American; I, like a Briton. The result may well have been the worst of both worlds.

Given the troubles now plaguing Third World universities, I would like to advance two notions of what ought to be done. Of course, the range of things that need to be done far exceeds the two efforts I would like to have considered. One notion points in the direction of selectivity; the other, in the direction of inclusiveness. By selectivity, I refer to such matters as rigor in the choice of research programs to be maintained at a given university or university system. This is what Professor Irele recommends. He knows how difficult it is to concentrate all effort on a few targets instead of spreading it over many, important and unimportant, that have political support of some kind. Beyond that, I suggest that in the short term there ought also to be selectivity in the choice of certain universities to be supported in reaching the status that would entitle them to be called national research universities. If in a given country or region such selective designation and support were to be decided upon—the intellectual aid that Professor Irele mentioned in his oral remarks—and if such an effort could be made for a number of years, at least a few intellectual centers would be lifted above the flood. Otherwise, I fear that intellectual aid, even if increased, when confined to the "refreshment" of individual scholars and scientists, will fall far short of its most effective use.

Now, to the second suggestion. Soedjatmoko, in the brief remarks that he has sent us, speaks of the fact that the population is still increasing more rapidly than literacy; the absolute number of illiterates is still rising. Some of the situations that one discovers, particularly in those places where approximately half the national budget goes into education, lead me to ask whether we have been radical enough in optimizing the quantum of learning that can be secured for a fixed financial investment. Let us suppose that a government is able to appropriate an amount that, divided by the number of pupils coming along, is sufficient to assure each child four years of education. Is it self-evident that those years ought to be between ages six and ten? There is a limited literature, but not an unconvincing one, which shows that the rate at which an eleven-year-old can become literate and numerate is at least twice the rate of a six-year-old. Yet, today's practice, inherited and imitated from an earlier day, assumes that everyone is going to attend school for eight years, with perhaps a good proportion going further.

Such practice never raises the question of how much learning could be achieved if the optimal entry age were lifted. I see at least two advantages in considering this. Let us hypothesize again. A government would be saying, in effect, you are entitled to four years of education; they need not necessarily be the first four years; we are providing national schools, funded through a national tax, which offer eight grades of instruction. The point at which you enter the system will depend on whether or not you have learned anything before you arrive. We will not let you in before you are eleven. The pupil, the family, and the village would be encouraged to make a local educational effort that would supplement what the nation could afford to do with its tax system.

Should such a system be set up, you would almost be assured that a higher proportion of the citizenry would reach the present sixth-grade learning level than is now the case, with the present truncated efforts to imitate a full European system. I ought to add that I tried to persuade UNESCO to consider this proposal; they published it with great reluctance in some journal—I have lost my copy—and then went out of their way to dissociate themselves from what they thought to be a harebrained scheme. It has never been given a trial. It haunts me because I do not think we ever did raise the question of how much learning it is possible to get for a fixed amount of money.

ROBERT A. LE VINE: I think that in education, as in the other areas of development, there are both success stories and disaster stories to be told, and we have heard both. I find it useful in thinking about development and education to make a distinction—it may sound pedantic—between schooling and education, because only in the first case are we talking about kids going to school. We do not know what goes on there; we do not know whether in fact they get the kinds of competence they are supposed to be getting when they attend. We do know that schooling has all sorts of unintended effects on other aspects of life, like health and family, especially if girls go to school. I think it is important to distinguish between schooling and years of school attendance, which in quantitative studies is all the information we have. We simply know the number of years in the aggregate that a particular population or population sample has gone to school. That has all sorts of effects, even when the individual involved may not emerge as literate. It is likely to be a very important problem in the future.

On the other hand, education means also the acquisition of some forms of competence that the society values, that it has set up schools and educational institutions to achieve. This is where we hear the disaster stories. Schooling still seems to have positive effects; even the broadening of access to schooling continues to have effects, which I think are somewhat underestimated in the Birdsall paper. I think that if you are going to ask schooling to guarantee a mortality decline as great as the one that went on between 1945 and 1970, there will be a sense of diminishing returns. If, however, the choice in the future is between expanding female school enrollments in places like India, where there is still a great deal of room for expansion and where there is a high infant mortality rate, and using other measures, not specified, I am not convinced that new measures would be better than expanding female schooling.

Kamla Chowdhry

Poverty, Environment, Development

INDIA'S POVERTY IS CLOSELY CONNECTED with its increasing land degradation. Out of 329 million hectares of land mass, as much as 175 million are considered degraded in one form or another. What is even more alarming is the rate at which land degradation is taking place. Satellite imagery has indicated that we are losing forest cover at the rate of 1.5 million hectares a year. Further, with bad agriculture and irrigation practices, bad road building in fragile hills, bad mining practices, wind and water erosion, water logging, urbanization, and industrialization, possibly another million hectares a year is going out of productive use. In a country with a population of 760 million the amount of land per capita declined from 0.9 hectares in 1951 to 0.5 in 1981. And cultivable land declined from 0.48 hectares per capita in 1951 to 0.26 in 1981.

POVERTY AND THE ENVIRONMENT

The pressure on land is enormous. Marginal lands are being used for subsistence agriculture leading to further land degradation. With livestock herds of over 400 million grazing, communal lands are overused to the extent that they have hardly any productivity left. With half the forest cover gone, there are acute shortages of fuel and fodder. Illegal felling in reserved forests and illegal occupation of government and village community lands have become widespread, destroying the communal use of common lands and the related social fabric.

137

Because of deforestation, especially in the upper catchment areas, soil erosion has increased considerably. The soil erosion estimate for 1972 was 6 billion tons; it is now estimated at 12 billion. According to India's department of agriculture, the country is losing 30 to 50 million tons of food grains through loss of topsoil. Because of runoff caused by deforestation, underground water tables have been going down even where rainfall has been ample. Large numbers of ponds and wells are dry, so that the agricultural productivity, especially of the smaller farmers, has declined. Floods and droughts too have increased in frequency, severity, and extent, leading to enormous losses and to human suffering and poverty in rural areas.

Diverting scarce resources for unproductive disaster relief, the government spends crores of rupees on drought and flood relief. (A crore is an amount equal to 10 million rupees.) In 1985–1986 drought and flood relief assistance from government at the center alone was Rs 997.14 crores. In 1987–1988, the government spent over Rs 2,000 crores for drought relief. In spite of this assistance, human suffering and the loss of farm animals have been immense. Drought and floods are reminders of inappropriate land use and forest policies as well as the need to take a holistic view of land use and its productivity for the welfare of the people and the elimination of poverty.

The country has paid a heavy price for its neglect of the land, especially in the uncultivated half of India. Land policy is fairly well defined for the 143 million hectares of private agricultural land. The policy framework is built on expertise and decades of experience and analysis. Certain policy combinations have evolved to increase productivity at successive levels of difficulty.

The same cannot be said of the uncultivated half of India. Forest lands, grazing lands, community and revenue lands are almost all used as resources by the poor, and almost all are fast becoming wasted lands. Different administrative jurisdictions of common lands have provided land-management policies that often conflict with each other. Custodial jurisdictions dictate policies that do not always promote the highest contribution of such land resources to the social welfare.

If poverty in the country is to be tackled, then environmental issues such as deforestation, soil erosion, pollution, use of common lands, and fuel and fodder development need to receive the highest political attention. In the forty years of development planning since independence, every five-year plan has focused on the elimination of poverty.

And yet forty years later, we still find half our population below the poverty line.

The challenge in development is to understand the interrelationship of poverty, resources, and people. The poor are caught in a vicious downward spiral. They are forced to overuse resources to survive; the impoverishment of the environment makes their survival even more difficult and uncertain. Development thinking must take into account the connection between poverty and the environment as well as the need to empower the local people in relation to local resources and their equitable distribution. Development must be socially as well as environmentally sustainable.

DEVELOPMENT AND THE ENVIRONMENT

Jawaharlal Nehru, India's first prime minister, dreamed of a modern industrialized country that could produce steel, fertilizer, machine tools, and dams, that could irrigate the fields, update agriculture, and introduce a scientific temper in the country. He supported the Atomic Energy Program, the Council for Scientific and Industrial Research, the Council of Agricultural Research, the Institutes of Technology, and the Institutes of Management so as to produce the scientists, technologists, and managers to modernize India.

Today India can boast of its scientists, technologists, managers, and broad-based industrial infrastructure. In spite of these impressive achievements, India's progress in eliminating rural poverty has been poor. Floods and droughts, famine and hunger, unemployment and unrest and women's drudgery have increased.

In the pursuit of food security, the country supported large dams and irrigation projects but did not fully realize the implications of degrading the environment and uprooting the people. Substantial forest areas were submerged and large numbers of people were ousted during the implementation. The dams and reservoirs lasted less than half the time planned because of heavy siltation from upper regions. The cost of irrigating one hectare of land has been very much higher than the original estimate.

The rape of the Himalayas has also occurred in the name of development. Earlier, the colonial rulers deforested the Himalayas for their own use. But since then, development to meet the need for railway sleepers, paper and pulp, sport goods, and so on have continued the devastation. The consequent soil erosion and runoff, the acute shortage of fuel and fodder, the decline in agriculture and the migration of male workers, the deepening poverty and ecological damage are all related to a concept of development that ignores the environment and the needs and life-style of local people.

The famous Chipko movement was in effect an uprising of the women in Uttarkhand, a part of the middle Himalayas, a protest against government policies of development and against the diversion of natural resources for urban and commercial purposes. The deforestation of the Himalayas has also resulted in floods from the Alaknanda river and its tributaries, which have devastated the villages of Uttarkhand and threatened lives year after year. Many critical survival issues are related to such development policies.

Serious questions are being raised about development policies that ignore not only environmental concerns but also rural communities that have been living in harmony with their environment. Prime Minister Indira Gandhi, who was sensitive to environmental issues, once said:

> I have been critical of the methods adopted by industrialized countries, not because we are wiser but because we who call ourselves developing tend to imitate the developed countries and have not evolved a nonexploitative strategy for development. The need of the poor for livelihood, the greed of the middleman for quick profits, the demand of industry, and the short-sightedness of the administration have created ecological problems. . . . there is a need for a systematic campaign to educate governments, political parties, students, and others regarding the importance and relevance of conservation and the factors involved.[1]

A militancy is growing among the tribals and others affected by such exploitative development projects. Activists in the environment movement are questioning such development projects. Development, they argue, must be indigenous, matched to local needs. Large projects have the aura of success, power, and modernization, but there are better, cheaper decentralized options.

Amulya Reddy, an engineer at the Indian Institute of Science in Bangalore, brings out clearly the urban bias in conventional energy planning and the availability of decentralized options:

> The conventional wisdom on energy planning is as follows: Development is equal to growth, which is equal to energy, which in turn is equal to centralized electricity generation plus grid transmission.[2]

Most of the steps in this logic, argues Reddy, are highly questionable and patently false. In the conventional approach the only way of providing energy to scattered and remote villages is through large-scale centralized generation followed by grid transmission. This, of course, makes rural electrification almost impossible. In fact, claims Reddy, there are many viable decentralized options based on renewable energy sources that have been neglected.

GANDHI ON DEVELOPMENT

Gandhi emphasized bottom-up planning to get at the realities of rural development. He suggested that the Indian economy should be built by the a priori method of securing rock-bottom facts and therefore by a rigid process of reasoning and scientific observation that no amount of juggling could controvert.

To show the kind of data he thought should be collected for development planning, he sponsored a study of Matur Taluka (a county in Gujarat). The survey highlighted the need to harness the local natural resources and listed the following as developmental priorities: a detailed soil survey, bringing wastelands into production, improving the water distribution system, increasing the capacity of water tanks to reduce the brackishness of well water, improving grazing lands and fodder production, and promoting local production of cloth.

These measures were directed at improving the natural resources, generating additional employment and income, and making communities self-reliant. With decentralized planning based on local resources and local skills, the participation of the people was also ensured. This meant not only more realistic planning but the long-term involvement of the people.

To Gandhi, development planning meant focusing on the poorest of the poor—the concept of *antoyodaya* (unto the last). He proposed village republics—*gramsabhas* (village communities) and *gram panchayats* (village-elected bodies) as institutions to involve the people in decision making and implementation. In Gandhi's thinking, development success did not lie in the growth of the gross national product but in the removal of poverty and inequality, and in the productive use of all manpower:

> If I could produce all my country's wants by means of 30,000 people instead of 30 million, I should not mind it provided that the 30 million are not rendered idle and unemployed.[3]

Gandhi's focus was people—poor people—and his policies were people-centered. According to Gandhi, heavy industries too had a place and needed to be centralized and nationalized. But he said they would occupy the least part of the vast national activity, which would be mainly in villages. The emphasis was on "the *khadi* mentality," meaning the decentralization of the production and distribution of the necessities of life. He pointed out that:

> since the wanton destruction of this central village industry (*khadi*) and allied handicrafts, intelligence and brightness have fled from the villages, leaving them inane, lustreless and reduced almost to the state of their ill-kept cattle.[4]

Although 80 percent of India's population lives in rural areas and more than half of them are below the poverty line, the policies governing development, investment, education, training, infrastructure, and institutional support systems have all been biased toward urban needs. It is the biased structure of rewards and opportunities in urban areas that forces young men of energy and ability from rural backgrounds to migrate to cities to seek new opportunities of employment.

It is this kind of development that Gandhi tried to prevent. Addressing a gathering of economists in Allahabad, Gandhi said:

> I hold that economic progress is antagonistic to real progress. Hence, the ancient ideal has been the limitation of activities promoting wealth. This does not put an end to all material ambition. We should still have, as we have always had in our midst, people who make the pursuit of wealth their aim in life. But we have always recognised that it is a fall from the ideal. . . . I have heard many of our countrymen say that we will gain American wealth but avoid its methods. I venture to suggest that such an attempt if it were made is foredoomed to failure. We cannot be wise, temperate and furious in a moment.

Gandhi talked of the fourfold ruin that India suffered at the hands of the colonial rulers: economic, political, cultural, and spiritual. The interrelatedness of these provided the traditional modes of cooperation, of sharing and control over common resources. With the fourfold ruin, the very essence of communal life was eroded. The customary ways of doing things began to fail, and all restraint in the exploitation of people and natural resources diminished.

In *Gandhi's Truth* Erik Erikson points out that the fourfold ruin did "irreversible damage to the people's identity wrought by colonial masters who often felt with justification that they have advanced the very people whom they damage in their identity." While Gandhi spoke of a fourfold ruin, Erikson diagnosed the processes that aggravated each other: economic and psychological ruin, which erode the very essense of communal life and common resources.

Gandhi's concept of development was to deal with the fourfold ruin, not merely economic development. His strategy was to benefit the villages and the rural masses first. He emphasized village councils, self-sufficiency in basic needs at the community level, focus on the rural poor. This approach to development was a far cry from Nehru's dream of a modern India with emphasis on industrialization, large dams, and atomic plants. The gap in the two dreams was, to use Gandhi's language, "as wide as the Ganges in flood."

Commenting on the current development scene, Lakshmi Jain writes,

> Seen from Gandhiji's window, development appears to be proceeding along a collision course vis-à-vis the poor; it is recklessly destroying even such means of subsistence as nature has long afforded them. . . . in addition to causing such wide-spread ecological damage, development has succeeded in driving a large wedge between different segments of Indian society.[5]

Ultimately, development is not merely economics or technology or social issues but a moral force that does not accept poverty, does not accept the widening disparities between the rich and poor, and does not accept the overexploitation of natural resources. Gandhi himself lived a life of austerity because, as he said, "He who has made the ideal of equal distribution a part of his being would reduce his wants to a minimum, bearing in mind the poverty of India."[6] Rich nations too need to be conscious of the overexploitation of natural resources, the widening gap between the rich and poor nations, and the need for some measure of austerity. Sustainable global development will also require more equitable sharing of resources: a voluntary giving up of affluent life-styles so that we can live within the planet's ecological means.

PEOPLE'S PARTICIPATION

A policy of participation requires concern about the people, people-centered policies, and people-centered institutions. Bureaucracies have not been very successful in reaching the poor. In the 1950s Nehru introduced the Community Development Programme for integrated rural development to enhance the economic base and improve the quality of life in rural areas. To provide the necessary political and administrative support, a national-level committee was set up with the prime minister as the chairman and with ministers of planning, agriculture, and cooperation as members. Similar committees were also set up at the state and district levels. Initially, the program was located in the planning commission, but later a separate ministry of community development and cooperation was established to strengthen it. The program was, however, given up after Nehru's death, partly because of its lack of success and partly because of a trend toward centralization of power.

The 1970s too saw an emphasis on antipoverty programs to reduce rural poverty. Institutions such as the Small Farmers Development Agency, the Marginal Farmers Development Agency, the Tribal Development Agency, the District Rural Development Agency, the Desert Development Agency, the Drought-Prone Area Program, and the regional rural banks were established. Like the Community Development Programme earlier, these institutions increased the lower levels of bureaucracy, but the delivery of services did not take place to any extent. The failure is attributed to bureaucratic inflexibility, organizational weakness, faulty delivery, and the technocratic approach. At the core of such bureaucratic institutional mechanisms lay lack of people participation and systems that frightened people away from government offices. The very bureaucracy hired to service these programs drained development funds from people who were too weak to protest.

The Social Forestry Programme, initiated largely in the Sixth Plan, meant to enhance fuel wood, fodder, and small timber for the rural poor, also shows that the schemes have largely benefited the big farmers and the paper, pulp, and construction industries, bypassing the rural poor. Large centralized nurseries for raising saplings were set up, and the government agreed to free distribution of saplings to encourage and benefit the rural poor. In fact, however, the bigger farmers collected the saplings, in their trucks and tractors. The smaller farmers could not benefit because of the distance, the difficulty of carrying saplings, and so on. The selection of species too was not on the basis of what the poor needed, but for a commercial market. The system of consultation or involvement of the beneficiaries in decision making is generally not part of the bureaucratic orientation. Although many of the antipoverty schemes as well as the social forestry schemes have a beneficiary orientation, the beneficiaries' perspective, the rural poor's point of view, is missing. The reality of the poor living on the margin of existence is often different from that visualized by the administrator. It is difficult for the administrator coming from an urban background to understand the fears, the hesitancy, the pain, and the labor with which the poor live and which therefore separates project formulation from its implementation. With a bottom-up approach and the involvement of the people in planning and implementation, the success of such schemes can be ensured.

People's participation in antipoverty schemes is more easily talked about than achieved in reality. Schemes are formulated by the central government and the state ministries, targets announced and implemented through conventional bureaucratic structures unable to be responsive to local needs and preferences. By its very logic and goals, the bureaucratic system becomes target oriented, subordinating local needs to a blue-print approach or guidelines determined from the top.

Government is beginning to realize that the involvement and participation of the rural people is essential and that bureaucracies are perhaps not the most appropriate structures for implementing antipoverty plans. They too seem to be reaching out to the nongovernmental organizations (NGOs) and the volunteer sector, especially in relation to rural and antipoverty programs.

NONGOVERNMENTAL ORGANIZATIONS

India has thousands of voluntary agencies, large and small, doing constructive work in remote and backward areas close to the rural poor. The largest number are Gandhian agencies. Gandhi inspired thousands of people to serve India by undertaking constructive work in the most remote and backward areas. Constructive work, according to Gandhi, was working for communal harmony, removal of untouchability, basic and adult education, village sanitation and health, *khadi* and village industries, economic equality, and women's equality. The aim of constructive work was to make local people and local institutions self-sufficient.

Besides the thousands of Gandhian agencies spread all over the country, two other kinds of agency have contributed to voluntary action. The first were the Christian missionaries who came in large numbers during the British Raj to work on education and health. Their numbers have decreased considerably after independence. The second were the Ramakrishna missions, inspired by Vivekenanda. Also spread all over the country, as well as internationally, these missions have contributed significantly to education, health, and culture. More recently, in the last decade or so, many young scientists and professionals have established NGOs for development work and act as intermediaries between government and the people. They have introduced improved hand pumps and smokeless *chullas* (stoves), solar energy for irrigation, television, lighting, and agricultural techniques. Other young professionals have devoted their energy to establishing village industries and market facilities, boring wells, and generally providing an interface with government.

The most significant emergence of young professionals in voluntary action in recent years has been in relation to environmental issues. In India environmental problems are closely linked with poverty and women's issues. To protect the poor and the environment, these voluntary agencies have often confronted the government. In Karnataka a number of voluntary agencies have challenged the Karnataka government's leasing to industry of C and D degraded lands, customarily used by local communities for grazing. Mining in the Mussorie hills has devastated the hillsides, endangering the water supply and health of local communities. Environmental NGOs took up the issue and obtained a stay order from the Supreme Court. The agitation by local groups in Kerala to save the Silent Valley from so-called development is another such example. In a recent march organized by voluntary agencies to focus attention on rehabilitation in the Western Ghats, some 150 voluntary groups took part. There are protests organized by many voluntary agencies against the government-approved Narmada and Tehri dam projects, which threaten to uproot thousands of people and submerge thousands of hectares of prime forests.

At the nexus of poverty and environment and its manifold manifestations in floods, drought, famine, unemployment, unrest, violence, women's drudgery, health, and the disappearance of flora, fauna, and grazing lands, the interests of many voluntary agencies have converged. The convergence has produced cooperation and synergism in dealing with these issues. The environmental concern, with its other face as poverty, has been a great unifying force.

Baba Amte, a social worker known for his work with lepers and the disabled, organized a bicycle march of young people from Kanyakumari to Kashmir, a distance of over 2,000 miles, to focus attention on national integration and environmental concerns. Thousands of young people from all over the country joined the march to spread the message of environmental conservation and to participate in afforestation activities with communities en route.

The Chipko movement, the protest spearheaded by the women of Uttarkhand in the Himalayas, was against the government policy of contracting forest trees for industrial purposes when the people's survival was at stake. The movement received support from Gandhian voluntary agencies in the region and from students, teachers, scientists, and other local groups. The Chipko movement has inspired environmental groups all over the country. With similar tactics learned from Chipko, the Apiko movement in Karnataka has also been fighting government forest policies. In general, the various environmental groups have adopted Gandhian tactics to protest and change existing laws and policies in favor of conservation, sustainable growth, and protection of the rights of the poor on common property resources.

Without decentralization of power to local agencies, people's participation and involvement does not take place. In the Community Development Programme, a three-tiered *panchayat* system was suggested, but not many state governments were willing to share political power with local agencies and leaders. The program did not succeed. In the Communist state of West Bengal, the state government has recently strengthened the village *panchayats*. They have effectively distributed surplus land for productive use and have protected forests in return for sharing gains. Group farm forestry has been supported and is doing well. Karnataka too has decentralized powers to elect county *panchayats* for local projects and schemes enhancing people's involvement.

Some government policies can be a barrier to people's participation and development. For instance, the Forest Conservation Act of 1980 is meant to stop the diversion of forest land to nonforest purposes. But guidelines from the government of India prevent people's groups such as voluntary agencies and cooperatives from participating in afforestation activities in degraded forest areas. There is a custodial approach to the management of forest lands irrespective of the welfare of the people. In such situations only voluntary agencies can act as counterplayers in the fight for change. In this regard we have much to learn from the inspiring and challenging campaigns of Gandhi—and of Martin Luther King in the United States.

The funding of protest campaigns, the *satyagrahas* (social and political reforms through passive resistance), is a point to consider. In the Champaran campaign, Gandhi said he would collect funds only from Bihar since the issue was not an all-India one but related only to that one state. It was also a method of involving the Biharis in their local issues. The members of the Chipko movement too have been careful not to accept outside money. Many voluntary agencies are dependent on government funds for their constructive work. Such a situation makes the confrontation role difficult to undertake. If they lose favor with government, the flow of funds is likely to stop. Under these circumstances, few voluntary agencies can afford to question government policies openly. The voice from below gets stifled, and yet there is a strong need for developing a countervailing force.

ONLY AS MUCH AS ONE CAN PUT BACK

There is a growing realization that poverty and environmental degradation are two sides of the same coin, and development strategy must reflect these realities. Deforestation threatens to alter the face of the country. If the present trend continues, there will be no forests left by the turn of the century. It is clear that many critical survival issues are related to deforestation and increasing land degradation. They have resulted in unprecedented pressures on land, water, forests, and other natural resources.

There is an upsurge of interest in environmental and poverty issues. Voluntary agencies of different hues and colors are coming together and motivating people to participate in dealing with these issues. Young people are especially in the vanguard of this movement. During the last few years hundreds of new voluntary agencies have emerged to protect environmental resources, to involve people in their regeneration, and to protest government policies that ignore environmental and human concerns.

The NGOs both in India and abroad seem to be veering toward Gandhian thinking. They are questioning the very concept of development based on the use of more and more natural resources for growth. As Gandhi said, "There is enough for everyone's need but not enough for everyone's greed." It is sustainable growth that is being emphasized.

People's participation is not a slogan or a magic word. It requires hard political decisions to move toward decentralization of powers, people-centered policies, and people-centered institutions—NGOs, cooperatives, locally elected institutions such as *panchayats,* water users associations. There is an important distinction between government acting to meet a need of the people and government acting to create enabling structures within which people can be more effective in meeting those needs themselves. Such local agencies have provided a territorial perspective emphasizing direct links between people's uses, the environment, and personal consequences of such uses. Knowing the ravages that can be caused by the misuse of resources, the Chipko women have safeguarded their ecosystems and their villages through afforestation. The logic of self-reliance is the logic of place, people, and resources bound into locally self-sustaining ecological systems. It is in this context that Gandhian thinking and the environmentalists converge.

The environmentalists, like Gandhi, share the idea of austerity, of not having affluent life-styles, of equitably sharing resources, of bearing in mind the limited natural resources of the planet. The ancients in India recognized that one should take from the earth only as much as one can put back. In the *Atharva Veda,* in the hymn to the earth, they chanted:

> What of thee I dig out, let that quickly grow over.
> Let me not hit thy vitals or thy heart.

ENDNOTES

[1]Indira Gandhi on the environment, Department of Environment, Government of India, 1984.

[2]Amulya Reddy, "New Approach to Energy Planning," *Times of India*, 1987, sec. 25, 27.

[3]Vijendra K. R. Rao, *Indian Socialism, Retrospect and Prospect* (New Delhi: Concept, 1982).

[4]Pyare Lal, *Towards New Harijans* (Ahmedabad: Navjivan Publishing House, 1959).

[5]Lakshmi Jain, "Poverty Environment Development—A New View from Gandhi's Window," unpublished paper, Institute of Social Studies Trust, July 1987.

[6]Krishna Raj, "Nehru-Gandhi Polarity and Economic Policy," lecture at Nehru Memorial Museum Library, 15 November 1977.

Comments on Kamla Chowdhry's Essay

LINCOLN C. CHEN: The paper by Kamla Chowdhry raises three critical questions. First, what has been India's development experience over the four decades since independence? Second, what were the driving ideological forces, and the historical origins, behind these developments? Third, what is the role of government and private institutions, including popular participation?

In more human terms, these questions may be rephrased. How do "Chipko women"—Himalayan women who must walk miles for firewood and who have literally hugged trees to prevent government officials and commercial timber truckers from cutting trees down, as described by Kamla—fit into India's development? Or what about the Indian government officer who travels from farmer to farmer with new varieties of "miracle" seeds for rice or wheat? What about the Gandhian *khadi* worker in a voluntary agency who spends much of his or her time propagating adult literacy in sanitation for the villages?

In terms of socioeconomic development, however defined, India has had success as well as failure. Over the past forty years she has experienced an average economic growth rate of 4.5 percent, now has a large middle class of 100 million people, has developed a strong scientific and industrial base, and is producing well-educated people sufficiently talented for export around the world. In spite of the famine crisis of the 1960s, India has achieved food self-sufficiency. The country has emerged as a regional military power with nuclear capabilities.

Shortcomings cited in Kamla's paper relate to the damage done to the environment and the natural resource base upon which India's food production depends. India has experienced flooding for two years, drought for four. These may reflect longer-term climatic changes brought about by poorly understood environmental shifts. India's biggest failure, of course, is the sheer magnitude of continuing absolute poverty, 35 percent of the people. Three hundred million people still live without the basic essentials of life! And as pointed out by Champ Ward, India's illiteracy level is still at 65 percent; in absolute numbers, India has more illiterates today than she did at independence.

There are also the institutional failings. The great Congress party that carried India from colonialism into independence is generally seen as unable to govern, faction-ridden and corrupt. The great bureaucracy, a heritage of colonialism, is so procedure-bound as to be unable to execute and implement key programs. There has also been an increase in violence, a new and distressing phenomenon. Violence has become more common in everyday life; strains between ethnic, linguistic, and social groups are increasingly being expressed in violent terms. The Punjab represents only the most visible dimension of these conflicts.

India's progress is a "glass half empty or half full" depending upon the viewer. Kamla's paper challenges the Nehruvian vision of Indian development, which she holds accountable for these failings. That vision aimed at democracy, secularism, and socialism through social modernization using science and technology. While the strategy may have been expedient for economic growth, it was not necessarily conducive to harmonious social relations nor for sustainable development. Kamla praises the Gandhian vision of people-oriented development—bottoms-up, decentralized, village planning; full employment; poverty alleviation; and social harmony with justice. Ultimately, as Kamla says, it was not just about economic development but about a struggle that relates to moral issues, a moral force that refuses to tolerate ethnic tensions or social disparities.

What about the third question—governmental versus nongovernmental action, including popular participation? We should avoid overromanticizing either side, nor should we become disenchanted prematurely. India's poverty-alleviation programs, in fact, contained both Nehruvian and Gandhian visions. Science-based extension programs to promote food production and health care services reflected the former, while integrated, rural community development is consistent with the latter. In many cases, the Nehruvian and Gandhian visions were joined, but in all cases, government, especially at the center, created a plethora of bureaucratic agencies. Kamla lists five or six; dozens more could have been added.

It is important to recognize that government in India is not monolithic. It is pluralistic, as is Indian society. Government, however, has become an independent force in a nonrevolutionary society. No longer can government be viewed simply as an expression of the political process or an instrument of the state; in many cases, government has become an actor with its own powers, traditions, and vested interests.

Nongovernmental agencies have as their origins diverse ideological roots-:Gandhian, Christian missionary, Ramakrishnan, and others. Some private agencies have positive attributes: innovation, flexibility, local responsiveness. They may also be ideologically intolerant and bureaucratically entrenched. They may operate development programs with mixed efficiency and effectiveness. Some are outstanding; others less so. None are large in scale, considering India's needs. Nearly all are poor, and few have the legitimacy that government commands. Voluntary agencies perform many different kinds of functions, providing welfare services but also serving as models of experimentation. They may be confrontational to government and other entrenched interests.

Most important, in my view, is that as a group they have been sentinels to the development experience. It was from the private voluntary sector, for example, that the environment issues, which will certainly dominate much of India's development agenda into the next century, originated. It was the private groups that first identified the plight of India's vast underprivileged in the urban "informal" sector. And, as Kamla mentioned, it was the nongovernmental sector that initiated and that sustains the women's movement.

Both government and nongovernmental institutions represent expressions of popular will. In India, popular participation will take on characteristics particularistic to Indian society—pluralism, distinctive-group and regional identity, and hierarchical social relations—all historical legacies of a rich and enduring civilization.

JUDITH TENDLER: I want to say a few things about the issues raised in this essay because, not only in India but in various places in Latin America, Africa, and Asia, there is much interest in nongovernmental organizations, issues of participation, decentralization, and local control. I think that we really need to understand better what this phenomenon means, what the proliferation of NGOs can signify with respect to our concern about getting better performance from government in the area of poverty remediation.

It is important to understand that decentralization and local control are not necessarily equivalent; NGO control is not always synonymous with helping the poor or creating more democratic processes. Indeed, they may do just the opposite. I would cite two examples, each from Kamla Chowdhry's paper. One has to do with the progress made in poverty-oriented programs in West Bengal. That was the result of a highly centrally organized Communist-party government that pursued at the same time a decentralized strategy while maintaining strong central control and displacing local leaders and replacing them with its own cadres. What is interesting about this is that it combines decentralization and centralization. I think that the concern with NGOs, the hope that NGOs can somehow replace government in poverty remediation, really does not recognize this aspect, so characteristic of successful programs.

The other example from Kamla's paper has to do with Martin Luther King and the civil rights movement in the United States, which indeed was very much a phenomenon of grass-roots mobilization, with continuing pressure on government. But it was accompanied, again, by a strong centralizing effort on the part of the U.S. government, which took away control from local governments, forcing local governments and local leaders to follow what the central government wanted. In this case, the government sought desegregation, and after that the implementation of voting rights legislation. And so, it is ironic that today decentralization is seen as being automatically synonymous with improved situations for the poor and more democratic processes. Twenty years ago, we portrayed things in quite the opposite manner: local control was seen as the source of conservatism and exploitation, and local elites were thought to appropriate unjustly the benefits of projects.

I am not saying that either view is wrong, only that we need to understand the combination of strong central support and decentralization that lies behind those cases where something important was accomplished. This puts the issue in a more complex way than those who imagine that decentralization or centralization is the answer. I regret that we do not have more time to discuss issues of equity and income distribution, because I think they are going to be more important in the future.

One other point, again with examples from Kamla's paper—the issue of village power and village elites, and the problem of village elites and exploitation. Again, studies show that elite control will sometimes result in exploitation and expropriation of benefits; sometimes, however, it is just the opposite. The example from Kamla's paper has to do with environmental issues where communities protect themselves against violence or invasion by outsiders who would denude their forests or pollute their rivers. In these cases, you have communities uniting across, rather than along, class lines to defend themselves against outsiders. In that instance, decentralization works; it does not have to be democratic. You can depend on the elite; in such a case, it will protect the poor. There are other cases, however, where that will not be true. With land reform, the provision of agricultural credit and other services in respect to agricultural production, control by village elites will generally undermine the purpose of the program. I think we need to make these kinds of distinctions and be very careful when we laud, uncritically, NGOs and local elites.

Mohamed Naciri

Urban Systems and Development Strategies

T HE PROCESS OF DEVELOPMENT pursued by the industrialized countries—both, capitalist and socialist—has produced
an enormous extension of the urban system. Thanks to
industrialization, there have been decisive transformations of the
socioeconomic and political structures of both city and countryside.
The revolution, with its different modalities and rhythms in different
countries, has resulted in a progressive or radical reduction of rural
societies. The demographic growth of rural areas has been eased at
the same time as their productivity has been raised and their societies
modernized.

The urbanization of the rural areas of the Third World has been
perceived more and more as a similar process resulting in the
elimination of peasantries. The same phenomenon can be found in
Africa, Asia, and Latin America. Rural people remain, however, the
majority in the first two continents; even in the countries of Latin
America, where the majority of the population lives in the cities,
many rural communities remain relatively stable and only slightly
penetrated by modernization. The poverty of rural areas seems even
more irreducible than that which exists in urban peripheries.

Two perspectives exist today on the role of the city. Either it is seen
as an absolute evil, the source of irremedial disorders that destroy
communities living in harmony with nature and reduce them to
poverty; or the city is considered the motor of innovation, the
impelling force of the positive transformation of rural society.[1]

This Manichean representation originating with the social reform-
ers of the nineteenth century and borrowing much from the urban

155

utopias that appeared after the Industrial Revolution, inspires reflection about the place of urbanization in strategies of development.[2]

To grasp at once the differences and similarities in the forms of transformation of rural societies, it seems necessary to start with an analysis of the "urban system," which is not only the city and its functioning, its socioeconomic and political mechanisms, its reciprocal interactions with the countryside, but also the nature of the state and capital that intervene in its field of action. The state and capital seek to integrate as fully as possible the whole population, the state with its structures of command, capital with its relations to production.

There is not a single urban system but a plurality of systems. Their nature, evolution, and variety explain the differences of impact that urbanization has had on rural areas.

Do urban systems appear as systems of concentration of power and income, reinforcing cumulative disparities to the advantage of a single group, to the detriment of other categories of the population, or do they tend to limit social differentiation by the widespread participation of numerous actors in the decisions and results of collective effort? How does the modernization of rural areas, the extension of the physical signs of urbanization, carry the process of integration for one part of the population, excluding others from the benefits of growth?

What roles are assigned to "local elites" in the changes that affect rural societies in the Third World?[3] Are these elites skirmishers for the centralized state or the authentic expression of a local power in gestation? In effect, the existence or not of a strong rural community, well structured and enjoying basic autonomy and decision-making power at the local level, has a profound influence on the evolution of the urban system itself.

There is reason to distinguish between two fundamental choices: the importance given to rural communities as intermediaries in decisions taken concerning their own economic, social, and political future, by recognition of their right of negotiation; and the nature and priority given to economic growth, where financial and economic equilibria are the determinants of the model of development. These choices are never entirely explicit. However, they influence profoundly the nature of the urban system.

The manner in which effective choices, decision making, and their implied powers are set to work, ideologically, politically, and economically, will determine the several types of evolutionary place given to urban models in the process of transforming the rural world. This can take the form of favoring population on the norms of city dwellers or of a path based on alliance between peasants and urban dwellers, determining the options for priority and the exchanges between the rural and urban worlds. Finally, the urban system may be questioned fundamentally, and the development of rural areas is then envisaged as the promotion of a peasant egalitarianism that is generalized to the whole of society.

The preceding considerations raise more than theoretical questions. They ask whether the urban system is a constituent part of the system of power, and in what measure the changes that occur in their relations affect rural policies, determining the orientation of rural areas. Stated otherwise, is there a correspondence between the urban system and the power system which is so perfect that they constitute one and the same system, or are these two distinct but interdependent systems? In the latter hypothesis, does the elimination of the urban system bring fundamental changes to the power system, and does it provoke profound transformations in the evolutionary conditions and transformation of rural areas?

Two cases illustrating different types of rupture enable us to grasp the circumstances in which a disjunction between the urban system and the system of power occurs. The Cambodia of the Khmer Rouge and the Iran of the shah are both examples worthy of exploration.

From 1975 on, a quasi-experimental attempt at radical transformation of rural areas was undertaken in Cambodia. It took the form of an organized ruralization of the whole society after the evacuation of the cities and the forced exodus of their populations to the countryside. This experiment, which lasted nearly three years, took the form of a countermodel to the general evolution of societies in the Third World, where there had been an increasing reinforcement of the hold of the cities on the rural world.

The evacuation of Phnom Penh and the setting to work of all levels of the population in the fields was an ideological decision to create an egalitarian society on the basis of the production of a new man, but it had political and economic objectives as well. Food self-sufficiency was to be secured, and independence of the country guaranteed. This extreme choice was made in reaction to the policy pursued by the Americans during the war, which had brought about a massive urbanization by radical depopulation of the countryside for strategic purposes, and led to an influx of rural folk into the cities. The American policy was intended to weaken the resistance of the countryside and permit more effective control of the urban populations destined to serve as a reserve army for the war and ultimately as a reserve of labor. The circumstances at the end of the war, in particular the risks of famine but also the will to power of a victorious army made up overwhelmingly of peasants, and the temptation to take a historic shortcut toward a completely new society also played into the choice.

Behind these explanations there were other realities: the narrowness of the political base of the victorious army, the consciousness among its leaders of the difficulties in building a new state on an urban system swollen artificially by the war, posing insoluble problems of a political and economic order. In destroying the urban system, in reducing its institutions to nothingness, a form of the state and a system of power were also destroyed, with relations of production, social relations, and cultural symbols having to be substituted. This extreme solution, involving the liquidation of all the representatives of the fallen state that had been assimilated to urban power, brought in a "politico-administrative apparatus, strictly hierarchical and organized on the military model." The territory was divided into six geographic zones and society into three categories of "forces of production"—the young, adults, the aged.[4] Such an organization implies a double control—of geographic movements of the population and their numerical size. The extreme mobilization of "peasants" for productive work, the strict control of marriages, and the affirmation by the Khmer Rouge that a million or two young people would suffice for the reconstruction of the country shows the intent to effect a violent reduction of the population. It is not surprising that it would result in the dramatic diminution of the Cambodian population by half. Three million inhabitants were the price paid for this ideological madness.

This radical restructuring occurred in a rural society that had undergone neither advanced proletarianization nor a massive rural exodus before the war. The close, oppressive, and rigid control of the peasantry (by the Khmer Rouge) was accompanied by a technological choice: the permanent mobilization of the population to ensure its food self-sufficiency. Producers were to count only on their own labor; the utilization of machines was excluded; they were perceived as opposed to the type of society that was in the making. The cost in human lives through forced labor became intolerable and was followed by the collapse of the system, independent of the external causes that precipitated its fall.

The "Angkor" organization aimed to resolve all the contradictions of Cambodian society at the same time, passing beyond the urban-rural cleavage, class opposition, demographic problems, technological constraints, and their implications, as well as the food supply impasse—a set of acute problems present in virtually all countries of the Third World. But the organization aimed further, if not above all, to resolve its own contradiction in Cambodian society, to wit the narrowness of its political and social base, by the elimination of the system of urban power that dominated the country until the fall of Phnom Penh.[5] Do the conditions in which this "experiment" of radical disruption of an old peasantry occurred authorize us to view the strategy of liquidation of cities as exceptional and unprecedented? One is tempted to reply in the affirmative.[6]

At the opposite pole of the strategy for the destruction of the cities is an *inverse strategy*, that of consolidating the power system by extending the urban system. The most pronounced expression of this is the attempts by the shah of Iran to create original institutions that would integrate the traditional influence of the cities in the country-side of a Muslim country, both on cultural and religious planes, but also at the level of exchanges and services, with modernizing actions and the reinforcement of the power of the Iranian state in the rural world. Armies "of God," "knowledge," "hygiene," "development and reconstruction," were created to ensure the triple aim of consolidating under the cover of Islam, the imperial ideology.[7] It was intended to extract the peasants from networks of traditional power, putting them into direct relationship with the state and its institutions, extending the mechanisms of an urban system articulated with world markets into defined zones of the Iranian countryside through radical modernization .

Such a strategy consisted of the programmed liquidation of rural communities by means of an agrarian reform that aimed at the dismantling of a network of traditional powers. Initially, it gave birth to a peasant power that was quickly stifled and replaced by other powers of control, closely centralized in a state bureaucracy, supported by an emerging aristocracy. The objective was to break the rural armature of the villages, the number of which was to be considerably reduced, suppressing the intermediate feudal powers that had existed between the peasantry and the central power.[8] The rural population was to be reduced, subordinated to technocrats and businessmen, to coercion and control through state organizations.[9]

The modernization of agriculture was based on the introduction of agribusiness in the frame of "poles of development,"[10] circumscribed in number and location, concentrating men and investments in favored zones. This called for the abandonment of vast spaces that were considered unprofitable (steppe zones and small irrigated areas). The undercutting of vast pastoral areas and the condemning of small-scale irrigation, paradoxically, only emphasized the incapacity of the favored zones of development to ensure the food supply of the country because of their orientation toward export products.

In this context, exchange between city and countryside became more and more unequal; agricultural prices remained unchanged, while the price of urban products soared, increasing the disparities between the rural population and urban dwellers.

The policy provoked an uprooting of the rural people and gave rise to a particularly wild urbanization, with the creation of enormous dormitory cities. It was the source of violent spatial disequilibria, producing poverty zones that drove the rural population toward the cities. Transfer of new structures to the countryside and of destitute rural people toward the urban centers—through a process of modernization that produced waste and poverty, the decay of structures, the exacerbation of social disparities and regional inequalities- —ended up by changing the very nature of the urban system. Industrialization was not able to compensate for the destruction of preexisting social relations or the penetration of unemployment and poverty, induced by the combined effects of modernization, demographic growth, and explosive urbanization.[11]

This strategy, born of an excessive will to power and supported by the extension of an urban system closely subordinated to "centers of decision, conception and research and to technical management and commercialization bureaus, to producers of capital goods"[12] located abroad, ended by collapsing because the social, economic, political, and cultural disruptions it produced in the rural areas as well as in the cities became intolerable for a people who had been subjected to them for more than twenty years.

This was more than a flawed model of development; it was a manifestation of structural divorce between the nation and the state in Iran.[13] The Pahlavi dynasty thought it could obtain the legitimacy refused to it because of its foreign origins by radically reconstructing society. In seeking to generalize an urban system into a countryside with feudal structures, this exercise of power unleashed a shockwave that struck the cities with full force. Unwittingly, it introduced the Trojan Horse, which permitted the urban revolt to carry it away, bringing to an end a power which, for want of a consensus on the part of the nation, sought support outside the present time and the national area.

In the preceding cases rural development policies have had one of two objectives: ensuring the increase of production and political and ideological control of the rural population, or modernizing the rural areas by extending the urban industrial system.

Other strategies have also been tried, which, while pursuing all the preceding objectives, seek to remodel the urban system itself—which, while dependent on the rural areas for food, holds the monopoly of services and collective facilites. The project is to create in the rural world human and socioeconomic units that combine the advantages of ensuring their own subsistence while enjoying facilities and services indispensable to agricultural production and to peasants' daily consumption.

Two experiments show the difficulties of this strategy: these are the communal (*ujamaa*) villages of Tanzania and the communal villages (*aldeicomunais*) of Mozambique. The transformation of the villages was supposed to permit these two neighboring countries, weakly industrialized and urbanized, to satisfy the essential needs of the peasants within society, free of the links of dependence.

In Tanzania, the *ujamaa* village program was elaborated by the state's planners in reaction to the reinforcement of dependency after the three- and five-year plans of the 1960s, and the failure of the agricultural policy based on concentration of investments in more favorable zones.[14] A policy of opening colonization zones in the frame of a plan for populating uninhabited regions had no more success; it resulted in neither the augmentation of production, nor the creation of a dynamic agricultural sector controlled by a category of rich peasants. As a consequence, the state nationalized the vital sectors of activity in the cities and colonization lands, and created *ujamaa* villages, which regrouped a population of small holders living in subsistence agriculture to work together on common lands.[15]

The *ujamaa* villages evolved according to their own capacities and the will of the peasants to collectivize their production and consumption activities. With the economic crisis of 1973, due in part to drought but also to structural failings of the economy, coercion prevailed over persuasion in the formation of villages. It was the "villagization" policy that regrouped the dispersed population in villages to which services, schools, dispensaries, and water were brought.[16] This reshaping of the rural space was accompanied by a reduction in the collective forms of exploitation that were rejected by the peasants. Only a single collective field, worked by labor provided by the villagers, continued to procure the means to finance services and equipment for the villages.

This reordering of the rural development sector took the form of a regaining of powers at the local level by the administrative hierarchy of the state.[17] Regional cooperative organizations of state farms were dissolved in 1975 when there was a reinforcement of the state farms and a relaunching of an urban private sector. A policy of industrial development around basic industries recentered the new economic strategy on the urban industrial system.

The existence of a village sector comprising nearly 8,000 villages posed problems with regard to management of space. The peasants' villages are very far from their fields. Thus, plans were made to reduce the concentration of villages and take part of the inhabitants closer to their private fields, while reinforcing the equipment network by favoring village centers for the location of services. With the creation of village managers, the concentration of local power in the hands of planning agents and of equipment and services in the village centers surreptitiously introduced the logic of the urban system to the countryside. Successes were registered in education, health, adult literacy, and production.

What is striking in the development model chosen by Morocco is its constant unity of inspiration. The state opted to favor the countryside over the cities. Its refusal of an industrial policy, perceived as a potential risk toward the reinforcement of the urban system, was inspired by the same principle; it was considered as a corollary to the necessity of limiting the weight of the cities in the social and political equilibrium of the country.[18]

This option had historical foundations. During the precolonial epoch, the two major protagonists on the scene were the state (the *Makhzen*) and the tribal communities. The city represented a stake that was sometimes of great symbolic value, but it did not constitute an autonomous force able to dictate its law to the *Makhzen* or the tribes.

During the colonial period, resistance to the occupation (from 1912 to 1934) made the countryside at first a place of weakness for the state. Only subsequently (with the Dahir Berbère of 1930) did the city become the principal actor in the struggle against colonialism. It emerged triumphant in 1956 with independence.

The rural troubles of the High Atlas and the Rif (in 1959) made political power sensitive to tensions in the rural world. Because the colonial power had favored the city, the countryside remained relatively disadvantaged. Thus the plan of 1960–1964, which reflected choices made by the urban elites for industrial development, was corrected after its promulgation to make it lean toward options more favorable to the agricultural sector.[19] This tendency remains the foundation of the model of accumulation put in place during the 1960s. In this model, social investments (housing, education, health) are considered unproductive.

The successive coups d'état of 1971 and 1972, however, attracted attention to the urgency of what was going on in the cities. The rise of a middle class for which independence was to open the way to the realization of its aspirations obliged the state to readjust the policy to accord more possibilities to these rising strata, so that they could benefit from employment, housing, schools, and hospitals created in the cities. For the planners, "the rural exodus is at the same time the sign and guarantee of development."[20] Has there been a manifest change of attitude toward migration from the countryside to the cities? In reality, it is a question of a "policy" that has been progressively elaborated, step by step, in the framework of a global action. The 220,000 houses foreseen for the rural world were declared beyond the capacity of the state.[21] The readjustment was designed to respond to the demand of an urban social stratum that occupies a critical place on the political chessboard and to the outbreak of massive urbanization. From 1971 to 1982 the cities increased 4.5 percent annually and tensions multiplied.

The social movements of January 1981 again tipped the balance toward the countryside. A severe drought lasting several years aggravated the crisis of the rural world, which only heightened the urban crisis and that of the state's finances. From 1984 on, the year when the troubles extended to the cities of the northern part of the country, Casablanca and Marrakech, equal attention was accorded the cities.[22] How is it, then, that this flexibility in the adjustment of economic and social policy has not given the results expected in either the control of the urban system or the transformation of the countryside?

A major contradiction has marked the chosen strategy. Concern with sociopolitical equilibria has dictated the maintenance of traditional structures. There has been no notable upsetting of land tenures, only limited distribution of lands and the maintenance of poorly productive collective lands (20 percent of the lands). Local elites in the rural areas continue to be supported. The stratifying power of the community moderates the integrationist tendencies of the state while also expanding them in the long term. This strategy, combined with an effort to limit the rural exodus and extend the urban system very moderately, has had the effect of slowing down the momentum of urbanization.

The economic necessity of increasing food production led the state to multiply its organizations for intervention in the countryside. But these state apparatuses (offices of agricultural development, provincial agricultural authorities, central ministries) have another logic— that of economic and technical rationality. They encourage production directed to the external market (vegetables and citrus fruit) much more than production for internal consumption (cereals and legumes). After thirty years of this strategy, Morocco has been falling progressively into food dependency. It exports with more and more difficulty what it produces, and it imports more and more of what it consumes in agricultural products. Exports cover only two-thirds of imports.[23]

The major part of the peasantry is caught in nets of traditional organization but shows remarkable initiative in modernizing production. Nonetheless, it is constrained by a lack of credit, the prices of agricultural products, the cost of inputs, and the circuits of commercialization. Also, 56.5 percent have less than 24.5 percent of the arable land,[24] and the World Bank estimated in 1977 that 45 percent of the rural population, that is to say, 5 million peasants, were living in "absolute poverty."[25]

The enormous investments conceived by the state have benefited only 7 percent of the arable lands. The irrigated areas appear as islands having no relationship with dry-land agriculture (90 percent of the lands and 85 percent of the rural population), which accounts for the overwhelming majority of the cultivated areas in the countryside. It is not surprising that in these conditions the rural exodus has intensified, although it shows a tendency to diminish in relation to the growth of cities. In spite of all this, the urban system has not dismantled the peasantry, which remains active and anchored in its setting.

Investment in hydraulic works, production subsidies, partial or total fiscal exemptions to the benefit of the farmers (to the 9 percent of the farms that occupy 55 percent of the lands and receive 40 percent of the disposable income[26]) explain at once the efforts of the state and the beneficiaries of its manna. How does it happen in these conditions that, with half of the population still in the countryside, the development strategy for agricultural production has failed?

To this question must be added another. The strategy of the state is to oppose the inexorable growth of the cities. However, the activities of urban government (in providing employment, sociocultural infrastructure, and services) role and influence in the countryside, thereby promoting rural exodus. How is it that the state, which wishes to master the urban system, works against its own policy of stabilizing the peasantry?

One must seek the answer to these questions in the persistence of a whole nebula of small farmers. They show signs of great adaptability to the modernization of cultures. They dig wells and change their agricultural techniques in the quest for survival and gain. Through seasonal migration from countryside to city, the peasants engage in supplementary activites that give them enough income to maintain their farms.[27] Many newly arrived urban dwellers continue to live on small incomes from plots of land they own in villages. Successful emigration to the cities or abroad permits going beyond the survival level to invest in modern production on their farms.

It is not only through complementary incomes that small farms are maintained. The system of patronage practiced by the elite permits some redistribution of resources. The social hierarchy remains functional because to continue acquiring resources, those at the top must in turn distribute some resources.

The central problem is to see to what degree this hierarchy limits or accelerates production. Morocco's debt is so great ($17.5 billion dollars in 1988) and its economic crisis so profound that creating any practical way to deal with the demographic increase and ensure the food self-sufficiency of the country lies well beyond this century.

Is there a difference in nature or simply in levels of development or degrees of evolution of the urban system's contradictions between these cases and other countries? Does a model of the evolution of city-country relations and of the system of power underlying them exist?[28]

The city is an expression of the urban system. Into this space where social, political, economic, and cultural antagonisms are interwoven, the state does not operate simply as a factor of regulation. In constructing the nation-state, the phase most countries of the Third World are experiencing, the state is itself a part of the struggle among the competing interests. In these conditions the state is a component of the urban system.

Conversely, in a situation of conflict—the disjunction of the power system and the urban system or the identification of one with the other—the true stakes become the existence of the established power. Then the urban system is condemned to destruction because it is perceived as a totally antagonistic element serving the objectives of the existing power. The disappearance of the city becomes necessary to the establishment or the survival of a new power.

A number of characteristics distinguish each urban system—its history, the unfolding of its urbanization process, its distribution and territorial radiation, its relationship to the rural communities, and the nature of its commercial, cultural, and political networks.

Set within a definite territory, dominated by a state and articulated with other fields of state activity, the urban system develops two tendencies, each in contradiction with its specific nature. There is, on the one hand, the rapidity and similarity of its process of growth across continents and, on the other hand, the autonomy the system acquires vis-à-vis the state. As urbanization develops, the social and economic contrasts within the city and the migratory flows intensify; the rural areas lose their structure through the departure of their best-trained and most dynamic elements, through the loss of their resources and the erosion of their communal institutions. The urban system acquires in this way an autonomy against which the state cannot act, because of impotence, resignation, or fear of putting civil order at risk or of damaging the interests it protects. Thus, policies of struggle against rural exodus, by fixing peasants on the land, have failed to slow down urban concentration. There is a manifest inability to stem the "invasions," to move or eliminate substandard housing. Rural people living in the city have the tenacity to manage, innovate, improve housing, and constantly create situations about which the most coercive state can often do nothing. These people represent between a quarter and a third of the population of the cities, sometimes more. The urban system thus tends to function autonomously in both cities and countryside, outside the power of the state.

The urban system thus appears to the population as an effective system, a supplier of employment, services, equipment, and infrastructure, and as a place for the social and economic advancement of individuals. The state, however, in the conditions of socioeconomic and political evolution of most countries of the Third World, is not able to face these aspirations. Demands develop for rights to the enjoyment of advantages and the utilization of public goods seen more and more as indispensable—health, potable water, roads, education, services, leisure facilities. Dearth manifests itself within the interior of the cities themselves, and when the state undertakes to satisfy these new needs, it only increases the attraction of the urban system. In attracting rural people, and in tending toward a concentration in a few large cities, the urban system increases its inertia and rigidity.

There develops at the same time a propensity to diffuse and multiply the activities of exchange and of services more easily than activites of production. Tasks and occupations fragment, adding to the multiplicity of circuits and forms of distribution. On the one hand, the enormity of the needs for equipment and infrastructure is paralyzing; on the other hand, the urban economy is malleable; it adjusts to the multiform demands for goods and services, ranging from the utilization of avant-garde technology to the salvaging of the most miserable materials for housing and the necessities of daily life in the most deprived layers. The conjunction of these two tendencies, contradictory in appearance, determines the margin for autonomous functioning of the urban system with respect to the state.

Cutting across the state's policies and playing on the contradictions of a poorly mastered urban development, capital is invested and gives structure to domains left explicitly to its initiative. It extends its action into areas left at the margin of state activity, or it tends to reoccupy terrain that had been reserved for urban government, thanks to exploitation of gaps in institutions or by their diversion or manipulation. It deploys its own strategy to effect decisions which affect the functioning of the urban system with a view to orienting it to its exclusive profit.

The state itself does not master the outcomes of its policy; a massive industrialization program may create upsets in the agricultural sector. In provoking tensions over employment, it affects activity, production, and housing in the countryside, unleashing a flow of migrants to the cities, which acts in turn on the problems of housing, employment, and services. The whole urban system is thus paralyzed, and its subsequent management becomes costly and its growth irrational.

This model of evolution has functioned perfectly but inversely. That is to say, we have had:

Accelerated urban growth.

Limited industrialization.

Deterioration of the rural areas.

This reverse evolution in the functioning of the model is not due uniquely to the constraining factor of demography: countries low in rural population density have experienced the same evolution. What, then, has blocked the model in its functioning? In the historic conditions of its application (colonization, domination, hegemony), disequilibrium has been created in space, exchanges and flows, and power.

The literature on the urban crisis and economic research has been preoccupied with the disequilibria between north and south. It has focused less on other relationships, such as that between city and rural area. Certainly, north-south relations are decisive as an element in the explanation of the crisis, but the relationships of city and rural area are no less so. The city is the place where dominant and dominated rural relations are articulated. The city serves, in its turn, as a relay—it rules the rural area that it dominates. This linkage space that is the city (and the apparatus of production and exchange organized there) functions in the last analysis as a system. At its entry and exit one finds flows of energy, capital, products, and people. Set in a favored, even strategic, position, the growth of this system has blocked the functioning of the model of development and inverted its mechanisms.[29] The system escapes any mastery because it acquires a species of autonomous functioning. The social and political actors are unable to contain it. They can neither discipline its growth nor prevent some of the consequences of this growth— poverty, insecurity, and violence.

The complex interactions among its different components, therefore, make the urban system a giant mechanism of social and economic transfer through the aspirations for rise in the social scale of more and more definite social categories. Actions and initiatives designed in the beginning to improve the living conditions of populations in the city as well as in the countryside are caught in this mechanism. Through the complexity of its workings, the urban system evolves as a mechanism for multiplying disparities through two movements: the one pressing the majority of the urban population toward situations beset with insecurities and excluding them from equitable sharing in the incomes created by the city, the other attracting a minority toward decision centers that permit them to dispose of income and ensure the best conditions of existence in the city.

In such a system, the state represents a decisive factor. Either it accelerates the movement toward more disparity by political, economic, social, and cultural choices; or it tries to reduce the contrasts in standards of living and to attenuate social cleavages. In the former case, the rural areas disintegrate; in the second case, the impact of the urban system changes.[30]

In these conditions, the urban system has a primordial significance. Through it, the state gives concrete content to its policy with regard to the rural area, whatever may be its original motivations, ideological options, or professions of faith about social choices. In designating the rural areas or the city as the vital locus of its strategy—a policy of "rural development" or of "industrial development"—the policy either accentuates the contradictions of the urban system and its impact on the countryside, or it attenuates them according to the capacity of the state to prevent ruptures and avoid the risk of bringing its own survival into question. Radical strategies underestimate the contradictions that develop in the urban system itself because, when it is condemned or manipulated as a simple instrument of power, it behaves like a boomerang. The objectives of public policies of readjustment are to take into consideration the mechanisms of the urban system, the reality of its relative autonomy, and to attempt to ease the conflicts and reduce the contradictions that develop in the system or in the places it dominates.

The fundamental choice for the state is between a strategy based on long-term urbanization of the society in its totality and a strategy that adapts to the functioning of the urban system as it has resulted from a more or less long evolution, without seeking or being able to bring about a solution to the problem of urban development. The state then shifts its vigilance and effort to the rural world because the countryside is seen as the essential place of its fragility.

Do these schemes of differentiation of urban systems give a better appreciation of their impact on the rural areas? Physical urbanization, equipment, types of rural development, modes of incorporation of the peasantry, the industrialization of the countryside, and the consequences on the volume of employment have meaning in reference to the particular characteristics of an urban system. A road, a piece of equipment, the organization of a market, the introduction of new techniques of production or training, an extension of the infrastructure of transport and service will have quite different significance according to which type of urban system they are attached to.

Policies of transformation of the rural world must always affect the cities. Any attempt to stabilize rural populations and restrain the exodus toward the urban centers must be seen for what it is. The alternative to urbanization appears as a utopia. A certain mastery of urban growth remains possible only if the increase of productive forces is not the ultimate aim of the evolution of production. If, on the contrary, the latter is only a means to ensure the largest possible distribution of goods and services to all categories of the population—urban and rural—then it becomes viable. The development of the rural world would then take the form of a reduction of disparities between town and country through control over the process of modernization by the rural population itself, in the framework of negotiations that make possible bargaining between local requirements and national imperatives.

The optimal rate of urbanization will vary according to how long urbanization has existed, the state of economic evolution, and the resources of a country. In creating a balance of power between countryside and city, central power recognizes implicitly the validity of a counterweight to its own authority. This dynamic equilibrium ought not to involve only the claims of the urban and the rural. It is equally a function of relations of the urban system with the outside world, of forms of dependence, of political will and possibilities, and therefore a question of commercial exchanges, international credits, and access to the technology of industrial powers.[31] On the totality of these variables the productivity of the urban system depends, that is to say, its capacity for mastering the economy and demography of regional spaces and at the same time ameliorating the living conditions of rural populations generally. These relations must be the object of constant negotiation between city dwellers and peasants.

This readjustment can only come about to the degree that regulating institutions function. It must take into consideration the political realities of the rural areas, so that the only basis for political functioning is not the existing social hierarchy. Economic effectiveness may come about through a new manner of organizing demand that rests on the existing social structures yet inclines toward a more democratic evolution. A utopian society without a hierarchy leads to a sharp change of structure and, in consequence, to an economic impasse (through restraining production) and political crisis.

For this strategy to succeed, the preceding condition is necessary but not sufficient. It presupposes a dual orientation. At the level of the urban system, there is the necessity to give the rural communities sociocultural equipment and infrastructure adapted to their own situations, which will attenuate the appeal of the city. The extension of the urban system would function then as a vaccine and not as a virus that destroys the social fabric. At the demographic level, controlling population growth is fundamental to mastering the relationship of resources to population and of city to countryside.

Above all, in Third World countries, no development is possible without the prior development of rural areas.

ENDNOTES

[1]B. Taylor, "Savoir et pouvoir dans l'urbanisme colonial," *Les Cahiers de la recherche architecturale*, no. 9 (January 1982).

[2]C. Taillard, "Les Représentations étatiques des espaces ruraux," in report of the Colloquium on Change in the Rural Areas of the Third World, *Action thématique programée* (France: Centre national de la recherche scientifique, 1980).

[3]C. Taillard, "Pouvoir et espace au Laos," in *Etat, pouvoir et espace dans le Tiers-Monde*, written under the direction of C. Bataillon (Paris: IEDES-Tiers-Monde, Presse universitaire de France, 1977).

[4]F. Ponchaud, "Le Cambodge, année zero," *Document Juilliard* (1977).

[5]"Vider ainsi, Phnom-Penh de sa population ne repondait à aucun mobile écologique ou économique; il ne s'agissait ni de requilibrer les rapports ville-compagne, ni de changer la ville, mais prendre le pouvoir. Privé de la base urbaine qui aurait permis son éventuelle reconstitution, l'Etat qui était mis en place pour Sihauouk s'effondra." (George Boudarel, P. Brocheux, and D. Henry, "Craquement un Asie," *Le Monde diplomatique* [February 1979]:4.)

[6]Equatorial Guinea had the same experience: a country with weak urbanization, a sparse population (on 300,000 hectares in 1968), but strong basic literacy. It underwent—under a dictatorship that lasted more than a decade—a veritable withering of the urban system. Malabo and Bala became villages of unrest, and 60,000 persons were reduced to forced labor; the political class was physically eliminated and the cultivation of cacao fell apart. (See I. Ramonet, "Guinée équatoriale: l'état des supplices," *Le Monde diplomatique* [December 1978]: 4–5 and Elisabeth Becker, *When the Was Is Over* (Paris: Presse de la Cité).

These two limited experiences of Cambodia and Equatorial Guinea had two small countries as a laboratory. Would they have been able to succeed in a large, well-populated area? The spatial dimension of the area population size, and the size of the villages make manipulation of the urban system problematic. For these reasons, the Cultural Revolution in China, in spite of its struggle for urban power, could not emerge above these two extremes.

[7]P. Vieille, "Transformation des rapports sociaux et révolution en Iran," *Peuples Méditerranéens* (July-September 1979):25–58.

[8]In fact, the dislocation of traditional powers was unequal: at one time the large landowners were spared (khorassan); at another a distinction was made between large grain producers and producers of tea for export who had maintained their ownership. In the villages the elimination of large landowners had been compensated for by the maintenance of administrative chiefs, middle-size landowners, or former accountants of the wealthiest landlords. (Communication with J. Dresch.)

[9]The Ve Plan (1972–1976) forecast the reduction of the rural population to 25 percent of total population. In Khuzistan 38,000 families were pushed off

57,000 hectares. (See Thirry-A Brun, "Les Echecs du développement a l'Occidental accroissent les difficultés du régime," *Le Monde diplomatique* [July 1978]:18.)

[10]Outside these privileged zones, according to an official circular, there was neither credit nor subsidy. Neither was there agricultural extension or mechanization; nor were schools, clinics, highways, or electricity established outside the poles of growth: "Ainsi, la migration des populations vivant en dehors des pôles vers ceux-ci pourra être envisagée." (See *Revue Iranienne d'économie*, no. 56 [1978].)

[11]According to statements of former Prime Minister A. Hoveida, this urbanization was to be organized in forty-three cities with fourteen metropolises between the end of the 1960s and the end of the century (proposal reported by J. Lacouture in *Le Monde*, 2 November 1967). In the same statement the ex–prime minister assigned the Iranian economy the objective of "catching up with Europe in thirty years" and to be "the Japan of the Third World." (See E. Rouleau, "L'Opulence et la force," *Encyclopédie Universalis*, 1974.)

[12]P. Vieille, 40 ff.

[13]P. Vieille, ibid.

[14]Peter Temu, "L'experience 'Ujamaa'," *Ceres: Revue de la FAO sur le développement*, special issue on Africa (July-August 1973):71–75.

[15]D. Martin, "Le socialisme Tanzanien: de la critique à l'action," *Le Monde diplomatique* (June 1978):6.

[16]Thirteen million residents were regrouped in this way. See D. Martin, "Le socialisme Tanzanien aux prises avec la dépendance," *Le Monde diplomatique* (April 1979).

[17]J. K. Nyerere, *Le Declaration d'Arusha dix ans après, bilan et perspectives* (Paris: L'Harmattan, 1978). See also Martin.

[18]M. Naciri, "Pouvoir de commandement, espace rural et modernisation au Maroc," in *Etat, Pouvoir et Espace dans le Tiers-Monde* (Paris: IEDES–Collection Tiers-Monde, Presse Universitaire de France, 1977).

[19]Rural development must in its first phase ensure "la constitution de nouvelles unités de groupement en milieu rural par l'equipement des centres ruraux." (*Plan quinquennal 1960–1964, Royaume du Maroc* [Ministère de l'économie nationale, Division de la coordination et du plan, November 1960], 261.)

[20]*Plan de développement économique et social, 1973–1977, Royaume du Maroc*, vol. 2, "Développement sectoriel" (Premier Ministre, Secretariat d'état au plan et au développement régional), 442.

[21]*Plan de développement économique et social, 1973–1977*, 452. See also "L'Exode rural peut être un facteur de progrès," in vol. 1, *Plan quinquennal 1968–1972, Royaume du Maroc* (Ministère des affaires économique du plan et de la formation des cadres), 87. See R. Escalier, "Maghreb-Machreq, La Documentation française," *French Quarterly Review* (no. 118) (fourth trimester, 1987):20–45.

[22]C. W. Stockton, "Drought, Water Management, and Food Production," in *Current Research Progress Toward Understanding Drought,* proceedings of conference (Agadir, Morocco: Kingdom of Morocco, 1985).

[23]N. Akesbi, "Sur le Maroc: de la dépendance alimentaire, à la dépendance financière," *African Development* 10 (3) (1985):40–62.

[24]N. Bouderbala, "Les structures agraires," in *Agriculture-pêche, La grande encyclopédie au Maroc,* 1987, 12–28.

[25]*Maroc, Rapport sur le développement économique et social* (Washington: World Bank, October 1979).

[26]N. Akesbi.

[27]F. Alioua, D. Benatya, and L. Zagdouni, *L'Impact socio-économique des projets d'irrigation, Dokkala I et II,* reports: *Les Ressources de l'exploitation, Relations de l'exploitation avec son environment socio-economique, L'Impact socio-economique de l'irrigation sur les femmes* (Rabat, Morocco: Direction du développement rural, Institut agronomique et vétérinaire Hassan II and World Bank, 1988).

[28]The "urban preference" restrains the development of the Third World. See the elements of reflection in "La Primauté du rapport inegal ville-campagne sur la differenciation interne de chaque secteur," *Le Monde diplomatique* (June, 1978): 13. See also B. Kayser, "Pauvreté urbaine, pauvreté rurale, le pillage des miettes," *Revue du Tiers-Monde* 20 (80) (October-December 1979):695–702.

[29]M. Naciri, *La crise urbaine,* introductory report to the scientific records of URBAMA (Tours, France: Centre national de la recherche scientifique, 1984).

[30]See World Bank, "Le Rôle de l'état," chap. 4 in *Rapport sur le développement dans le monde,* 1987 (Washington, D.C.: World Bank, 1988), 68. The authors indicate that "l'inégalité dans la répartition des revenus peuvent s'aggraver au cours des premières décennies du développement" even if the real income of the poorest classes increases. The present realities of the underdeveloped countries show that the tendency is to aggravate and not to reduce inequalities.

[31]C. Bataillon.

Translated by Francis X. Sutton.

Comments on Mohamed Naciri's Essay

HOLLIS B. CHENERY: Discussions of the urban problem have gone through various stages: sometimes they are very theoretical; at others they are very empirical. Ten years ago the World Bank surveyed the needs for research in various fields, and the urban problem came out near the top of its list. The bank has now published what we call a new look at development research; rapid urbanization is again near the top of the list of problems.

I would ask first, how do you know when urbanization is too rapid. Most people seem to think that the problem arises from having a too rapid growth of cities. The way economists go about their analysis, the sort of semi-modern way, is to think of an urban economy with one kind of technology linked to a rural economy by trade and migration. All this presupposes the existence of markets. How well do these markets work? If the markets work well, if people, goods, and capital move in response to interglobal price mechanisms, then the system is thought to be working. If the system does not work well, or if improvements are thought to be necessary, you have to identify where the markets are failing.

For example, I would refer to two studies on Colombia financed by the World Bank, which has become one of the leaders of research in this area. The bank searched the world for a representative country and picked Colombia; it spent a couple of million dollars in its inquiry. I find the case interesting because, though this is one of the best studies in the field, most of the guesses made about overurbanization have been misleading. Instead of finding great bottlenecks, as the Arthur Lewis hypothesis about surplus labor in the countryside might have suggested with large differences in wages and so forth, Bogotá, in fact, was not growing too fast. It may still not be growing too fast, given its infrastructure. In fact, if anything, the growth may be too slow.

A more recent study of the Colombian economy, concentrating on the urban areas, looked at the labor markets. If labor markets have been working well, it is difficult to know why the government would wish to intervene. The Colombian study suggests that the case for intervention was much less strong than the urban experts had been prepared to maintain.

There is also a similar study of India, using the same sort of methodology, which tends again to support the idea that less intervention is necessary for the economy to work well. The only reason I bring this up is that such study provides a framework for asking questions. If you are interested not only in gross income but in income distribution, you may be surprised that the differences in wages and incomes are not as large as they were expected to be. Yet the economists' approach is not always welcome. The argument, for example, that you do not need to intervene in all urban transport, as governments usually do where private transport works, is not always welcome. Edmar Bacha can tell us whether the private transport system works or does not, and the questions need to be put in those terms.

In other aspects of the urban setting, where decisions have to be made on how to spend money, as in the housing sector, government intervention is typically unsuccessful and expensive. It may be part of the political strategy of governments to sponsor public housing projects, but such housing is rarely part of an efficient program of economic interventions.

MIGUEL URRUTIA: One of the interesting things about Colombia is that the absence of capital-city overurbanization may be explained by the political system. Given the structure of political parties in Colombia, the periphery has tremendous political power. By the time Hollis and his employment experts got there, there had been ten or fifteen years during which the central government had made no subsidy transfers to support investment in infrastructure in Bogotá or any of the other major cities. The national budget, therefore, did not create incentives for urban centralization.

This particular political configuration is very different, for example, in Mexico. There we find tremendous subsidies and substantial central intervention in favor of the people in Mexico City. The structure of political power may have something to do with some of the results you find; perhaps Colombia is not as difficult to explain once the political situation is taken into account.

CLIFFORD GEERTZ: I would like to say something about the generalization problem, and about the comment that Cambodia and the shah's Iran are not typical cases. They are not. The Cambodian case is extreme by anybody's measure, but the shah's case I am not sure is so extreme. At least one of the principal sources of the shah's policy was his American advisers. Undercutting the traditional structures upon which one needs to rely, so that when difficulties arise one has no power structure to call upon, is not exactly an ungeneralizable case. It is unique in its particulars, but it is the sort of thing that the ruler wants to avoid by keeping political rural structures in place, so that when the cities become rebellious, he has something to offset them with. The tendency to think that there cannot be too much overurbanization, that there cannot be too much emptying of the villages, is politically dangerous advice to the health of rulers. The other thing I would say is that whether urbanization is too fast or not fast enough is not really the whole question. Urbanization *is* very fast, and that raises very serious internal problems. In the town I study in Morocco, over half the population has been there fewer than ten years, and there are cultural differences as well. So you have an internal structural problem that is extraordinary. It is not just a question of going too fast or too slow; the town is growing very fast, and combined with other kinds of convulsion, that does put urban policy and structural policy right at the center of the political map. But it does not seem to me that either slowing down or speeding up urbanization really states the issue properly.

NANCY BIRDSALL: Hollis is saying that markets are working, that it is difficult to conclude that there is overurbanization. But I think that much of the research to which Hollis has referred shows only that labor markets are working. People are acting rationally, given the circumstances, when they move from rural areas to urban areas. It does not make sense to intervene with all kinds of planned interventions to try to stop that flow. But the problem with the argument, which I know Hollis is aware of, though he chose not to focus on it, is that other markets are not working properly. Foreign exchange regimes favor the industrial areas, with all kinds of subsidies given to capital to favor urban areas. So, even though you do not want government to step in to reduce people's freedom to move or do other foolish things that would cost money and be ineffective, in preventing people from moving, you might wish to change the distortions in the other markets that are contributing to what may be—depending on the extent of those distortions—overurbanization.

I think an issue that economists have not looked at, which I suspect geographers are investigating, is the issue of scale. This comes out when you start looking at the problem—so-called—of cities from a population point of view. What you see is that in ten or twenty years, many cities in developing countries will be even larger than Mexico City is now, which means that they will be larger than the size cities ever attained in industrial countries. Twice as big, three times as big, four times as big. By 2020, the ten biggest cities in the developing countries will probably be the ten biggest cities in the world. They will all have more than 20 million people, or even 25 million people. I do not believe that development communities, let alone urban planners, know how to cope with such numbers. How to organize transportation, housing, working space, and the like when you have these numbers is something that we have not even begun to consider.

Paul R. Krugman

Developing Countries in the World Economy

D EVELOPING COUNTRIES have never been a unified group. Yet there was a time when they shared more than their economic backwardness: they shared a common role in the world economy. Even twenty years ago, the division of the world into manufactures exporters and primary exporters was a pretty good match for the division into advanced and developing nations. So was the division of the world into capital exporters and capital importers. As recently as the mid-1970s, North-South debates still focused on the traditional issues raised by this seemingly permanent functional division of the world. The South wanted higher commodity prices; it wanted curbs on the freedom of Northern capital to do as it pleased in the Third World.

At the end of the 1980s, all this has changed. The developing countries still share the common feature of being relatively poor; but they have fractured into at least four groups occupying very different places in the international division of labor:

1. *Inward-looking primary exporters.* Much of the population of the developing world lives in nations that still play a role in the global economy that was nearly universal two decades ago. In South Asia, in the more affluent nations surrounding the Indian Ocean, and in China (though perhaps not for much longer), the economies are inward looking. Their manufacturing sectors are oriented toward the domestic market and sheltered by protectionist policies from international competition; partly as a result, these manufacturing sectors

178

are often highly inefficient and uncompetitive at world prices. For goods they cannot produce at home, they trade primary products. Their foreign debt is modest, much of it owed to official institutions; the role of foreign multinationals is limited, largely because of government restriction.

2. *Wards of the international community.* An unfortunately large number of people in the developing world live in another set of countries, one for which the term *developing* is, alas, a euphemism— as in sentences like "Per capita income in the developing countries of sub-Saharan Africa has fallen at an average rate of one percent annually since 1974." Several hundred million people now live in economies that essentially fail to provide even bare subsistence on a reliable basis, so that economic collapse is avoided only through resource transfers from the advanced nations. These nations are a reproach to the world; the aid they receive, though critical to their survival, is tiny compared with the resources available elsewhere. In terms of the world economy, however, these desperate economies are too poor to matter much.

3. *New manufacturing exporters.* At this point the shift of manufacturing production to Asia's "four tigers" as well as to a number of less spectacular manufacturing exporters is a staple of discussion in international affairs. The developing world as a whole is still a substantial net importer of manufactured goods—manufactures were 64 percent of developing-country imports in 1985 and only 41 percent of exports—but the share of manufactured goods in developing-country exports has doubled in the past two decades. One measure of the newness of this phenomenon, or at least of the perception of it, is that the now universal phrase "newly industrialized countries" and the associated shorthand of NICs dates no earlier than a 1978 report of the OECD (Organization for Economic Cooperation and Development).

4. *Problem debtors.* The years 1973–1981 were marked by a great wave of bank lending to middle-income developing countries. When this wave suddenly receded in the face of world recession and high real-interest rates, a number of countries were left stranded with high levels of debt that they could service only by running large trade surpluses. Consequently, for this group of countries, capital flows— as measured by the transfer of resources rather than the accounting

measurement of changes in debt—has actually strongly reversed, with the countries sending substantially more resources to the North than they receive in return.

These are not neatly defined categories. In particular, the new developments that are most visible in categories 3 and 4 overlap in some countries, and are present in some of the countries I have assigned to categories 1 and 2. Mexico is a problem debtor that has become a major exporter of capital, 5 to 6 percent of its resources going to its creditors each year; it is also, partly by force of necessity, a rapidly expanding exporter of manufactures, which now account for 60 percent of its foreign exchange earnings. India and China remain inwardly oriented economies, but both now rely on manufactures for about half of their export earnings, and China appears to be shifting toward export orientation. Sub-Saharan Africa has a severe debt burden; the dollar amounts are tiny in comparison with Latin America's debt, but given Africa's poverty its debt is just as large relative to its income, and the debt service eats up most of the new loans and aid that the continent receives. Each country occupies a place on a continuum in terms of each category rather than fitting neatly into one category or another.

The important point is that the old division of the world into a North that exports capital and manufactures to the South and that receives raw materials and IOUs in exchange has broken down. The role of the developing countries in the international economy is therefore more complex than it used to be, and it is fast changing.

The purpose of this article is to survey two new aspects of the changing role of developing countries in the international economy—the large-scale export of manufactured goods and the emergence of the debt problem.

THE GROWTH OF MANUFACTURES EXPORTS

In 1965 manufactured goods accounted for 20 percent of the exports of developing countries and for 66 percent of their imports. In 1985 the corresponding percentages were 41 and 64. Equally important, manufactured exports seem to have been the engine of growth for several countries that have grown with extraordinary speed, belying the widespread pessimism about the ability of less developed countries (LDCs) ever to graduate into the ranks of advanced nations.

The emergence of export-oriented industrialization as a growth strategy for development raises several questions. First, why was the apparently permanent division of the world into affluent manufacturers and poor primary producers replaced with a seemingly inexorable trend toward internationalization of manufacturing? Second, why has manufactures export seemed to work so well as a development strategy when import substitution has not? Third, can this strategy of exportation spread throughout the developing world, or is it subject to severe limits?

Why the surge in manufactures exports?

Ask a manufacturer what the advantages of producing or sourcing in a developing country are, and the answer will be stark and simple: low wages. So there is no mystery about why manufacturing has moved south. The mystery instead is why it did not happen sooner. After all, wages in South Korea were even lower in relation to U.S. wages in 1955 than now. Why didn't Korea begin exporting automobiles until three years ago?

The answer to this question goes to the heart of the mystery of underdevelopment itself. For a host of reasons—poor social environment, a dearth of infrastructure, unreliability of power supply and transport, high turnover, lack of skilled workers—companies have often found that overwhelming wage differentials cannot be translated into low costs. Even now, U.S. businesses occasionally move production facilities to Mexico or Southeast Asia and then sheepishly shift them back to the United States after several years' experience shows that the advantages of low wages are more than offset by the difficulties of operating in a less than fully modernized environment.

But if there are enduring disadvantages to producing in less advanced countries, why did these disadvantages become less important in the last two decades? The disadvantages are still there: despite its low wages, South Korea is reported to be exporting its automobiles at a loss, its labor cost advantage more than offset by low productivity. But something has made the obstacles to manufactured exports less overwhelming now than before.

The usual answer is technology. Improved transportation and communication indeed make the world smaller now than it was in the past. However, transportation costs have been a minor obstacle to trade in manufactured goods for a long time now, and pretty good communication has also been available since the late nineteenth century. Furthermore, technology does not always encourage the internationalization of production. Modern production systems, with their emphasis on close coordination between plants and minimal inventories (e.g., the "just in time" system made famous in Japan), have created a new incentive to locate production in existing industrial complexes. We cannot quantify the effect of technology in causing or inhibiting the spread of manufacturing to the developing world, but my guess is that improved transportation and communication are not a major factor in the rapid rise of South-North exports of manufactures. Instead, I would argue that the main sources lie in changes in the trade policy of the developing nations themselves and in a sort of "contagion" effect as successful manufacturing ventures breed followers.

The essence of the trade policy argument is that import substitution regimes discouraged exports and that, as increasing numbers of developing countries have shifted either to more open trade or to explicit export promotion, they have made it more attractive for firms to take the risk of trying to export manufactured goods. The proposition that import substitution policies inhibit manufactured exports has several strands. First, there are the direct effects: foreign exchange licensing of raw materials and intermediate goods, local content laws that prevent low-cost assembly operations, tariffs that raise exporters' costs all discourage exports directly. Second is the competition for resources: import-substituting manufactures may compete with potential exports for scarce supplies of capital and skilled labor. Third, and perhaps most important, there are the macroeconomic effects. Most developing countries tend to run higher inflation rates than the industrial world, necessitating periodic currency devaluations if they are not to price themselves out of world markets. Limits on imports allow these devaluations to be postponed for long periods, leading to exchange rates that are on average less favorable for all exporters. The upshot is that import-substituting nations are low exporters as well as low importers.

Since the early 1960s certain trade policy moves in developing countries have removed barriers to exporting. Some countries have simply liberalized trade. More frequently, countries have replaced import quotas and foreign exchange controls with tariffs, which usually involve a lower level of effective protection and also increase the flexibility of the economy, allowing successful exporters to bid raw materials away from traditional industries. Countries like Brazil and Korea have introduced explicit export promotion schemes, which to some extent undo with the right hand what the protectionist left hand is doing. And there is a proliferation of sophisticated schemes that loosen the rules for exporting firms: firms may substitute exports for local content in domestic sales or create special trade regimes for exporters (the Mexican *maquiladora* program is a spectacular example). There is little question that these changes in trade policy have contributed in an important way to the rise of manufactures exports from the developing world.

There is also little question that thinking of rising exports of industrial goods as simply a response to an exogenous change in attitudes about trade policy is not sufficient. In crucial cases the response of exports to changes in policy has been startling, out of all proportion to the apparent policy shift itself. Korea certainly did change its policies in the early 1960s, but nobody imagined that the result would be a quarter century of double-digit export growth. Furthermore, the changes in policy have not simply dropped from the sky. Admittedly, policy responds to swings in intellectual fashion, which may have little relation to experience and evidence. But trade policies have changed largely in response to perceived facts: the success of export-oriented development has been extraordinary in a few cases. In 1955 the Soviet Union was widely perceived as a model of economic transformation; in 1988 its place has been taken by Taiwan and Korea.

Let me briefly suggest a way to think about the process of spreading manufactures exports from developing countries and then go into more detail.

The basic story can be described by the word *contagion:* successful inroads of export-oriented manufacturing into developing countries generate futher inroads. Each firm that succeeds in exporting manufactures from a developing country makes the same process attractive to other firms.

One reason for this contagion is that a firm that invests in manufactures exports usually generates knowledge that other firms can use. If the firm is a multinational from an advanced country, it will need to learn how to adapt its production technology to a less advanced environment, how to establish a labor pool, and how to deal with local suppliers. This knowledge cannot be kept entirely proprietary; other firms considering a move into the country, or even into other countries, will benefit from the ability to imitate the actions that have worked for the first firm. If the firm is instead a local business, in exporting it will have to learn how to apply foreign technology, how to establish marketing and distribution links in the industrial world, and so on; again other firms can follow its path more easily than if they had to start the process.

The point, then, is that it is easier for manufactures exports from developing countries to grow once they have been established on a modest scale than it is for them to get started in the first place. Multinational firms now think routinely about the possibility of producing or sourcing in developing countries; entrepreneurs in many developing countries now think routinely about the possibility of selling in industrial countries.

There is also contagion at the policy level. The first set of moves to export-oriented industrialization may have been accidental, rooted in the particular circumstances of particular countries. Since the mid-1970s, however, the drive to export has been based on the desire to emulate the success stories.

But why have manufactures exporters been so successful? Despite the intense attention given to the newly industrialized countries, this is a question that is rarely seriously posed.

Why do manufactures exporters thrive?

One view—institutionalized at the World Bank and widely accepted elsewhere—is that the success of manufactures exporters has nothing to do with their emphasis on manufactures per se. Instead, the export of industrial goods is viewed as a by-product of a turn to free-market policies, especially on foreign trade, and these market-oriented policies are seen as the source of growth.

It is important to understand that while there may be some truth in this view, it cannot be the whole story. Leave aside the question of how much of an example of market-based policies Korea may be (it is certainly more market oriented than, say, India). Still, the standard arguments for free markets cannot explain the nature and extent of success in some developing countries. Protectionist policies, according to the usual economic models, distort the allocation of resources among sectors. Removing them should produce a once-and-for-all gain in the efficiency of the economy because of a reallocation of resources to the sectors where they are most productive at world prices. Such a reallocation can explain only a one-time gain, however, not a continuing process of growth. It cannot explain why the efficiency of resource use *within* sectors should rise, as it clearly has. And quantitative measurements of the conventional costs of protection never find that they amount to more than 10 percent or so of the gross national product (GNP), and usually a good deal less—that is, all the conventional gains from freer markets can explain only about one year's growth in the fast-growing economies of East Asia.

Clearly, something more is at work. The gains from the shift to manufactured exports must go beyond the straightforward Ricardian gains from specialization to a dynamic process that produces much greater gains.

Part of the explanation lies in the spillovers between manufacturing exporters. Consider the following typical story of how a manufacturing export operation is set up in a developing country. A multinational firm decides to open a plant. To do this, it hires domestic contractors and teaches them how to build structures to its specifications. It hires foreign contractors and suppliers of capital goods and pays the costs they incur in learning to adapt their methods and products to the developing-country environment. Finally, it hires and trains a local labor force. In doing all this, it greatly eases the path for subsequent entrants. The next firm to open a plant can turn to the contractors and suppliers of the first firm and get their services at lower prices since these contractors and suppliers have already incurred the sunk costs of getting into the business; and it may even get part of its labor force by hiring the workers already trained.

As any economist recognizes, the first firm to enter pays the cost of breaking the ground and the companies that enter later reap the benefits as free riders. Only if the first can hope to have a temporary monopoly, or if it has an established market position elsewhere that precludes entry by new competitors, will it potentially find entry profitable, and even then it may not enter. A shift in trade policy that encourages exports may tip the balance, inducing the first set of firms to begin exporting; once they have done so, they will have a wave of followers.

Perhaps equally important, what a manufacturer can do for a country is to demonstrate that profitable exporting is possible, and thereby induce many followers. I refer to this as the "It" theory. As I have noted, the reasons why it is not always profitable to produce in developing countries, in spite of their low wages, are complex and subtle. Firms may not know whether they can produce profitably in a country until one of them tries it. That is, some countries have "It," the ability to produce manufactures competitively, while others do not, and the only way to find out if a country has It is to try producing there. Yet to try producing, a firm must make a significant investment, much of which cannot be recovered if a country doesn't turn out to have what it takes. Countries that really have It do not get a chance to prove it if nobody takes the risk.

A shift in trade policy can produce a sudden, startling surge in manufactures exports. Suppose that a country has what it takes to be a NIC but that nobody knows that it has. (For example, Korea in 1960 had, as we know now, the level of education and entrepreneurial drive to create spectacular growth, but nobody saw this potential at the time.) Suppose that a change in policies makes a few businesses—domestic or foreign—willing to try exporting manufactures. Then the country may suddenly find itself "discovered" (or may discover itself). Suddenly everyone knows that the country is a place where low wages can be translated into low costs, and rapid industrialization follows.

Of course, it might turn out that the country doesn't have It after all. In that case, the gains from an export-oriented trade policy will be modest. This leads us to the next question: how far can export-oriented industrialization take us?

The limits of manufactures exports

Let us start by acknowledging that the success of export-oriented growth in some countries is the best news development economists have had since the origins of the field. We now know that development is possible; the nations of Europe and North America did not, it turns out, take up all the good seats before other countries had a chance to go to the box office. Still, we need to ask whether the great achievements of a few countries can be widely repeated.

If the key to export-oriented success is simply that free markets work, so that any country that liberalizes its markets can expect to become another Taiwan, then the answer would be that we have now found the recipe for dramatic world development. Unfortunately, this is almost surely not the case. The dynamic effects that export-oriented policies produced in some countries will not always follow when other countries try similar policies.

Somewhere Lee Kwan Yew gave an interview in which, asked for the secret of Singapore's success, he responded frankly; instead of praising his own policies, he cited the "inner dynamism of East Asian man." In my own less elegant terminology, he was asserting both that Singapore had It and that other (non-Chinese) countries probably didn't. And it is surely true that not every country has It. To take an example, Chile has followed policies under Pinochet that have radically opened the economy to foreign trade, so that the share of exports in GNP in 1985 was more than twice what it was in 1965. Yet the export surge has been concentrated in agricultural products rather than manufactures, which still accounted for only about 7 percent of total exports in the mid-1980s. This is not to denigrate the desirability of selling off-season grapes and peaches if that is a profitable business but simply to point out that outward-oriented policies do not always lead to the kind of economic transformation we have now been accustomed to expect. At the very least, we should not base our expectations on the assumption that very rapid growth can be automatically summoned with an invocation of free-market principles.

Notice that if my It theory is correct, there is an important bias that tends to make export-oriented growth look better as a strategy than it really is. When a country that has It turns to export orientation, there is an explosion of growth that attracts widespread attention. When a country that does not have It tries export-led growth without much success, there is a fizzle that gets little notice. In effect, our picture of the prospects for manufactures export comes from looking only at the cases where it has worked.

Still, there are probably important countries that have It yet have not so far taken much advantage of their potential. Judging from recent trends, I see two likely candidates. The first is Mexico. Geographical closeness to the United States, relatively easy cultural links with the increasingly multilingual society north of the border, and political stability (cross your fingers) make Mexico a favorable place for manufactures exports. With the combination of marked trade liberalization and sharp depreciation of the peso, there has been rapid growth in manufactures exports, which have transformed Mexico in the space of a few years from being mostly an oil exporter to being mostly an industrial exporter. (The collapse of oil prices of course helped shift the percentages.) I believe this process is irreversible. The feasibility of profitable manufactures exports from Mexico is well established, the knowledge of how to make such exports work is now widespread both in Mexico and elsewhere, and as a result these exports will continue to grow even in the absence of any further incentives.

The second likely candidate is China. Perhaps China should not be regarded as consisting of fifty potential Taiwans, but even if it contains only ten Taiwans' worth of export potential, it will quickly become a major factor in North-South manufactures trade.

The interesting question is how the world will adapt to the emergence of new NICs, especially NICs that have much larger populations than the existing ones. Will the United States be willing to absorb Mexico's rapidly rising manufactures exports? (Yes, probably, national security issues plus the strong role of U.S. firms in the process will no doubt counteract the temptation to shut the Mexicans out.) Will the United States then be unwilling to accept manufactured goods from other Third World nations, and close itself up in a trading bloc with Mexico the way that the European Community seems to be doing with the southern European nations? (Probably yes again.) If so, who will accept the massive number of manufactures exports that China will probably seek to use as its engine of development? Is a Chinese-Japanese trading bloc a real possibility?

THE DEBT PROBLEM

The growth of manufactures exports from developing countries was on the whole a happy surprise. It presents problems, but the problems are those of unexpected success rather than failure. The other major change in North-South economic relations, on the other hand, represents a stunning negative surprise. The debt problem has essentially arrested development in most of Latin America and probably eliminated the possibility of significant capital flows to developing countries in this century. There may be a few shreds of silver lining to this cloud, as I will argue shortly, but at least at first sight the whole affair has turned out worse than anyone might have imagined ten years ago.

Much has been written about how the nations of Latin America came to be so deeply in debt and about whose fault the debt crisis was. Was it the fault of the countries, who borrowed irresponsibly? Or the fault of the banks, who lent recklessly? Or the fault of God (perhaps in his earthly incarnation as Paul Volcker), who subjected debtor countries to a series of adverse shocks nobody could have predicted, turning what should have been sound loans into unsound? At this point it really doesn't matter. In September of 1982 it was simply clear that the debt of a dozen or so countries was now more than their creditors wanted to hold, so that no more lending would be forthcoming on a voluntary basis. At the same time it was also clear that the ability of the debtor countries to service their debt was contingent on a continuing infusion of new credit that covered all of the principal and at least part of the interest due. The debt problem as it has unfolded since then represents the struggle to reconcile the debt overhang with the limits on countries' ability to pay.

Strategies for dealing with the debt problem

When any debtor cannot pay its debts out of current income, its creditors have three basic options: (1) they can try to seize whatever assets of the debtor they can; (2) they can postpone some of the debtor's obligations, hoping that it will be able to pay later; (3) they can offer a settlement that reduces the obligations. Now that the age of gunboat diplomacy has passed, there is essentially no possibility that the first option will be exercised. So in dealing with debtor nations, creditors have the option of either postponing their obligations or offering to reduce them in return for a settlement. In short, we can describe this as a choice between *financing* and *forgiving* a debt overhang.

The orthodox debt strategy since 1982 has, of course, been one of financing rather than forgiving. This strategy has been widely misunderstood, denounced as simply throwing good money after bad; it is not as foolish as that. There have turned out to be major problems with the strategy of financing, but it is necessary to understand its virtues in order to judge how it might be replaced.

The first key point in a financing strategy is that it is possible in principle for a country to grow its way out of a debt problem even while continuing to have an expanding nominal debt. Suppose that world prices are rising at an annual rate of 3 percent and that a debtor country can grow in real terms at an annual rate of 4 percent. Then as long as its debt grows at a rate of less than 7 percent per year, the ratio of debt to income will be falling, not rising, over time. If debt grows at 3 percent a year, then after a decade the ratio of income to debt, and therefore presumably the country's creditworthiness, will have risen by 50 percent.

The second key point is that lending money to a problem debtor is preferable to a default as long as the new money is less than the payments of interest and principal. Suppose that a country has a debt of $100 billion and that its interest payments on this debt are $9 billion. Suppose that as part of a debt package creditors reschedule all the principal and provide $4 billion in new loans. They still receive $5 billion in net payments—that is, $5 billion more than they would receive if the country were to break relations with its creditors and declare a moratorium.

Thus, a strategy of financing is essentially one of playing for time, one that is preferable to creditors over an immediate confrontation. It is easy to justify quite substantial lending on this basis. Again, consider a country that owes $100 billion. Suppose that if no new lending is provided, creditors can expect to receive only 50 cents for each dollar owed. On the other hand, suppose that by lending $40 billion more over a period of several years, the same creditors can buy time, raising the expected payment to 75 cents on each dollar of debt. Is this worth it? The new lending takes place at an expected loss of 25 cents per dollar, so it costs $10 billion; but it raises the expected payment on existing debt by $25 billion, making it well worthwhile.

Notice two things about this argument. First, the usual argument that lending should take place only when a country is illiquid, not when it is insolvent, does not apply; lending is worth doing then, despite the substantial remaining risk that the country will fail to pay in full. Second, the new lending makes sense only in terms of its effect on the value of existing debt, not in isolation. Each new loan takes place at an expected loss, so that no lender who does not already have a stake in the country will be willing to lend more, and indeed each creditor would prefer that someone else do the new lending.

The point that lending is in creditors' *collective* interest, but not in any one creditor's *individual* interest, is the well-known "free rider" problem. In the basic debt strategy to date, the main effort has been to overcome the free-rider problem through pressure from central banks and the International Monetary Fund, exerted through bank advisory committees, aimed at producing "concerted" lending. Implicit in this effort is the understanding that the usual market criteria for lending do not apply and that the choice to lend or not is not and should not be voluntary on the part of the banks.

I hope that this description shows that the strategy of financing developing-country debt is reasonable at the conceptual level. After almost six years of the debt problem, however, there is widespread dissatisfaction with the results of this strategy. Next we need to consider the alternatives.

Problems with financing and the case for forgiving

The strategy of financing is one in which concerted provision of new capital gives debtor nations time to grow out of their debt problem. In practice, unfortunately, neither end of the equation has worked out as intended. The capital has not been provided on the scale envisaged, and the countries have failed to grow much. As a result, the process has very nearly worked in reverse: the debtors have received little new money, yet their indebtedness relative to income has risen instead of fallen.

Sample calculations suggest that it might make sense for creditors to expand their exposure by 25 percent or more over the course of a five-year program for a problem debtor. In fact, the exposure of commercial banks in Latin America has risen by only about 8 percent since the end of 1982. That is, very little concerted lending has actually taken place. Nevertheless, most indicators of indebtedness as measured by ratios of debt to income or exports have worsened since the onset of the debt crisis. The main reason is the sharp slowdown in growth. Before the debt crisis, Latin America routinely grew at annual rates of 5 to 6 percent in real terms; since 1982, the average has been only about 1 percent, far short of the rate of population growth. Income per capita in problem debtors is now 10 percent or more below its peak.

At least so far, then, we have not been making progress. The countries appear further than ever from being able to regain normal access to credit—an impression confirmed by the fact that debt trades at huge discounts on the secondary market. Meanwhile, development is running in reverse. Thus, there is a strong case for an alternative strategy. The only problem is to come up with one.

One strategy would be to look to advanced-country governments to resolve the situation: buy out the banks, then forgive a substantial part of the countries' burden. We need not discuss this possibility at any length, since it seems politically out of the question. At the moment, we must restrict ourselves to schemes that do not require a large inflow of money from third parties.

Now one appealing argument is that it is in everyone's interest to have the banks forgive part of the debt. The debt already sells at a large discount in secondary markets, and banks have recognized the likelihood of less than full payment by establishing loss reserves. Why not recognize this reality by reducing countries' obligations to what they can actually pay? The reduction in the debt burden would then, so the argument goes, increase the countries' growth prospects and thereby secure the payment of their remaining obligations.

Unfortunately, this argument is too good to be true. To see why, consider again a hypothetical example. A country owes $100 billion; it might be able to pay in full, or it might be able to pay only $40 billion. If these outcomes are equally likely, the expected payment will be $70 billion. We may suppose that the debt will sell on the secondary market for 70 cents on the dollar. Suppose that the creditors now recognize reality and reduce the country's obligations to $70 billion. Then the country will pay the $70 billion if times are good but can still pay only $40 billion if times are bad, reducing the expected payments to $55 billion—not what the creditors had in mind. The point is that debt forgiveness takes away the creditors' option to participate in any good fortune the country may have.

Now there is a possible counterargument. What if reducing the debt burden increases the probability of a good outcome, so that the country is more likely to be able to pay? Surely this relationship must hold to some extent; if it is a large enough effect, then debt foregiveness will be in the interest of both sides. This need not always be the case, however.

A useful way to think about the relationship between debt and expected repayment is in terms of the curve CD shown in the figure on page 198. On the horizontal axis is the nominal value of a country's debt; on the vertical axis, the actual expected payments. At low levels of debt, nominal claims may be expected to be fully repaid, so that the outcome lies along the forty-five degree line. At higher levels of debt, however, the possibility of nonpayment grows, so that the expected payment traces out a curve that falls increasingly below the forty-five degree line. At a point such as L, the ratio of expected payment to nominal debt may be measured by the slope of a ray from the origin; ignoring risk and transaction costs, we may regard this as approximating the secondary market price of debt.

Value

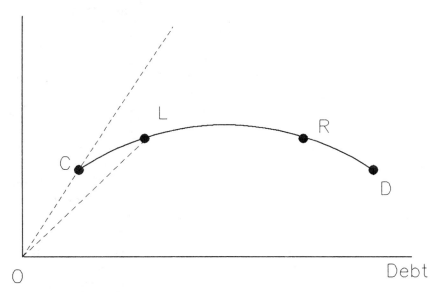

O   Debt

Although increased levels of debt above point C will be associated with lower secondary market prices, at first the total value of debt will still rise. At high enough debt levels, however, the disincentive effects discussed above may be large enough so that the curve actually turns down.

We may now ask under what conditions a reduction in nominal claims—debt forgiveness—will leave the creditors better off. Many authors have suggested that when debt sells at a discount on the secondary market, creditors should recognize reality and reduce their claims on the country correspondingly. However, it is clear from the figure that this is not necessarily the right conclusion. At point L there is a secondary discount, but a reduction in the claims of creditors would still reduce what they expect to receive overall. The reason is implicit in the discussion above. Given the uncertainty about the future, a reduction in claims deprives creditors of the option value of sharing in good fortune. Only if this option value is outweighed by the improved incentives offered by a debt reduction do the creditors gain by passing on part of the secondary discount to the debtor. This is going to happen only if the debt burden is very large, so that these incentive effects predominate, at a point like R.

The curve DRLC should by now be a familiar sort of object. It is the debt-relief Laffer curve. That is, just as governments may sometimes actually increase tax revenue by reducing tax rates, creditors may sometimes increase expected payment by forgiving part of a country's debt. In both cases the proposition that less is more depends on an initial extreme situation, whether of taxes that provide extreme disincentives or of a debt burden that is crippling in its effect on economic growth. Arguments that debt relief is in everyone's interest are, in effect, arguments that countries are on the wrong side of the debt-relief Laffer curve.

Now of course in practice it is very difficult to ascertain which side of the curve a highly indebted country is on. There is a consensus that hugely indebted countries with weak governments like Bolivia are on the wrong side, and this agreement has led to granting debt relief with few arguments. But for the major debtors the question is anybody's guess.

Debt forgiveness, then, is not an idea that is obviously and clearly in the interest of creditors as well as debtors. If it comes, it will almost surely have to be forced on reluctant creditors; they may in the end be grateful, but they will not volunteer.

Prospects for the debt problem

Can anything be done to resolve the debt problem? At the moment there are two widely discussed options. One of these is, I will argue, largely illusory; the other will require more nerve and determination on the part of the debtors than they have yet displayed.

The option that I would argue is largely illusory is the use of clever financial schemes to achieve voluntary debt relief. Such schemes include buyback of debt on the secondary market by the countries themselves, exchange of debt for "exit" bonds, and exchanges of debt for equity. Each of these is intended to harness the existing discounts on secondary market transactions to the country's benefit and yet to bypass the problems we have just seen in straightforward forgiveness.

Without going into detailed analysis, the basic point may be stated bluntly: there is no magic in market-based schemes for debt reduction. The secondary market discount on developing-country debt does not automatically constitute a resource that can be harnessed to provide free debt relief; in many circumstances repurchase of debt on the secondary market, whether through reserve-financed buybacks or through creation of new, senior securities, will hurt existing creditors. There is a mutual benefit from such repurchases only when a reduced debt burden strongly increases a country's likely ability to repay—the same situation in which unilateral debt forgiveness is in the interest of creditors in any case.

The most heavily advertised scheme for market-based debt reductions is the use of debt-equity swaps. Such swaps are in principle a kind of securitization, like the issue of exit bonds. In practice "round-tripping" and other leakages tend to make them degenerate into buybacks financed by reserves, and they are usually both disappointing in terms of their ability to capture the secondary market discount and costly in their effects on countries' fiscal positions. While there are potential advantages as well, the claims made for debt-equity swaps by their sponsors are clearly exaggerated.

Market-based debt reduction, then, cannot serve as an alternative to the orthodox strategy of rescheduling and concerted lending. Schemes that benefit the debtor at the expense of the creditor—such as buybacks and exit bonds for countries not on the wrong side of the debt-relief Laffer curve—will be opposed by existing creditors when they become more than marginal. Schemes that benefit the creditors at the expense of the debtor—such as debt-equity swaps that fail to capture the secondary discount while allowing firms to make investments they would have made in any case—will be opposed by the debtors as the effects become clear. Mutual agreement on schemes will come only when, as in the recent Bolivian case, there is more or less universal agreement that the debtor is so heavily indebted that a reduction in claims actually increases expected repayment.

It seems, then, that creditors are likely neither to offer forgiveness to the debtors nor to be induced to provide much forgiveness through the backdoor of voluntary debt-relief schemes. Yet the financing

strategy seems increasingly unsatisfactory, with the countries growing more and more restive about their failure to resume acceptable
rates of growth. This brings us to the other possibility for a change in
the way international debt is handled: unilateral action on the part of
countries.

It is actually one of the mysteries of the debt problem that
unilateral reductions of debt service have been so rare. After all, the
basic bargaining power would seem to be on the side of the debtors:
if there is a breakdown in relations with the creditors, the debtor does
not pay and the creditors do not get paid. The new money provided
by creditors falls far short of the interest payments, so that access to
capital is not an issue. Essentially, debtors have been induced to
continue paying out of fear of sanctions other than that of a cutoff of
further lending.

What are these sanctions? A cutoff of trade credit would hamper
international trade, forcing it to be conducted on a cash basis: this
would be an inconvenience and a cost, although perhaps not a fatal
one. In principle, creditors could try to attach assets of deadbeat
countries abroad, including bank accounts and export cargoes: this
would be serious, but it is somewhat implausible and has not
happened yet. Defaulting countries would presumably get worse
treatment in the foreign policies of creditor countries, receiving fewer
trade privileges, less support for their security, and so on. When all is
said and done, however, the penalties against a country for declaring
a moratorium on debt payment seem mild in comparison with the
cost of making sustained net transfers to creditors of 5 percent or
more of GNP each year.

Yet confrontation with creditors has not so far been a widely tried
strategy, and Brazil, which seemed to lead the way, has now
retreated. The essential reason, I would argue, is not the external
sanctions imposed on bad debtors but the internal problems of
conducting responsible domestic policies while confronting creditors.
What Brazil found was that its debt service was only part of its
economic problem; it still needed strong domestic austerity, even if it
was not paying its foreign debt. It is very difficult, however, simultaneously to pursue a policy of repudiating obligations abroad while
tightening belts at home, to be orthodox internally while being
heterodox externally. Brazil succumbed to the inevitably strong
temptation to have a party and thereby discredited its own stand

against the banks. Other countries doubt whether they can do any better. Could Mexico hold to its current fiscal austerity and stern anti-inflation program in the face of the wave of populism that a debt repudiation would create?

Even more serious is that the current sentiment for market orientation on the part of debtors is difficult to reconcile with a debt moratorium or repudiation. It is not easy to reconcile reassurances that property rights will be respected and the market allowed to operate with actions that expropriate a major class of asset owners, even if they happen to be foreign; domestic investors may well imagine that they are next.

So the debtor countries have been extremely reluctant to confront their creditors. Yet this is the only way that debt relief is likely to come. If the strategy of financing continues to work as badly in the future as it has so far, an eventual unilateral declaration of unwillingness to pay in full on the part of the countries seems inevitable. Whatever they say, the banks think so too; that is what those huge discounts on the secondary market are telling us.

THE END OF THE THIRD WORLD

The subject of this paper is the role of developing countries in the world economy. The message of the paper is that there is no longer such a thing as one role for developing countries; there are several roles, played to varying degrees by various countries. They have few issues in common. There are the traditional developing countries, their economic fate still tied to the prices of commodities; the desperate countries living year to year on a trickle of aid; the manufacturing exporters, crowding into advanced-country markets that may be increasingly closed by protectionism; the debtor countries, bargaining over the size of the resource transfer they must, perversely, make back to the North. It is hard to imagine restarting the new international economic order debate on anything like the terms that made sense even ten years ago. What are the demands? Whose interests are to be represented?

This paper has offered a quick tour of two of the new issues that affect subgroups of what used to be the Third World. As we might expect, the issues are almost completely different, overlapping only to the extent that some manufactures exporters are debtors (though

Korea will, at present rates, pay off its debts within four years) while some debtors hope to expand manufactures exports. But this disparity may be the main point. Relative to the rest of the world, all developed countries are alike; but each group of less-developed countries is underdeveloped in its own way.

Comments on Paul Krugman's Essay

EDMAR L. BACHA: I want to tell another story. Paul said that creditors decided to buy time for the debtors to get out in a fortunate way. I would suggest that there is another way of looking at it. The strategy of financing was a way of buying time for bankers to get out of it. If it had not been done that way in 1982, the whole banking system of the United States might have gone into bankruptcy. So, time had to be bought for that. I think that was the main issue. Once time was bought, banks got some interest payments, more than the money they put in. With that money, they could increase reserves. The hope was that in time there would be reserves enough.

German and Swiss banks—and maybe the Japanese, although we do not know much about them because they do not publish their accounts—apparently took the lesson seriously. But not the money-center banks in New York and California. Why is that? I want to present four possibilities. One is the "trust effect," a moral hazard, a consequence of official intervention. The other, their belief in Bill Cline's optimistic projections, which explains their misconception of what was going on. The third relates to taxation. They have no tax rebates in the way that European banks have on general reserves. Finally, banks' profits were not sufficient; they had been left with too many bad domestic loans. The money-center banks were under the threat of being written off.

We saw what happened last year in the wake of the moratorium by Brazil. The money-center banks moved to increase their reserves. Once the floodgates were open, there was an attempted second wave to move up reserves. It started last November here—with the Bank of Boston and American Express—but also in Chicago and California, where reserve ratios went up 50 percent and more in order to match the level the market discount showed was needed.

And then all this stopped because of the open intervention of both the Bank of England and the New York Federal Reserve Bank. The reason is quite clear. Manufacturers Hanover, for example, would have to commit 131 percent of its total equity in order to satisfy this reserve provision. So you still have a problem. There are four major banks here (and two more in England) that need to be restructured, that need to be taken over. That, I think, is the main issue. Bank restructuring in this country is what it is really all about.

Another point: Why did developing countries not behave otherwise? That has always surprised me. In a paper that I wrote with Carlos Diaz just before the debt crisis erupted, we imagined that the scenario of the 1930s would be repeated. Countries just wouldn't pay, and the problem would be transferred to the creditors. We were totally wrong in that.

Still, there are some lessons to be learned when you look at the Brazilian experience last year. The total foreign liabilities of Brazil are roughly 60 percent long-term bank debt, 25 percent official credit, 5 percent trade credit, and 10 percent direct investment. We had a net negative financial transfer with the private banks but not with the rest of the group, except for one year. Then, as far as trade credit, official credit, and private investment are concerned, we are potentially on the plus side. What happened last year, clearly, is that there was a ganging up on Brazil. We saw the interruption of flows from the World Bank, the interruption of trade credit. We had for the first time negative direct investment.

I shift back to the idea that what is basically needed is to have something done with the banking system here. Banks have taken collective action in lending; now they need to take collective action in forgiving. For a bank, individually, is worse off if it forgives; that action does not by itself improve the capacity of the country to pay.

JEFFREY D. SACHS: Paul Krugman's very interesting and provocative paper has two main parts: a discussion of trade policy and trade performance in developing countries, and an analysis of the ongoing developing-country debt crisis. As we have come to expect with Krugman's papers, we are treated to provocative hypotheses that are original, thought provoking, and clearly stated. There is much to learn from Paul's analysis of the trade and debt issues, but I also believe that Paul leads us a bit astray at certain points. Let me explain.

I will begin with the issue of trade policy. Krugman's emphasis is on the emergence of major manufacturing exporters in the developing world, particularly in East Asia. He rightly indicates the fundamental importance of this phenomenon, not only for the changing relations between developed and developing countries but also for our most basic thinking about the processes of economic development.

For the first couple of decades after World War II, the "standard" approach to development stressed the goal of shifting workers from agriculture to import-competing industry. In the dominant import-substitution model, the industrial sectors would produce for the domestic market, thereby substituting for imports that were formerly paid for by primary commodity exports. This strategy was justified on many grounds, including the famous Prebisch-Singer hypothesis that primary commodities prices would inevitably experience a secular decline in world markets, thereby rendering primary commodities a major drag on the development process.

As Krugman stresses, the remarkable surprise of the past twenty-five years has been the emergence of manufacturing exporters in the developing world, who have boomed on the basis of rapidly growing exports to the industrial world. The emergence of superexporters such as the "Gang of Four" in East Asia (Hong Kong, Singapore, South Korea, and Taiwan) and many of the ASEAN countries (e.g., Indonesia, Malaysia, and Thailand) have led to a shift in development theory, to a new orthodoxy which stresses the advantages of outward-orientation and export promotion and which emphasizes the heavy costs of import substitution.

Krugman outlines some of the reasons that have been identified as the advantages of the outward-oriented strategy: the ability to enjoy economies of scale by producing for a large world market, the greater ease of technology transfer, the productivity gains from learning by doing that follow the introduction of new manufacturing processes, and so on. Krugman himself has contributed in earlier work to the development of many of these ideas. The surprising part of Krugman's discussion is his scepticism about the ability of other developing countries to follow the examples of the East Asian economies. In Krugman's view, some countries simply have "It," and others don't, in regard to their ability to export industrial goods in world markets. Only those countries that have "It" can benefit from a shift to outward orientation. Krugman cites as a putative case of failure the example of Chile, which has liberalized trade but has not developed an industrial export base. Liberalization has instead spurred new sectors of nontraditional agricultural exports. (On the whole, despite Krugman's negative comments, Chile's recent economic growth is quite impressive, even though it is based on agricultural rather than industrial exports. Wages, employment, and living standards have been rising steadily for several years as a result of the new policies.)

I find Krugman's theory of "It" quite troubling. The theory rather casually divides the world between innate successes and innate failures, and seems to bolster the hoary myth that cultural superiority (or race or religion, according to some observers) can explain the economic success of some parts of the world and the failure of others. It was this attitude, after all, that fundamentally misled many observers in the 1950s into predicting that

Korea and other Asian countries could never succeed (since East Asian Confucian and Buddhist traditions were supposedly inimical to capitalism). Now, in the updated form, it is Korea that has "It" and Chile that does not.

I would rather have Paul look more systematically at the various economic and political factors that have contributed to the relative success of some countries and not others, without the appeal to a mystical "It." In this regard, we can point to fundamental differences such as: the direction of economic policy over long periods of time (Korea's export promotion strategy has been around almost thirty years; Chile's has lasted less than half that time, in much more conflictive political circumstances); the endowments of the main factors of production in the various economies (e.g., land, labor, natural resources, educational attainments of the population); the distribution of income, with its effects on political stability and entrepreneurship (Latin America has much greater inequalities of income and wealth than do the Asian economies).

The relative supply of land versus labor in Latin America and East Asia is one of the most important differences between the two regions, a difference that has played an important role in their distinctive paths of development. It is a difference that Krugman fails to mention, surprisingly in view of the importance that economists have long attributed to the linkage of factor endowments and trade patterns.

In Hong Kong, for example, there are about 5,000 people per square kilometer (and in Korea, about 400 per square kilometer), whereas in Chile there are only 16 people per square kilometer. The vast availability of land per person in Latin America in comparison with the dense population in East Asia has naturally made Latin America a region of agricultural exports. Also, Latin America is resource rich (Chile has copper, Peru silver, Mexico and Venezuela oil), while most of East Asia is resource poor (the Southeast Asian countries of Indonesia, Malaysia, and Thailand are exceptions). Thus, it is natural, indeed virtually unavoidable, that Latin America would be an agricultural and resource exporter, while East Asia would not.

If it is true that manufacturing exports offer special benefits to an economy (through economies of scale, opportunities for learning, technological advances), then a large endowment of land and resources can sometimes be, paradoxically, a hindrance rather than a help to rapid growth. With Argentina's productive pampas producing meat and grains for the world and Chile's copper supplying much of the world's needs for that metal, for example, the exchange rate in those countries has traditionally been too strong to give their manufacturers a chance to compete in world markets. Historically, it is only when copper and food prices are low in world markets, so that the peso is weak in Argentina and Chile, that manufacturers in those countries have been able to gain a tenuous foothold in world markets. Ironically, subsequent commodity price increases have then squeezed the nascent manufacturing exporters out of business once again until the next commodity price collapse!

Of course disastrous trade policies and an unstable political environment added significant damage to the manufacturing export capabilities of Argentina, Chile, and most other countries in Latin America. Immediately after World War II, when Prebisch and Singer made their pessimistic forecasts of future commodities prices, the inward-looking process of import substitution (based on high tariffs, which punish potential exporters) added to the natural bias against manufacturing exporters. Until Japan and other Asian economies showed the way, there was little confidence among most development specialists that the poorer countries could possibly compete in the world market for manufacturers, even if they tried.

The battle over income distribution also played an important role in Latin America's choice of inward-oriented development strategy rather than promotion of manufacturing exports. Policies to make the exchange rate competitive and to lower tariffs would not only benefit new manufacturing exports but also the existing agricultural exporters. Since these exporters were part of the old and rich oligarchy (or at least were perceived to be so), political parties based on urban workers, such as the Peronists in Argentina, fought virtually all policies that tended to promote exports. Export promotion of any kind was seen as good for the rich and bad for the urban workers. This kind of distributional battle was virtually absent in the peasant-based East Asian economies, where urban workers had little political power.

With the benefit of hindsight, we can now identify a set of policies in land-rich Argentina and Chile that would have been consistent with the Prebisch pessimism about raw materials but that would also have allowed for the development of manufacturing exports. Rather than pursuing a policy of high tariff barriers and import substitution, policymakers could have taxed agriculture and natural resources (at a moderate rate), thereby limiting the dependence on primary commodities while at the same time encouraging labor-intensive manufacturing exports. In countries like Argentina and Chile, this combination of policies could well have helped to spur growth and improve income distribution at the same time.

Let me now turn to the debt crisis. What I miss in Paul's interesting discussion is the kind of power politics that has underlain most of the management of the debt crisis in recent years. Contrary to Paul's analysis, the debt crisis is not mainly a process of negotiation between debtor countries and their creditor banks but a process of negotiation between debtor countries and creditor *governments,* led by the United States. The United States and other creditor governments have set down the terms that the debtor countries must follow. Those terms have been ridiculously harsh and thereby very shortsighted.

So far, the United States has insisted that the debtor countries continue to pay interest to the banks, even if that contributes to the collapse of the debtor country (note that Argentina, Brazil, and Peru, among others, are now experiencing virtual hyperinflations, in large part because of their debt burdens). These countries have continued to pay their debts, on the whole, because to do otherwise would be to risk a foreign policy rupture with the United States, which would threaten these countries in many areas other than finance, including trade relations and military security.

One easy way, therefore, to resolve the crisis would be for the United States government to state, simply, that it is no longer standing behind the banks and that it recognizes the need for the commerical bank debts to be renegotiated on more favorable terms. The banks would then be forced to come to new terms, since the main bargaining power of the banks comes not from their own leverage but from the active support of the U.S. government.

While serving in recent years as one of Bolivia's debt negotiators, I watched at close range how the process can work out this way. When the Bolivian economy collapsed in the mid-1980s and the U.S. government judged the situation to be sufficiently desperate, the U.S. government simply looked the other way when the Bolivian government suspended debt-servicing payments. The U.S. government continued to deal sympathetically with Bolivia's needs (e.g., by supporting an IMF agreement for Bolivia) despite the suspension of debt payments. When the banks realized that the U.S. government would not "enforce" their contracts with Bolivia, they entered negotiations with Bolivia. These were based on the notion that Bolivia required a fundamental reduction of its debt burden. By mid-1988, about half of Bolivia's debt has been canceled through Bolivia's repurchase of its debts from the banks at a very deep discount.

Krugman is undoubtedly correct that there are no easy solutions to the crisis and that all suggested policy alternatives to the current approach have serious risks. But I would strongly urge that the risks of the various new approaches (particularly those stressing debt reduction) are much less than the risks that confront us if we continue on the current path.* The risks of the current approach are a continuing descent of the developing countries into poverty and political instability, as well as the risks of large taxpayer expenses at the end of the road, as the creditor governments finally bail out both the banks and the debtor countries. Already many of the Latin

---

*I have shown the feasibility of some of the alternative approaches in "New Approaches to the Latin American Debt Crisis," a paper prepared for the Harvard University Symposium on the Debt Crisis, September 1988.

American democracies (such as Argentina, Brazil, and Peru) are in jeopardy over the sharp deterioration of their economies. It should be stressed that the alternative approach of debt reduction no longer poses any serious risks to the commercial banking system, since almost all banks are now out of danger with regard to their developing-country exposure.

DAVID E. BELL: I would like to introduce a different line of discussion at this point. What I want to do is tie the classification that Paul uses in his paper back to the discussion of development aid that we were having a little while ago. You all realize, of course, that development assistance and developing countries have come to refer to two different communities. Development assistance is concessional aid. This recent discussion has been about countries that do not receive concessional aid except in the case of a write-down of debt.

Twenty-some years ago, when Hollis and I were in AID, we began to distinguish to whom development aid in the traditional sense ought to go. We developed a theory on the basis of which development aid was a temporary investment process; when countries reached a certain stage of economic strength, development aid was to be brought to an end. Development aid terminated for Taiwan and Korea, for Iran, Mexico, and so on, in country after country. Development aid, therefore, was seen correctly as a temporary process. I refuse to accept the idea that some countries are wards, permanent basket cases. I personally know no such country. I think this theory of development assistance as a temporary investment process is entirely consistent with world reality and would fit well into a new formulation of a development assistance program.

It does not mean, however, that there would not be a lot of international economic issues, debt issues, trade issues, and the like that would have to be considered in different forums, on different terms. I think our terminology has not caught up with all that. The World Bank refers to all Third World countries as developing, whether or not they are the recipients of concessional aid. So this way of looking at differentiation among the Third World countries may be seen as a contribution to designing a stable development assistance program. But the terminology, the semantics, are blurred today; they have to be addressed.

NANCY BIRDSALL: I would like to comment on something that I thought was missing in the discussion of debt, particularly in Jeffrey Sachs's remarks. Let me preface this by saying that I am newly impressed with how extraordinarily confused I am about the whole business. The thing that I thought was missing was any discussion of the ability of these countries to make the internal adjustment changes that are required. The failure of stabilization policies, particularly in Brazil, for example, is critical. I would not agree that the World Bank, for example, did not lend very much to Brazil recently, in the period of the moratorium, because there was some direct causal connection between the moratorium policy and reluctance to lend on the U.S. side, as opposed to the failure of stabilization efforts. I think the difference between Brazil and Bolivia is not only what you suggested in your remarks but also that Bolivia did take on some difficult internal adjustment policies, which made it easier for the concessional development flows to recommence. In the period of Brazil's moratorium, the constraint to lending in the lending program of the World Bank has been the difficulty faced by the Brazilian government in making the necessary policy adjustments, structural policy adjustments.

So I think it is not just a problem of negotiations between the countries and the other side—be the other side the bankers or the wider international community. I think there is a question of the ability internally to deal with the fiscal deficit problem, the internal debt problem, in Brazil and many other countries that have an external debt problem. That goes back to all of the other issues we have been raising about the role of government, good government, and to what development is all about.

Soedjatmoko

Education Relevant to People's Needs

I N WRITING THIS PAPER, I have become very much aware of how vast the subject is, how difficult it is to buttress the assertions made with available empirical research. This article should therefore be read as an impressionistic statement based on visits to universities in a number of developing countries.

Modern knowledge, understood to be science-based knowledge of man, society, and nature as well as the concepts, theories, metaphors, and worldviews derived from it, has, as we are all aware, become possibly the most strategic asset in the development effort. In the final analysis, development turns on the capacity of a nation to use science and technology to meet the challenges and opportunities it faces. Without this knowledge, the modernization of society —and of the soul—involving the freeing of the individual from the conventional social constraints of tradition and religion, in favor of the internalized constraints shaped by a personal conscience, which may or may not be rooted in religion or in a philosophical ethical configuration of values, may not be possible. The powerful and continuing impact of the third industrial revolution—of biotechnology, microelectronics, communications, and materials technology—as well as recent advances in the basic sciences has made that even more true.

There is no way in which the developing countries can hope to catch up, whatever meaning of the term is used, with the industrial countries and their accelerated productivity growth without the developing countries themselves participating actively in this revolution. The converse is also true. If they do not succeed in being part of that revolution, they are doomed to fall outside the circle in which the major decisions affecting the future of the world and of their own nations is being decided. The excluded countries will inevitably fall behind and lose their autonomy.

This challenge to the developing world occurs at a time when, except for the newly industrialized countries (NICs) in East Asia and Latin America, the process of industrialization of the South and the transition from a traditional agrarian economy have moved beyond their initial phases. These countries already find it difficult to keep up with the rapid changes in their comparative advantage as commodity exporters, with a shift from commodities—now being replaced by substitutes through advances in materials technology—to manufactured goods. And this is only part of the technology-driven changes in the international division of labor, which are not only affecting relative, competitive positions among the industrial countries but also the relationship between the North and the South. In fact, the widening gap between the North and the South has now become a knowledge gap almost as intractable as the poverty gap.

Access to modern knowledge should, however, not be seen only in terms of access to the state-of-the-art knowledge abroad, or of the need to enhance the capabilities of developing countries in science and technology so that they may catch up or become more internationally competitive. Industrial and developing countries alike will have to deal with the global problems of population and of the maintenance of the global life-support systems that will determine the governability of the human community and the habitability of the earth in the near future. Mass migration across national boundaries and across continental divides has already begun to create social and racial tensions, as on the border between the United States and Mexico and between the northern and southern riparian states around the Mediterranean basin. This trend, impelled by disparities between living standards and economic and population growth rates, confronts the affluent industrial nations with three options: (1) to revive and significantly enlarge the scale of the flagging international development effort, (2) to allow the free movement of people across national boundaries, as is already the case in large measure with the free movement of capital, or (3) to accept the inevitability of multiethnic societies and develop carefully calibrated policies governing the scale of intake so as to reduce the likelihood of racial or ethnic conflicts.

Another problem concerns the inadequacy of the international response to global environmental degradation caused by the cumulative impact of human action. Even though one may dispute the claims of certain environmentalists on the greenhouse effect by, for example, acknowledging the smallness of the probability that the American Midwest and the Soviet Ukraine may by the middle of the next century have turned into scrub desert, that by the end of the next century all coastal cities in the world may well be inundated, such probability cannot be summarily dismissed. Given the long lead time necessary to mount any concerted international effort and the even longer time for any set of policies to show its effects, it will require adequate and timely collective technological as well as political interventions on an unprecedented national and international scale to produce results.

It is no exaggeration to say that the educational systems of both the industrial and the developing countries are unprepared for this new set of tasks. The instruments for the effective management of global interdependence—a complex, fragile, pluralistic system in which no single country or group of countries is in control—are not in place. Access to modern knowledge as such may not be enough. What is needed is North-South cooperation in bringing about cognitive and attitudinal changes on a massive scale; this will happen only through education.

To draw from modern science new ideas on societal evolution and on development is to shoot at a moving target, for science itself is in transition. The new concepts that have emerged in the natural sciences concern the evolution of complex unstable systems. Studies owing a great deal to the Nobel prizewinner Ilya Prigogine show the roots of innovation and the unification of the physical and human sciences in a wholly new evolutionary vision. Some of these new concepts have already been applied to the study of urban systems, population movements, and the management of fisheries; they may well prove extremely useful for a deep understanding of the dynamics of the development process, of the growing complexity of issues both at the global and the local level. It will, however, most likely be quite some time, if at all, before we can expect the articulation of new theories of social evolution in the manner of the great but now exhausted ideologies that dominated the first part of this century. Access therefore must include participation at the cutting edge of scientific advance. Those countries which in the 1950s followed the wrong advice, ignoring the basic sciences and concentrating on the applied sciences, were condemned to remain perpetual consumers of the research of others and of their applications.

Against this background, what, then, does access to modern knowledge for developing countries and their educational systems mean? It means first, access to state-of-the-art scientific knowledge and second, participation in work at the expanding frontier of science, participation in the process of conceptualization and consensus building of the framework and instruments for the management of global interdependence. In practice, this means access to first-rate universities and research institutions abroad, unlimited access to scientific and scholarly and professional journals as well as to data banks. It means participation in the informal and formal networks of scientists and scholars and in scholarly exchanges.

Study abroad, as we all know, is not without its problems. They are too well known to warrant discussion here. Very often a graduate leaves a host country with little knowledge of its culture, of how the scientific attitude and enterprise is imbedded in that culture. Having concentrated wholly on his own research, he often returns home without having internalized the ethos of scientific inquiry, its intellectual rigor and commitment. If such a person were given the opportunity to stay for another year at a research institution, to see how research is in fact organized and managed, this experience might stand him in good stead on his return when he is entrusted with research management responsibility himself. Also, studying in an affluent and stable country, for all the analytical skill and disciplinary rigor acquired, may not always prepare a student intellectually or psychologicallly for the multiple complexities of underdevelopment, its politics of instability, or the interrelationship between his discipline and the broader questions of institutional development and societal evolution with which he will have to work back home. While such problems do not in any way detract from the overall beneficial effects of serious study at good universities abroad, they need to be considered.

Against this background, the narrowing of access to scientific information through training and exchange now taking place in several major industrial countries is disturbing. The increased cost of study abroad is only partially compensated for by scholarships. It would be unfortunate if fear of competition, the commercialization of scientific knowledge, or considerations of military security were to limit access for developing countries' scientists and scholars. It would be extremely difficult ultimately to contain the pressures toward a global redistribution of population or wealth without a more evenly distributed scientific and technological capability worldwide—which is after all a wealth-creating capability.

Historically, countries seem to go through cycles of openness, on the one hand, and closed-mindedness and self-centeredness on the other. Developing countries too are subject to these cycles. Domestic problems may be so overwhelming as to demand total and exclusive attention. Concern for national and cultural identity (in part a reaction to the communications revolution), considerations of security, the fear of contamination by Westernization or alien political ideologies and of the resulting alienation are very real. They have led, for instance, to setting age limits below which scholarships through government agencies are not available. There are often other restrictions as well. There are cases of extreme, often misplaced, self-satisfaction with the progress made, and a corresponding lack of interest in enlarging access to the outside world. All these and other such factors have contributed to the underutilization of available opportunities to have access to the sources of modern knowledge.

Important as unimpeded and broad access to external sources of knowledge is, the awareness of the need for modern knowledge, the internal capability to utilize opportunities, to create additional ones, to expand knowledge, to reach out, digest, adapt, improve, integrate, and use knowledge are also important. It is the strength and vigor of the national scientific establishment that constitutes the strategic factor in the overall learning capacity of a nation. Ultimately, I think, a nation's graduate schools, hopefully of international quality, may be able gradually to lift the educational system as a whole and may develop the in-depth international competence that guarantees a nation's competitiveness and autonomy.

In many developing countries, universities are seen as the seedbeds of political unrest by the national authorities. A great deal of energy is expended in keeping universities and their students under political control. This results in the suspension of free scientific inquiry and of the nurturing of intellectual curiosity. Independence of mind and intellectual and scientific creativity are devalued for the sake of political conformity. In several countries, universities have been reduced to institutes of higher vocational training for narrow-gauge technicians, capable of handling certain research techniques but incapable and often not wishing independently to define and analyze the problems of their nation. Creativity, a very fragile flower, can only blossom in a climate of academic freedom. Freedom has its risks; without creativity, no nation can hold its own in an increasingly crowded, rapidly changing, and highly competitive world. Nations that are not respectful of the political and social space that creativity requires are bound to discover later—perhaps too late—how high a price they have paid for the impairment of what may be the nation's most strategic asset.

Universities, especially in the large, populous, developing countries, have paid a high price in terms of quality for their expansion, in response to popular demand for more higher education. They have paid a price also for the expansion of the educational system as a whole, an unavoidable concomitant of political independence. The lowering of standards that followed the inevitable shortage of qualified teachers was ultimately reflected in the quality of university students and university teaching. The weakness of the private business sector in many developing countries turned the universities into almost the only channel for entry into the elite. This brought into the university a type of student whose main interest was a degree, rarely the pursuit of knowledge. Underqualified teachers, uncertain of their ground, accepted mediocre student performance. Their feeble authority was often buttressed by feudal notions of the subordinate position of students in relation to a "guru" and by the power of student herd instincts, rooted in traditional collectivist notions. Some students were always ready to ridicule and otherwise discourage any sign of nonconformist intellectual curiosity on the part of more talented colleagues. The failure to abandon deeply ingrained habits of learning by rote, apart from its generally recognized weaknesses, has reinforced the concept of knowledge as something static, to be transferred as is. The notion that knowledge is in constant flux, needs continuous review, and must grow to stay alive has remained alien to many transitional cultures. That many of these cultures have managed to produce some very good minds probably says more about the natural intelligence of the people than about the quality of their educational systems.

Many universities in the developing countries have followed the models of their former colonizers. These models, however, have evolved in the countries of origin and continue to evolve in response to new demands. This has rarely been the case in developing countries. There, Eurocentrism, reflecting the persistent colonization of the mind, continues to rivet academic expectations in many developing countries to the intellectual orientations and fashions of the major academic centers of Europe and America. Recently, it has started to dawn on some that the universities have been educating their students away from the pressing problems of their own countries. Confronted with the constant dilemma of how to keep up with scientific developments in the industrial world to meet the needs of the modern sector and yet also to meet the needs of the majority of their own people, so often impoverished, the best minds have often been pulled in the direction of glamor and prestige, where the economic rewards are greatest.

The persistence of the problem demonstrates the need for modern higher education not to remain separated from traditional culture and the traditional knowledge embedded in that culture, the fruits of centuries of popular experience. The natural and social sciences, and the humanities especially, have to make the connection with traditional culture. In Africa, for instance, some universities have responded by establishing centers of African studies. Similar experiments have been made in Asia. Apart from linkages with the histories of their own national cultures and their various regional subcultures, the humanities will also have to develop linkages with modern technology. The more that developing societies use modern technologies, the more ethical and social judgments are required in the kind of decisions and choices that bear on the purposes for which a particular technology is to be used. The humanities must concern themselves with the social and ethical implications of technological choice. They must become technologically literate. The universities must also play a role in the self-renewal and reinterpretation of their own culture to meet new needs and possibilities, to integrate science in that culture. Universities must, however, not limit themselves to their own culture and their own problems. Developing nations will have to gain expertise on other countries, on their languages and cultures. It is through such programs that a nation's self-awareness is enhanced.

Modern communications technology has brought with it hints of the global village. But so far, the only inhabitants of that village have been the transnational elites, those who live in the industrialized North and those in the South who have access to the global communications network. The current pattern of communication and transportation, to say nothing of the commercial culture imparted chiefly by the mass media, has helped create a new stratification of the world's people into two classes that share little information, experience, or common concern. The wealthy transnational class is assimilated into a universe of communication and information that is not shared by the majority of mankind. The psychological distance between these two strata is in imminent danger of reaching a point where the only form of discourse between the top and the bottom is violence, punctuated by occasional spasms of charity.

The profound irony of this situation cannot escape us. The very communications and information technologies that have the potential to knit humankind together in ways never before possible are now contributing to its fragmentation. Similarly, while these technologies have the potential to contribute to democratization, to the decentralization of power, they are often used thoughtlessly in ways that centralize power.

We are challenged to consider the ways in which the poor and the marginalized people of the world can be brought into the communications revolution so that they gain independent access to modern knowledge. They, too, are decision makers in the development process. The aggregate of millions of decisions and choices by individuals and households can make or break population policies, maintain or exhaust the carrying capacity of specific environments, ensure or undermine the stability of political systems.

The fact is that, for all the expansion of education the world over, the total number of illiterates has increased. Educational systems have failed to keep up with population growth. Conventional schools and teaching methods cost too much. What is obviously needed is a learning system that is not classroom based, but community based, that would use a mixture of modern and traditional information sources and technologies. What is needed is "a poor man's learning system" in which modern knowledge relevant to people's needs is communicated, using multimedia approaches and interactive learning circles, providing information and entertainment in poor urban and rural communities.

Charles William Maynes

Coping with the '90s

I N HIS WHITE HOUSE MEMOIRS, former Secretary of State Henry Kissinger concludes that since 1945 Japan has been better led than any other major country. Over this period, he writes, Japanese leaders simply proved to be more "farsighted" and "intelligent" than their counterparts. Leadership, in other words, can make a difference. Less than 50 years after the nadir of 1945, wise leadership has brought Japan to its current pinnacle.

Today, the extraordinary developments in U.S.-Soviet relations, the Soviet withdrawal from Afghanistan, the apparent willingness of Vietnam to pull its troops out of Cambodia, and the announced willingness of the Cuban forces to leave Angola all give many Americans a sense that their country is on a roll. But it would be unfortunate if understandable pleasure over these developments continued to ripen into a form of national self-satisfaction, blinding Americans to longer-term and more important trends of economic, military, and political significance. For the contrast between America's position in the world today and its position only a few decades ago is sobering.

In 1960 the United States was responsible for nearly one-half of the gross national product (GNP) of the world's market economies. Today it is responsible for only about one-third. For a period after World War II the United States enjoyed a nuclear monopoly. Today the USSR enjoys a position of nuclear parity with the United States;

Reprinted with permission of Foreign Policy. *Originally published in its Spring 1989 issue.* © *1989 by the Carnegie Endowment for International Peace.*

U.S. influence in the Western Hemisphere—so enormous in the 1950s that Washington could overthrow a left-leaning Guatemalan government with a minimal covert effort—had so diminished by the late 1980s that the Reagan administration was unable to force out of office a minor-league dictator in Panama, a country actually created by Washington and controlled by American officials for decades. Perhaps the extent of the change in America's international position can be summed up in a fact and a question. Between 1948 and 1952, the United States provided in today's dollars roughly $100 billion in grant assistance to Western Europe under the Marshall Plan. Does anyone believe that a U.S. administration today could persuade Congress or the country to make an investment of that size to further the country's international agenda?

Why did this shift in America's international standing occur? Poor leadership obviously played a role. Few would contend that the United States was well led after about 1965. It was also inevitable that major states like France, Japan, and West Germany would regain a major place in the international system. Crushed in World War II, they nonetheless retained the basic source of their earlier strength—talented, hard-working, well-educated populations.

What is puzzling about the decline in America's global fortunes is a sense not of steady decline but of sudden discontinuity. Something happened in the early 1970s that appeared to alter permanently America's place in the international system, however much American political figures have tried to pretend otherwise, particularly in a presidential campaign. What were the factors at work? As the country moves into the first year of the Bush administration, it will be impossible to understand, much less master, the new diplomatic agenda unless an attempt is made to answer this question.

In retrospect it seems clear that the decisive changes—those that transformed America from the world's pre-eminent power into only the world's most important power—took place, or came to light, during the presidency of Richard Nixon. The three pillars on which the United States had built its postwar hegemony suddenly buckled in the early 1970s, and none of the compensatory steps taken by administrations since then have succeeded in repairing the damage.

The three pillars were America's basic nuclear superiority, its control of the world's energy industry, and the pre-eminent role the dollar enjoyed in international trade and finance. In the early 1970s the Soviet Union, though still some distance from numerical equality in strategic warheads, attained rough nuclear parity. Meanwhile, the Organization of Petroleum Exporting Countries (OPEC) took control of the world's oil industry away from America, and Western allies began to compete effectively with the United States in the field of nuclear power. Finally, the United States abandoned the Bretton Woods system of fixed exchange rates based on a dollar standard for a regime of floating exchange rates. The marketplace rather than senior American officials began to dominate the world's monetary system.

Such relatively abrupt changes in such critical areas would have adversely affected the international position of any country, however well or poorly led at the time. America was no exception. Yet physical factors alone cannot explain the transformation that was taking place with respect to America's role in the world. Psychological forces were also at work; they are often overlooked but deserve more careful examination.

One explanation for the early postwar successes of U.S. policymakers is a hidden diplomatic advantage that America alone enjoyed in the same full measure: the positive image of America and its system of government in world eyes and the resulting deference toward its policies that many felt in other parts of the globe. This deference helps to explain the special international role the United States was able to play.

Any order, domestic or foreign, requires a certain measure of deference to remain stable. Otherwise police or troops would be stationed at every corner to compel obedience. The issue is why deference develops. In past centuries deference arose from the authorities' willingness to use almost unlimited force to compel it. The British could rule half the globe with only 100,000 soldiers. Whenever colonial figures failed to show sufficient deference, British authorities moved quickly to punish them. The machine gun was always there, if necessary, to snuff out more widespread rebellion. The white supremacy that reigned in the southern United States for many decades after the Civil War also rested on deference. Whenever blacks failed to show the proper measure of subservience toward whites, the hooded riders of the Ku Klux Klan soon mounted up.

In the Middle East, until recently, the Israelis could control the occupied West Bank and Gaza Strip with only weekend soldiers. No longer is this possible. The Israeli army is now trying to re-establish deference—in the words of Prime Minister Yitzhak Shamir, to put the "fear of death" back into the minds of the Palestinians—through the brutal tactics that have convulsed public opinion not only in the outside world but in Israel itself.

Some governments are obviously willing to go much further than others to force deference from citizens or subjects who may feel that the authorities no longer merit it. In Central America and Eastern Europe, governments have at times in effect suspended the rule of law in an effort to make average citizens once again deferential in their approach toward those in power. That has been the purpose of officially inspired death squads in Central America and officially supported show trials in Eastern Europe. And the Syrian government re-established deference by using artillery to level an entire city, Hama.

THE REWARDS OF DEFERENCE

Like other empires, the postwar American "empire" also benefitted from deference. Yet it rested on an entirely different basis. Unlike more traditional imperial orders, until its disastrous involvement in Vietnam the American empire enjoyed the advantages of deference not so much because others feared the United States as because they respected it. The deference that existed in the British Empire, the American South, and the other examples cited rested primarily on brute force. The authorities had all the guns, or most of them, and were determined to use them if necessary. Except perhaps in areas like Central America, the postwar deference accorded the United States was quite different. Foreign observers saw America as the model of what a modern society should be. Their respect often bordered on awe because the attractiveness of the American model was coupled with phenomenal resources. Thanks to its overwhelming capabilities, America seemed in a position to accomplish whatever it set out to do. It could save Europe economically, block the Soviets militarily, and lead the world technologically. Most Americans do not reflect on the consequences of this deferential view of their country. Because it existed, for much of the postwar period challenges to American leadership and authority were fewer in number, less in intensity, and shorter in duration.

If the developments mentioned help to explain the relative decline in American power in recent years, are new developments likely to take place in the 1990s that will restore America to its earlier postwar role? In the military field some believe that the development of so-called smart weapons can restore the edge America once enjoyed. The U.S. Commission on Integrated Long-Term Strategy, whose members included such foreign-policy luminaries as former national security advisers Zbigniew Brzezinski and Kissinger, envisaged in its January 1988 report "dramatic developments in military technology" over the next 20 years. According to the commission, the exploitation of microelectronics and the development of directed energy will enable combatants through "greater precision, range, and destructiveness" to "extend war across a much wider geographic area, make war much more rapid and intense, and require entirely new modes of operation." The goal, will be "to use smart missiles that can apply force in a discriminate fashion and avoid collateral damage to civilians."

If such weapons were created with the requisite degree of precision, their political impact almost certainly would be greater in the Third World than in the First World. For even if it is assumed that the Soviets would be unable to make comparable advances—a hazardous assumption in light of the history of the arms race—it is difficult to see how "smarter" U.S. weapons could have any impact on the existing military stand-off in Europe except to reinforce it further. Even if it gained a military advantage, the West would be unwilling to exploit it except for defensive purposes. With regard to the Third World, however, smarter U.S. weapons might persuade some that the U.S. military would from then on be in a much better position to use force against Third World states whose policies angered American officials. With such weapons, for example, the Reagan administration might have been in a better position to strike Libya or Syria with impunity because of the support each apparently had given to terrorist groups around the world. Particularly in areas where there was slight possibility of escalation to a superpower confrontation, the United States, armed with smart weapons, could punish malefactors with few civilian casualties and no U.S. losses.

There are important reasons, however, for believing that, even if successfully developed, smarter weapons will not give the United States the edge envisioned. First, in this area the technologists often promise more than they can deliver. In other words, the weapons are unlikely to be as smart as their creators say they will be. It is not reassuring to recall that the United States used "smart bombs" to attack Libya and was embarrassed when they turned up in the French ambassador's garden and other civilian sites, killing large numbers of innocents in Tripoli. Second, it seems unlikely that intelligence will be as smart as the weapons developed. Probably no site was more carefully scrutinized than North Vietnam's Son Tay prisoner-of-war camp, which American commandos assaulted at great risk in November 1970, only to find that the North Vietnamese had moved their American captives before the commandos struck.

Third, it is vital to recognize that, precisely because America's earlier hegemony rested on a deference of respect, not of fear, efforts to use military force to restore the earlier level of deference are by definition bound to fall short of official expectations. Military force may cow a few radical states, but it is unlikely to have the anticipated effect on others. If an operation is carried out recklessly, the use of force can even reduce respect for the United States in the world at large. In this regard, many American commentarors overstate the meaning of the so-called Vietnam syndrome. They seem to argue that the key task of American foreign policy is to make others fear the United States again. On the contrary, the task is to make them respect America again. Placing as much emphasis on the use of force as some U.S. public figures do will serve not to increase the respect foreigners accord the United States but to lessen it. The image of the reckless, if well-meaning, cowboy will replace that of the benevolent, if firm, uncle. It is instructive to recall that respect for the Reagan administration was highest when it was negotiating with the Kremlin, not bombing Libya.

Are other, nonmilitary, sources of postwar U.S. power likely to be restored to their previous position of strength? In the eyes of a growing number of specialists, the financial capital of the world has shifted from New York to Tokyo as the Japanese propensity to save has outstripped that of any other major country. Any effort by the United States to regain its earlier financial position is hindered by its new position as the world's largest debtor. The United States must now tailor its economic policies to accommodate foreign creditors whose capital it cannot do without. It will take years to reduce America's trade deficit significantly. Even then, restoring the dollar to its earlier status in international financial transactions may be beyond America's reach, for Western Europe has regained its pre-World War II place in the international economy, and Japan has even gone beyond its earlier position.

America's loss of control over the world's energy supply also seems permanent. Indeed, if the United States does not manage its affairs wisely, OPEC may again achieve oligopolistic control over the world's energy markets. The National Petroleum Council has warned that net U.S. imports of crude oil and refined products are likely to rise from 27 per cent of consumption in 1985 to 30–40 per cent in 1990 and to 47 per cent in 1995. This oil will have to come from existing producers. For even if new oil fields are found, they take an average of 7 years to develop.

What about the factor of deference? Here there is room for constructive change because even though others have shown declining respect toward U.S. policies in recent years, many major opportunities remain to alter foreign perceptions. Events in even the last several months again demonstrate that the United States remains the critical link in the solution of almost all significant international problems. For that reason other states must be concerned with the American position. Wise leadership can enhance America's international image and the degree of its international influence. It will not be possible to return the United States to the extraordinary pre-eminence of the immediate postwar period. But the country should be able to improve on the record of the last few decades.

Past successes and failures provide the setting. Are there new realities that will alter this backdrop as the United States attempts to address its diplomatic agenda in the 1990s? There are, in fact, two: the resource gridlock and the information revolution.

Books by David Calleo, Robert Gilpin, and Paul Kennedy, among others, have opened up an important debate in the United States: Can America afford the international costs of its traditional postwar foreign policy?[1] On one side of the debate it is asserted that the United States is contributing to its own decline by channeling too high a percentage of its resources into the defense sector while its commercial rivals, primarily the West Europeans and the Japanese, are taking advantage of their lower defense burden to forge ahead economically. According to this argument, the United States must move more of its defense burden onto the shoulders of its allies so that the American economy can regain a sustainable level of international competitiveness.

On the other side of the debate are the alliance traditionalists who, while not disagreeing that the West Europeans and the Japanese should assume a larger share of the costs of maintaining the current international system, stress that, viewed historically, the American defense burden of the late 1980s is not excessive. In the words of the most prominant among the alliance traditionalists, former Secretary of State George Shultz, Americans enjoyed their highest economic growth in the 1950s and 1960s, precisely "when our military expenditures averaged 9.2 per cent of GNP, a much higher proportion than the 6.7 per cent we spend today."

Perhaps one reason neither side in this debate persuades the other is that the arguments of both sides are correct. It seems incontestable that, other things being equal, a country carrying a much smaller defense burden will have a commercial advantage over a country carrying a much larger burden. At least some talented people will be drained off into fields of endeavor valuable for national defense but not so valuable for international trade. And at least some of the money that the American government has spent on defense could have been channeled into areas like education and infrastructure that over time could have substantially improved America's ability to compete overseas.

At the same time, the traditionalists are right: America's defense burden, while significant, has not been so great that the United States could not have done what it needed to do in other areas by making an additional effort at home—for example, through economic policies that encouraged saving and productive investment. There is no fixed formula that determines when the size of the defense budget becomes counterproductive.

The key issue, in fact, is political. Both major party candidates for president in 1988 and leading pollsters agree that Americans are unlikely to make the same relative sacrifices for international affairs in the 1990s that they were willing to make in the mid-1950s. But this widely accepted point does not mean that the population has gone soft. Rather, various political sectors have become more conscious of their rights. In the mid-1950s the underprivileged members of American society were less likely to demand a fair share of the national income than they are today. Most blacks in the South in the 1950s did not even have the vote. Neither did many poor whites.

For many decades after Reconstruction southern political leaders skewed the electoral rules to disenfranchise blacks. But to avoid northern charges of discimination they also disenfranchised whites in comparable economic and social conditions. The result was that while black political participation virtually ceased, white participation also fell precipitously. By the 1920s black voting in the South had effectively ended, and white voting had fallen by more than 50 per cent from the 1876–1892 period. In some years, only a little more than 30 per cent of the white population turned out to vote in presidential elections. The South thus became a reactionary anchor for the rest of the country.

But those days are gone. The Reverend Martin Luther King, Jr.'s civil rights revolution enfranchised not only blacks but also poor whites. Those concerned with the defense debate would be foolish not to recognize the altered nature of the country in which they live. Not only do the poor have a greatly increased ability to press their claims on the federal government, but entitlements and other programs benefiting the middle class have also increased dramatically as legislators have shaped social programs to maximize political support. In an indirect way, therefore, the earlier disenfranchisement of blacks and the earlier high political support for larger defense budgets may have been related.

It will now take a major international crisis to galvanize the American people into making the same kind of defense effort in the 1990s that they made in the 1950s. And the threat will have to be real. Mere rhetoric will not be enough. For another recent trend in American politics has been the steady de-demonization of America's principal international foe. Even before Mikhail Gorbachev became general secretary of the Soviet Communist party, it was becoming ever more difficult for American policymakers, though some tried, to contend that the Soviet Union of the 1980s was the evil empire of Joseph Stalin's era. The sharp public criticism of the Reagan administration's initial harsh rhetoric expressed eloquently the change that has taken place in popular American attitudes.

In the 1990s American diplomacy will also find itself steadily constrained in its freedom of movement by the information revolution, which includes not only the development of new communications technology but also the growing ability of large numbers of people to receive and understand the information sent to them, thanks to education and urbanization. Literacy is key. Many Americans fail to see the enormous political impact that literacy has already had on the postwar world. In the United States, for example, it helps to put the civil rights revolution into perspective. In 1940 only 11.6 per cent of black adults between the ages of 25 and 29 had 4 years of high school or any university-level education. By 1970 that figure was 55.4 per cent. During those years blacks also poured out of the rural South into America's great cities where ideas flow back and forth more easily than in the southern countryside. From this politically fertile urban soil came the chief commanders of King's civil rights army.

Take another country and a completely different system of government. Gorbachev's revolution can be understood not simply by studying his powerful personality and political acumen but also by examining the levels of education and urbanization reached in his country. In 1987, 89 per cent of the Soviet adult population had at least a 10th-grade education. The comparable figure in 1939 was 10 per cent, and even in 1959 it was only 32 per cent. A rural society when Stalin died, the Soviet Union is now nearly as urbanized as the United States.[2]

Then there is the crisis in Central America. It has many sources, but certainly one is the rising level of literacy. In Central America between 1960 and 1976 the literacy rate rose from 44 per cent to 72 per cent.

In the remaining years of this century there is every reason to believe that the cumulative impact of education, communications technology, and urbanization will continue to revolutionize politics and diplomacy in virtually every country. Illiteracy will continue to fall. The communications revolution will continue on its accelerating trajectory and people will continue to flock to the cities. This does not mean that all countries will evolve in a similar fashion; nor does it mean that the results will always be peaceful or desirable. But everywhere, governments will find it harder to control the direction of change within their own societies. They will find it harder to prevent new voices from speaking out and playing a role in policy-making—whether these voices are found in the business community, the academic community, or the churches and mosques. The direct-dial telephone, the videocassette, the short-wave radio, and the personal computer all will facilitate a rising degree of cross-penetration of every political system. The development of the video telephone may even facilitate cross-border alliances without the necessity of travel.

A hint of the future can be found in such different developments as the role of foreign clerics in the politics of Central America, Eastern Europe, and the Middle East; the direct party-to-party negotiations between the West German Social Democratic party and East German Communist party officials; and the new ventures into foreign policy by more than 1,000 U.S. state and local governments.

Governments that try to stop or control these activities will fail. Those that understand their direction and make an appropriate adjustment in their diplomatic efforts may succeed. In the 1950s U.S. diplomats saw themselves as creators or builders. In the 1990s they will be navigators, trying to captain a ship of state whose new crew members are difficult to lead and may mutiny if they lose respect for the captain.

CHALLENGES OF THE FUTURE

Against that backdrop, four fundamental problems face the United States in the 1990s: the economic challenge, the security challenge, the Latin American challenge, and the global challenge.

• In the 1990s, for the first time since the interwar period, economic issues will rival political issues as America's number one diplomatic priority. This shift will radically alter American diplomacy as most observers have understood it in the postwar period. After 1945 America, unlike most countries, was in a position to elevate security issues to the realm of high politics and to relegate economic issues to the realm of low politics. This ordering of U.S. objectives permitted U.S. officials, almost alone among the officials of the major Western powers, to sacrifice economic objectives in pursuit of security objectives. The United States could tolerate trade restrictions against itself if such concessions helped to rebuild Western Europe and consolidate NATO. It could purchase disengagement agreements in the Middle East through massive increases in American aid to Egypt and Israel. It could also use aid and trade throughout the Third World to shore up American friends and weaken American adversaries.

Now U.S. diplomats will join diplomats of other major countries in according priority to economic issues. Can U.S. diplomats be as successful in the future as in the past when they will be losing a tool critical to their earlier success?

A key issue is whether the United States can persuade others to join in common sacrifices sufficient to preserve the postwar economic system. Among the tasks facing U.S. policymakers in the 1990s will be maintaining and improving an open trading system, solving the Third World debt question, establishing a more stable currency regime, and finding a new means of ensuring a reliable flow of capital to the developing world now that the United States is unable to fulfill this function.

Resource requirements are going to force the United States to link economics and security in a fashion that administrations have avoided for 40 years. Because the United States can no longer provide the capital and additional market access necessary to revive Third World, and thus global, growth, it must make clear to Western Europe and Japan that if they are unwilling or unable to assume a greater share of the military burden, the new security bargain requires them to take on a new role in the development field. Their willingness to assume new responsibilities is all the more important because the world economy needs a new source of growth, and revived development efforts in the Third World seem the principal hope in this regard.

Finally, in the 1990s the United States and its partners must find a way to integrate the communist world into the international economy. Whatever the future of the current reforms in the People's Republic of China, the Soviet Union, and other communist countries, there seems to be a systemwide determination among communist countries—except for Cuba and North Korea—to participate actively in the international economy so that they can become competitive economically and technologically. Over the long run, the West will be unable to deny them the right to participate; but it is not yet clear what conditions can be reasonably imposed for them to become full members of the international economic system.

- In dealing with security, the second challenge for the 1990s, American policymakers probably will have to work with their allies to develop a new defense structure in both Western Europe and

Northeast Asia. Nuclear proliferation, both vertical and horizontal, among states other than the superpowers is changing the balance of power in the world in ways still not fully comprehensible. For example, as a result of the nuclear arms modernization programs being undertaken by Great Britain and France, by the end of this century these two powers will have increased the number of land- and sea-based missile warheads they deploy from the current level of roughly 300 to approximately 1,200. Unless there is some serious breakthrough in national defense against missile attack, this increase will revolutionize the defense of the West. By 1995 France alone will be able to kill 80 million Soviet citizens and destroy two-thirds of Soviet industrial capacity. Britain may be able to inflict as many as 68 million Soviet fatalities and incapacitate one-half of the Soviet production base.[3] The commander of a single British or French nuclear submarine will have enough power under his command to wipe out every major and medium-sized city in the Soviet Union.

The momentous change the British and French modernization effort will bring can best be understood by recalling that in 1967 Robert McNamara, then U.S. secretary of defense, suggested that the destruction of perhaps one-fourth of the Soviet population and between one-half and two-thirds of Soviet industrial capacity would mean the "elimination" of the Soviet Union as "a major power for many years." Yet the 100 largest cities in the Soviet Union house one-fourth of the Soviet population and hold one-half of its industry. Thus, after their nuclear modernization programs are complete, Britain and France will have the capacity to destroy the Soviet Union many times over.

Meanwhile, according to the International Institutes of Strategic Studies, China has on order eight ballistic missile nuclear submarines, with more planned. The Commission on Integrated Long-Term Strategy has predicted that by the year 2010 China may become the world's second largest economic power. In addition, India and Pakistan seem to be acquiring nuclear weapons status as well as growing capabilities to deliver a nuclear device. These apparently include ballistic missiles. And Israel is believed to have more than 25 aircraft-deliverable nuclear weapons and has tested a missile with a range sufficient to hit southern parts of the Soviet Union. Other countries are undoubtedly engaged in similar activities. It is estimated that at least 20 countries currently possess or are striving to acquire ballistic missiles capable of carrying a chemical or nuclear charge.

Barring a degree of security cooperation between the United States and the Soviet Union that seems beyond reach, the United States has no interest in blocking the growing ability of Western Europe to defend itself. Indeed, in the 1990s the United States should do more to strengthen that ability. Although it should take no precipitous action, the United States should declare its intention over time—assuming appropriate developments in the Warsaw Pact—to limit its military commitment to NATO primarily to the air and sea, leaving only token ground troops in Western Europe. It should cut the special tie to Britain to end that country's illusion that it has an alternative to closer cooperation with its European partners; and, in continuing further nuclear cooperation with Britain, it should encourage Britain to work with France in nuclear targeting and acquisition.

The United States has an interest in seeing that the transition to a new security order is peaceful. It has a strong interest in preventing or slowing the proliferation of nuclear weapons to states such as Israel or Pakistan that face the kind of security threat that may someday tempt them to use their nuclear arsenals. For that reason, in the Bush administration and into the 1990s the United States should begin discussions, initially with allies and perhaps later with other major powers within the framework of the U.N. Security Council, on the contours of a new security order. Some observers may bridle at the mention of the United Nations in this highly sensitive field, but in September 1987 Gorbachev issued an important statement on common security in which he reversed traditional Soviet positions on such issues as U.N. peace keeping and the role of international law in settling disputes. He developed these ideas further in a remarkable speech before the U.N. General Assembly in December 1988. Key details are still lacking, but the United States has an important interest in exploring with the Soviet Union and other permanent members of the Security Council the seriousness behind his ideas.

Some might dismiss such discussions as utopian in light of the history of the earlier attempt at U.S.-Soviet détente undertaken in the Nixon administration. But it is time that Americans and others understand why détente in the early 1970s failed and why a new effort may have a greater chance for success. There is a tendency on the part of many who have assessed the wreckage of what might be called Détente I to search for scapegoats. The critics of the Nixon administration charge that officials of that administration oversold détente and practiced a deceitful foreign policy that finally destroyed public confidence. Former Nixon administration officials counter-charge that détente failed because the opposition exploited the Watergate crisis for partisan purposes and destroyed the ability of the executive branch to act decisively in foreign affairs.

In fact, the objective conditions for a lasting relationship of détente did not exist. This can be seen by looking at the nuclear arsenals of the two sides. At the beginning of the Nixon administration the United States was at the end of a major defense acquisition cycle. Under McNamara's direction the United States in the 1960s had increased its submarine-launched and intercontinental ballistic missiles eighteenfold. For many Americans who did not understand these realities, Détente I meant Soviet acceptance of the status quo, which in turn meant Soviet acceptance of the American build-up and the existing gap. For the Soviets, détente undoubtedly meant permission to catch up. But no American administration could publicly defend arrangements allowing the Soviet Union to catch up with the United States militarily.

By the early years of the Reagan administration, the Soviets had actually succeeded in their effort. The number of warheads deployed on systems with ranges greater than 1,000 miles was roughly equal—about 11,000 on each side. Therefore, objective conditions for a more lasting relationship of détente had arrived, provided the strategic arms limitation talks weapons ceilings remained in place. In general, they have.

• William Colby, the former director of the CIA, has contended that the major security threat facing the United States in the remaining portion of this century is more likely to be uncontrolled immigration from Latin America than a missile attack from the USSR. Clearly he is correct that the former will continue, whereas it seems almost inconceivable that the latter will happen. Yet uncontrolled immigration from Latin America can radically change the character of the American body politic, perhaps at a speed that will create political instability if effective measures to manage it are not taken in time.

Because of sharp reductions in the death rate, Mexico alone must create 1 million new jobs a year for the next 15 years if it is to avoid a political explosion. This is a daunting task, since there are only 20 million permanently employed Mexicans currently on the official job rolls. Moreover, such an achievement has no historical precedent. Mexico did create 700,000 jobs a year during the 1970s, but annual growth rates then were as high as 6 per cent. Now growth has virtually ceased because of the debt crisis. What will keep these young Mexicans from moving north when they reach the age of maturity?

If political unrest in Central America continues, another stream of immigrants will flow northward. Finally, the meager economic prospects for the people living in the Caribbean ensures that a third immigration stream will swell in the coming years. Stringent enforcement of America's new immigration laws will not keep out these millions with no other place to go except the bread line.

A major challenge for the 1990s, therefore, will be to create a political and economic order in America's southern neighbors of sufficient decency to persuade people to remain in their own countries. The Bush administration should develop with its Latin neighbors, particularly Mexico, a massive jobs program to provide employment opportunities to the new generations in their own countries.

Regrettably, barring a major change in Americans' attitude toward the national tax burden, it will not be possible for the United States to undertake this task unless it cuts back its profile and commitments elsewhere. At this point a reallocation of America's international burden can only mean cuts in funds dedicated to NATO and the Middle East, the major beneficiaries of America's current international priorities. The allies are able to shoulder a larger share of the burden even though this task is politically difficult. Israel is in a more precarious position, but in the past internal U.S. government reviews have concluded that U.S. military aid to Israel could dip below $1 billion without threatening Israel's margin of superiority. Such programs as U.S. support for the Lavi fighter, now canceled, suggest that the U.S. aid program for Israel could be more efficiently managed. Most observers harbor similar views with respect to the U.S. aid program to Egypt.

Also affecting U.S. views will be the evolution of the Arab-Israeli conflict. Originally internationalized, it is steadily being internalized.

This process can only lead to civil strife inside Israel. The U.S. government has repeatedly proved its willingness to finance Israel's security against outside aggression. Is it as likely to be willing for a sustained period to finance Israeli efforts to repress a large Palestinian minority insisting on its political rights? It seems unlikely that Americans will be comfortable supporting the permanent suppression of another people.

The Bush administration may have a last chance to develop a meaningful peace process in the Middle East before the process of internalizing the Israeli-Palestinian conflict has gone beyond the point of no return. If this negotiation effort fails, the United States should cut back its commitment to the Middle East in order to devote a greater share of its funds and energy to problems more pressing for American security. In this regard it should attempt to deal with international concerns about the security of Persian Gulf oil by probing more seriously Soviet proposals or those of former Secretary of Defense Elliot Richardson and former Secretary of State Cyrus Vance for a multilateral naval role. The Soviet withdrawal from Afghanistan should enable the United States to look at the entire region through a new optic. After all, America's major concern over the Soviet move into Afghanistan was the location of Soviet military bases closer to the Persian Gulf. Now these bases will close.

• In addition to nonproliferation, the United States and the world face a growing list of global challenges: apartheid, acquired immune deficiency syndrome (AIDS), the greenhouse effect, the international drug trade, acid rain, and the steady destruction of tropical forests, which serve as the globe's vital agricultural gene pool. Some of these issues pose a new challenge for international institutions: Formerly their main task was to facilitate the exchange of information and to encourage the establishment of global standards that member states would accept. Tomorrow their main task may be international regulation of economic behavior at the national level. This transformation will open a new chapter in the history of international organizations and will severely test their ability to assume new and daunting responsibilities. A symbol of the future was the treaty signed in 1987 to reduce the consumption of materials destructive of the atmosphere's ozone layer. In that treaty signatory powers accepted the obligation to reduce the use of materials that at the

national level are profitable but that at the global level are dangerous.

In addition, in the 1990s the world community will face a major
human and developmental tragedy in Africa. It is clear that many of
the countries on that continent will never be economically viable. If
millions are not to suffer or even die unnecessarily, the international
community in the 1990s will have to turn its attention to the task of
redrawing the economic map of Africa. Programs must be designed
to induce or compel African states to cooperate more closely with one
another. Special multinational programs must be launched to secure
the funding that will be necessary to save much of Africa from a
human catastrophe.

Few countries easily accept the need for a change in direction.
Most require a crisis of sufficient magnitude to force new thinking.
The 1990s may bring precisely such a crisis. In December 1987, 33 of
the world's leading economists met in Washington and warned of a
grave international economic crisis in the coming administration—
saying that "the next few years could be the most troubled since the
1930s"—unless key countries took actions that now seem unlikely.[4]
In the military field the 1990s could bring a dramatic increase in the
number of nuclear powers or in the number of powers armed with
chemical weapons on ballistic missiles. The 1990s seem virtually
certain to impose a serious social and economic crisis on Mexico and
Central America, which will adjust by encouraging more of their
people to move to California and Texas. Finally, as the AIDS crisis
demonstrates, new global problems can surface at unexpected mo-
ments.

In short, the challenges that seem likely to confront U.S. policymakers in the 1990s appear so urgent that it does not seem wise to
allow events themselves to set the country's agenda. Japan prospered
in the last four decades because its leaders faced up to new realities,
shaped a coherent national response to deal with them, and then
pursued with determination the long-range objectives they had set.
With wise leadership, America also should be able to protect its
security and enhance its welfare in the very different world that will
arise in the 1990s.

ENDNOTES

¹David P. Calleo, *Beyond American Hegemony: The Future of the Western Alliance* (New York: Basic Books, 1987); Robert Gilpin, *The Political Economy of International Relations* (Princeton: Princeton University Press, 1987); and Paul M. Kennedy, *The Rise and Fall of the Great Powers* (New York: Random House, 1987).

²See S. Frederick Starr, "Soviet Union: A Civil Society," *Foreign Policy* 70 (Spring 1988):28–29.

³John Prados, Joel S. Wit, and Michael J. Zagurek, Jr., "The Strategic Nuclear Forces of Britain and France," *Scientific American* 225 (August 1986):36.

⁴*Resolving the Global Economic Crisis: After Wall Street*, Special Report no. 6 (Washington, D.C.: Institute for International Economics, 1987), vii.

Comments on Article by C.W. Maynes

CHARLES WILLIAM MAYNES: I am interested in why American policymakers have had such difficulty with the Third World, why Americans have so many Third World hang-ups. Part of the explanation, I think, relates to the peculiar racial history of this country, which I think has left a feeling of hostility on the Right and a feeling of guilt on the Left. White settlers came here with conflicting purposes: to subjugate and to save, to conquer and to convert. There is, on the one hand, a missionary impulse in the American body politic; on the other hand, there is a history of conquest and hostility. I think white Americans in particular tend to overlook this history. It is not ignored by nonwhite Americans.

Several contemporary factors, I believe, make American approaches to the Third World difficult or controversial. There is, first, the whole American approach to the issue of development. The average American has a lot of trouble with the idea of development assistance. Disaster relief—one-time temporary help—is one thing. A form of international affirmative action designed to compensate for structural flaws in the international system is more difficult to accept, internationally as well as domestically. Such assistance is regarded as almost an unnatural act, something to be performed in the dark so that no one else can witness it.

If we look at the postwar period, the average American perceives a series of U.S. setbacks or defeats, which took place principally in the Third

World—militarily in Korea and Vietnam, geopolitically in Cuba and Iran, economically in OPEC and with the Asian tigers. This has left a bitter taste in the mouths of many Americans. Third World solidarity in the United Nations only contributes to this feeling. While there are good explanations for Third World solidarity, the average American notices that when votes are taken, it's 121 on one side and only a very few on the U.S. side.

And finally, though it did not start out that way, there has developed increasingly an image of the Third World as having only corrupt or brutal leaders. All these factors joined together make for a very difficult relationship between the United States and the Third World.

Still, there are positive trends, long-run in nature, that I think are going to make the relationship a more benign one, perhaps a more constructive one. To begin with, there is a change of racial attitudes inside the United States. I know that this is a contested point; we hear about racial problems on our campuses; we know what happened recently in the New York primary between Mayor Ed Koch and the Reverend Jesse Jackson. Still, if one looks at the growing number of black officeholders and the phenomenon of the Jackson candidacy, there is no question that the long-run trends are positive.

Also, there has been a change recently in the image of Third World leaders in this country. The leader in Central America that people are talking about is friendly to the United States. It is Arias, not Castro. In the Far East, it's Corey Aquino, not Ho Chi Minh. In Africa, it's Robert Mugabe, not Idi Amin. I think that this will have some impact on the average American's attitude.

The heroic age in the Third World also appears to be over. The period of political liberation and national political consolidation—both of which involved a process of sticking fingers in Western eyes—has given way to a new development agenda; that shift, I think, can only have a beneficial impact on U.S. attitudes.

Also, there is today more knowledge about the Third World in this country. Forty percent of our trade is now with the developing countries. More and more businessmen travel there and understand the Third World better. And 125,000 Peace Corps volunteers have served in the Third World. Many have gone into public service. Gradually, there is a body of knowledge developing in this country that did not exist before.

Finally, and I suppose this would be contested by some, if we look back over the last twenty-five years, although progress has been ragged, the East-West relationship is somewhat better. Today, with Gorbachev, there is a hope that it may become much better. I think this will allow us to look at Third World development through a less distorted focus than has been common in the past.

Changes in policy are clearly called for. In the field of aid, for a variety of reasons, we will have to do more with less. I think, for example, that we will need to consolidate more, emphasize performance standards more, give new attention to multilateral aid, precisely because it is more effective.

The trade issue is going to be much more important than the aid issue in the foreseeable future. We will have to find ways to pressure Japan and Western Europe to open their markets to the products of Third World countries, while we make certain to keep our own market open. Leadership from the White House will be crucial. While the outlook for the immediate future may not be bright, the longer-run future almost certainly is.

ALFRED STEPAN: Bill makes assertions that I find disturbing but not without foundation. He, like Frank Sutton, seems to argue that U.S. support for aid was originally based on the belief that aid was corrective—in short, temporary. The need for aid was obviously not temporary; but a massive fatigue with aid has set in. Furthermore, one of the few reliable arguments in Congress for aid has always been the Cold War, a policy intended to stop Communism. From this perspective, what is likely to happen to that security rationale if there is a real U.S.-Soviet détente? Also, amidst U.S. anxieties about our trade deficit, fears could grow that aid recipients might become truly competitive and take away our markets and jobs. Finally, there is Maynes's suggestion that there is no prospect of any significant improvement of U.S. official development assistance.

Notwithstanding all of this, however, I believe that there are some grounds for optimism, some bases for positive action in the development field, though not perhaps in the traditionally defined aid field. Indeed, my own belief is that we have just about finished the worst period of U.S. attitudes toward development. When I say this, I do not mean that good things will immediately happen. It is simply to assert that more realistic attitudes about U.S. trading interests, long-term needs for development, especially in the Western hemisphere, and possible support for new facilities for dealing with debt and development might emerge.

The whole issue of attitudes based on "corrective charity" rather than interest needs to be reexamined. We are told that 40 percent of U.S. exports now go to the Third World. If the Third World resumes economic growth, these exports could soon reach 50 percent. The fact is that we have lost 1 million jobs because of the debt crisis. To date, almost no private-sector industrialists have mobilized in any serious way to pressure Congress to alleviate the debt and development crisis, yet this situation could change as industrialists come to realize that their own real interests lie in the development of the Third World, especially in the Western hemisphere.

A possible U.S.-Soviet détente does not really erode the security interests in development. The United States is the only developed country in the world with a large, open border with a large poor country. England is an island; so is Japan; Scandinavia is virtually so; France and Germany are highly insulated from the poor of the world. For geographical reasons, therefore, the United States has permanent interests in the question of Third World development, interests different in quality and quantity from those of any other developed country. We need to start talking about these interests. We need a more serious understanding of the shared destiny of our hemisphere, an understanding which I believe would bring new supporters to development coalitions.

Where could some new financial resources for development come from? Twice in the last month I have had interesting conversations with a CEO of one of the largest banks in the United States. He remarks that it is time for us to rethink the doctrine that all trade and development banks be restricted to a one-to-one gearing ratio. He believes that a ten-to-one gearing ratio (which is still much lower than commercial bank ratios, some of which are as high as twenty-five to one) would be acceptable for trade and development banks, especially if a new debt and development facility were created. I think that some type of rethinking along these lines is long overdue. There is a huge amount of money circulating in the world; what is lacking is the political will, new institutions, and new programs to harness some of this money to alleviate our development crisis.

If Japan came in with $10 billion, something I do not rule out, if Germany came in with $5 billion, if we came in with $3 billion or $2 billion, and others did something, there would be $20 billion available for this new facility. If you changed the gearing ratio applicable to this new facility to ten to one, that would be $200 billion. Properly used, this $200 billion could go a long way toward providing real debt relief, relief that would not be a traditional form of aid but that would go a long way toward development.

JEFFREY D. SACHS: I must say that while I share the view that there are solutions to problems we have, we are not getting to those solutions as rapidly as is suggested. I am somewhat bothered by Alfred Stepan's remark about the CEO of the large U.S. bank. For the CEO to advocate more lending by the development banks is a measure of cynicism, not a measure of vision. Development bank money gives the debtor countries the resources they need to pay the interest to that CEO's bank. The bankers for the last five years have been saying yes, we need more development effort from the official community. Translation: the more official money we put in, the more money the banks can take out. I have seen nothing, frankly, that would lead me to believe that the banks are on the cutting edge of a solution to the debt crisis. We are still stalemated about how to share the burden of resolving the crisis. Mr. Stepan's proposal of a new international debt facility could make a lot of sense if the debt facility helped to extricate the banks with orderly losses rather than simply to bail out the banks with taxpayer dollars.

STANLEY HEGINBOTHAM: Is Congress really anti-international? I doubt it. The budget crunch at the moment stems in large part from a tactical failure of the administration. Anyone could have seen that 40 percent of the foreign-aid pie was going to Israel and Egypt. That was not going to change. Another 10 percent was also not going to get cut. This meant that everything else would be cut 20 percent if the average cut was 10 percent. That argument needed to be made in the budget committees, and it was not.

Congress is not likely to shape a foreign-aid strategy; it depends on an administration to shape one, and this administration has not done so. I sense that if an administration were to shape a strategy that took advantage of Congress's strong humanitarian instincts and concerns, its great skepticism about multilateral institutions, and its awareness of AID's institutional limitations, there would be a strong base of support in Congress for aid. Huge amounts of aid? No, but 25 percent, 30 percent, 40 percent more than we are now giving in development assistance? Yes. That is enough to make a difference. Does it solve the debt problem? No. Still, it would allow us to do substantially better.

But the debates about strategies in Washington over the last seven years have not been, for the most part, about what is likely to benefit Africa or Mexico. The concern has been with what will benefit the NGOs (nongovernmental organizations), the land-grant colleges, and other constituencies. I think the aid community needs to start thinking about a strategy that makes economic sense but that will at the same time appeal to congressional instincts. Aid has increased in two areas where there has been strong congressional support—first, in the Africa Development Fund; second, in the whole child survival area, where there is strong congressional enthusiasm for such aid. With a new president open to a new agenda, with a thoughtful aid community that helps to shape a politically sensible strategy, we ought to be able to do substantially better than we are now doing. I do not believe that the best strategy is to work through the multilaterals. Nor do I think that we ought to try to sell an aid policy based on its contribution to our strategic interests.

PETER D. BELL: I agree with Bill Maynes that blacks and Hispanics within the United States tend to view the world, particularly the Third World, rather differently from the way most middle-class whites in the United States do. I would caution him, however, that his historical arguments are probably oversimplified. The division he speaks of applies not only to the United States but to the entire New World.

In Bill's mind, there is a trade-off within the United States between increased attention to the problems of our own poor and disadvantaged, and support for development assistance abroad. I tend to think the opposite is true. While there may be some lag time between increased attention to issues of poverty within this country and in the developing parts of the world, I believe that the two are highly complementary. We have been going through a period in this country—not for just the past eight years but for more like twenty years—when the interests, the private purposes of people, have dominated. Even the advocacy of public purposes, moral purposes, has often had to be disguised in terms of self-centered interests. The pendulum is bound to swing; it may soon become respectable again to argue in terms of more public purposes.

I believe that there is a large wellspring of sentiment in this country and in much of the rest of the world—not only does it come out of our Judeo-Christian heritage, but it is strong in the Islamic tradition and other traditions as well—that waits to be tapped. The problem will be to find institutional mechanisms to express those values. We have a real problem in this country in terms of what has been happening to our so-called development assistance programs. The extent to which they have been bent to other purposes and corrupted in a moral sense obliges us to take a fresh look and perhaps to invent a wholly new set of bilateral institutions.

CRANFORD PRATT: As a Canadian listening to this discussion, I am struck by the major shift that seems to have occurred in the basic moral premises of much American thinking on development.

I recognize that there have always been, in American North-South policies as in the North-South policies of other states, important geopolitical and self-interested components. But there has also been a real commitment of the sort that Peter Bell just expressed, to the least-developed countries and to meeting the basic needs of the poorest peoples of the world. I felt yesterday that we divided into two, into those who were still concerned with development in these basic humanitarian terms and those who, though they focused on Third World issues, were concerned with the maintenance of the international system from which the rich countries benefit. The former have, however, been a minority. The resolving of such international problems— the international debt problem, international trade issues, environmental problems—is essential if the rich countries are to continue to prosper. The difference between the optimists and the pessimists within the majority group, in my view, is a difference over how hopeful individuals are about the stability of the international system and about the ability of the United States to contribute to the solution of problems in which they have a self-interest. What has happened to the deep concern that once existed to help the poorest countries and to reach the poorest people?

JUDITH TENDLER: I think that all discussions of what the United States should be doing in the future need really to be informed by asking the question, In what do Americans, or the U.S. AID agency in particular, enjoy a comparative advantage? The U.S. bilateral program is extremely constrained, not only by national security considerations but by the fact that it is controlled by a large civil service bureaucracy. If we want to come up with a bright new agenda for U.S. bilateral aid, it must be informed by a sense of what, over ten, twenty, or thirty years, we have shown ourselves particularly adept at doing. One always hears talk about the Scandinavians—how they are good at this—or about the Germans—how they are good at that—but one never hears about what the Americans are good at. It is impossible to make a politically convincing case for a significant, or even modestly expanded, role for aid in the future unless one can say that we have been really good in particular sectors, with particular types of programs, and that this is where we would wish to continue.

Amartya Sen

Food and Freedom

I FEEL DEEPLY HONORED to have this opportunity of paying tribute to the memory of Sir John Crawford and to his many contributions to agricultural research and economic development. Sir John was a powerful practitioner, but he was also involved in bridging theory and practice, and keen on investigating connections that may not be straightforward.

The links between food and freedom may at first sight appear to be rather remote to policymaking and far from central to practical concerns. I shall argue against that view, trying to discuss the various important connections that have to be recognized more fully as background to practical food policy. I shall not, of course, deny the fact that these connections are not typically taken to be straightforward preludes to practical policymaking, but I will argue that we have to probe deeper for an adequate background to policymaking.

FOOD FOR FREEDOM AND FREEDOM FOR FOOD

"Grub first, then ethics," thus runs a much quoted aphorism of Bertolt Brecht. There is undoubtedly some sense in this phased gradation. Ethics may seem like a much more remote and much less immediate subject than the command over food that we need to survive. Freedom too—as an important concept in ethics—may seem to be far less immediate than the compelling demands of grabbing grub.

Reprinted with permission of the World Bank. Originally a speech presented as part of the Sir John Crawford Memorial Lecture Series of the Consultative Group on International Agricultural Research of the World Bank, October 29, 1987.

But this contrast is quite artificial. The provision of food is indeed a central issue in general social ethics, since so much in human life does depend on the ability to find enough to eat. In particular, the freedom that people enjoy to lead a decent life, including freedom from hunger, from avoidable morbidity, from premature mortality, etc., is quite centrally connected with the provision of food and related necessities. Also, the compulsion to acquire enough food may force vulnerable people to do things which they resent doing, and may make them accept lives with little freedom. The role of food in fostering freedom can be an extremely important one.

On the other side, freedom may also causally influence the success of the pursuit of food for all. One consideration that has received a great deal of attention recently relates to the role of freedom to make profits in providing incentives for the expansion of food production, thus helping to solve the food problem. This consideration has often cropped up in the critical evaluation of agricultural policies pursued in many countries in Africa and Asia. For example, the rapid expansion of agricultural output in China in the economic reforms carried out from 1979 onwards has, with much justice, been seen to be closely related to the freeing of markets and the unleashing of productive opportunities connected with profit incentives. These experiences invite attention and scrutiny.

Other types of freedom may also have important instrumental roles to play in the guaranteeing of food for all. Insofar as public policy to combat hunger and starvation—including rapid intervention against threatening famines—may depend on the existence and efficiency of political pressure groups to induce governments to act, political freedom too may have a close connection with the distribution of relief and food to vulnerable groups. There are other possible causal connections—operating in both directions—which may be worth investigating, and some of these I will indeed try to examine and assess in this lecture. Freedom to make profits is not the only freedom the causal influence of which would have to be considered.

Thus, what may superficially appear to be rather remote connections between food and freedom can be seen to be, in fact, central in importance and extremely rich in the variety of influences involved, operating in the two respective directions, viz., from food to freedom, and from freedom to food. I shall try to supplement the conceptual and theoretical discussions with illustrations from practical problems with empirical content. Freedom and ethics are indeed very practical matters in the determination of food policy.

FOUR CONCEPTS OF FREEDOM

In a justly famous essay called "Two Concepts of Liberty", Isaiah Berlin[1] made an important distinction between "negative" and "positive" theories of freedom. The negative view sees freedom exclusively in terms of the independence of the individual from interference by others, including governments, institutions and other persons. The positive view, which can be characterized in many different ways, sees freedom not in terms of the presence or absence of interference by others, but in terms of what a person is actually able to do or to be. The distinction may be quite central to different approaches to the idea of freedom and its implications.[2] If a person is not free from hunger and lacks the means and the practical opportunities to feed himself or herself adequately, then that person's positive freedom must be seen as having been thoroughly compromised. On the other hand, his or her negative freedom may be completely unviolated, if this failure to acquire enough food is not a result of his or her having been stopped by interference from others.

There is another distinction which is quite central to the content and role of freedom, and this concerns the issue of *intrinsic* importance of freedom as such, in addition to its *instrumental* roles. That freedom must have instrumental importance as a means to other ends is obvious enough. Our freedom to choose one bundle of commodities rather than another may have an important effect on the living standards we can have, the happiness we can enjoy, the well-being we can achieve, and the various objectives of our lives we can fulfill. Similarly, the absence of interference by others may have important causal influence on various things that we can do and value doing. In the "instrumental" view, freedom is taken to be important precisely because of its being a means to other ends, rather than being valuable in itself.

In contrast, the "intrinsic" view of the importance of freedom asserts that freedom is valuable in itself, and not only because of what it permits us to achieve or do. The good life may be seen to be a life of freedom, and in that context freedom is not just a way of achieving a good life, it is *constitutive* of the good life itself. The "intrinsic"

view does not deny that freedom may *also* be instrumentally important, but does reject the view that its importance lies *entirely* on its
instrumental function.

It is easy to see that the two ways of categorizing different
approaches to freedom can be combined with each other, yielding
four distinct categories. It is indeed possible to look through the
history of ideas to see how different thinkers sharing a regard for
freedom fall into different categories, related to the *positive-negative*
distinction and to the *intrinsic-instrumental* classification. At the risk
of over simplification I might illustrate the distinctions involved by
referring to some particular examples.

For example, Milton Friedman and James Buchanan have both
tended to put considerable emphasis—indeed priority—on the negative view of freedom, related to non-interference by the state,
institutions and other individuals.[3] This contrasts with the emphasis
on the positive view of freedom that can be found in the writings of,
say, Bentham or Marx. On the other hand, within the negative
perspective, Friedman is much more concerned with the instrumental
role of freedom rather than its intrinsic importance, while Buchanan
constructs a "non-instrumental" normative case in favor of giving
priority to liberties and democratic rights. Whereas Friedman con-
centrates primarily on what he calls "the fecundity of freedom",
Buchanan goes largely beyond this role of freedom as a means to
other ends. Attaching intrinsic importance to negative freedom is seen
also in the writings of John Rawls, Robert Nozick and other
contemporary moral philosophers, and it is a position that was
broadly shared also by John Stuart Mill.[4]

Similarly, among the various theories concentrating on positive
freedom, some have seen freedom to be intrinsically important, such
as Adam Smith and Karl Marx, following a line of reasoning that
goes back to Aristotle in *Nicomachean Ethics* and *Politics*. In fact,
Aristotle had direct influence on Marx's writings on this subject.
Marx's philosophical focus included giving a foundational role to
bringing "the conditions for the free development and activity of
individuals under their own control", with a vision of a liberated
society in the future that would make "it possible for me to do one
thing today and another tomorrow, to hunt in the morning, fish in
the afternoon, rear cattle in the evening, criticize after dinner, just as
I have in mind, without ever becoming hunter, fisherman, shepherd

or critic."⁵ While his urban middle-class origins may have influenced Marx's evident belief that evening is a good time to rear cattle (he was obviously on more familiar ground with "criticize after dinner"), the placing of this general perspective of freedom in Marx's entire approach to economics, politics and society was altogether foundational.

While John Rawls' case for the "priority of liberty" attaches overriding importance to *negative* freedom, his advocacy of the importance of "primary goods" commanded by people reflects his basic concern for *positive* freedom as well. Primary goods include "rights, liberties and opportunities, income and wealth, and the social bases of self-respect". Possessing these things adequately makes a person positively more free to pursue his or her objectives and ends, and Rawls develops his political concept of social justice based on the efficiency and equity in the distributions of these freedoms.

In contrast, Jeremy Bentham's ultimate concern is with utility only, and positive freedom is regarded as important in the Benthamite system only because that freedom may be conducive to more happiness. This is, of course, an instrumental view. The Benthamite *instrumental-positive* view of freedom contrasts with Marx's *intrinsic-positive* view. And each in turn contrasts with the *instrumental-negative* view of Friedman, on the one hand, and the *intrinsic-negative* view of Buchanan and Nozick on the other. It is easy to find other examples to illustrate the contrasts, but perhaps the ones already mentioned will do. I ought to warn that these categories are often not very pure, and the same writers may have a certain amount of plurality within their overall theories (this was, of course, clearly seen in the case of Rawls in the preceding discussion).

FOOD POLICY AND ALTERNATIVE APPROACHES TO FREEDOM

This categorization is of crucial relevance even in understanding various demands on food policy, arising from different views of freedom. For example, the advocacy of greater freedom to earn profit in agriculture and of greater use of free market without much interference by the state and other public institutions (an advocacy than can, incidentally, be found in many documents of the host for this lecture, the World Bank) usually reflects an *instrumental-negative* view of freedom, applied to food policy. Freedom to earn profits without interference is advocated not because it is typically taken to be foundationally important on its own, but because it is seen to be conducive to such things as greater productivity, larger income and enhanced food output. In general, the perspective of *incentives* constitutes an instrumental focus, related to what Milton Friedman calls "the fecundity of freedom", and in this particular case this is applied primarily to the negative view of freedom, seen in terms of non-interference.

In contrast, the writings of some authors, such as Peter Bauer, have tended to go beyond the instrumental view even in the context of agricultural development, emphasizing the importance of people having the right to enjoy the fruits of their own creation, without interference by the state or by other institutions or individuals.[6] Bauer has seen this as a central feature of a good agricultural policy. The instrumental consideration of incentives is not denied in this perspective (far from it), but the ethical argument goes well beyond that, to intrinsic importance as well.

On the other hand, economic approaches emphasizing the need to fulfill "basic needs" for food and other essentials, or to pursue public policy to guarantee "freedom from hunger", and so on, take a positive view of freedom, concentrating on what people are able actually to do or be, rather than what they are prevented by others from doing or being.[7] The focus of this literature has often tended to be on pragmatic rather than foundational issues. Concentration on "freedom from hunger" and related objectives can indeed be defended either on grounds of their supposed intrinsic importance, or because of their instrumental role in serving other—allegedly more basic—goals, such as enhancement of happiness or welfare of individuals. The instrumental view can be seen clearly in the analysis presented by one of the earliest writers on "basic needs" (though he did not use that expression), viz. A.C. Pigou, in *The Economics of Welfare*.[8] For an example on the other side, Paul Streeten's approach is perhaps best seen in terms of intrinsic value being attached to these respective freedoms to fulfill the various "basic needs".[9]

The instrumental-intrinsic distinction relates to the foundational question as to what is regarded as valuable in itself, and what must be seen as important only as a contributor to other more basic goals. This is a question of deep philosophical interest, but it has pragmatic importance too, since instrumental arguments turn ultimately on the correctness of the cause-effect relationships postulated. For example, if it emerges that free markets and profit earnings do not provide much incentive for the expansion of production, or do not contribute to bettering living standards, the instrumental defense of these free market policies may well collapse, but this need not disestablish at all the view (e.g., Bauer's) that would see the right to earn these profits to be intrinsically important. In this sense, the intrinsic view is less vulnerable to empirical counter-argument, but it has, of course, greater need of foundational ethical defense.

The position is a little different as far as positive freedom is concerned. A policy of state intervention, e.g., in the distribution of food, is scarcely ever regarded as being of fundamental value of its own. The possibility of foundational valuation arises at a somewhat later stage (in this respect its contrast with the valuing of right-based *procedures,* as in the systems of Robert Nozick or Peter Bauer, is quite sharp), and valuing positive freedom has to be based on a good deal of instrumental analysis in moving from the means of state intervention to the realization of positive freedom.

The difference between the "intrinsic" and "instrumental" views of positive freedom lies, in this context, in the length to which the instrumental analysis has to be carried. In the broadly Aristotelian view, which sees the capability to achieve important functionings as being valuable in itself, the instrumental analysis can end at that point, but in those views in which positive freedom happens to be no more than means to other ends, e.g., in the pursuit of utility, the instrumental analyses have to go further into the translation of freedom into the fulfillment of other goals. In each case there is no need to examine the effects of policies such as public distribution of food on the positive freedoms that individuals can actually obtain, and the difference arises only at a later stage, in moving from freedom to achievement. In this respect the positive freedom view is basically more instrument-dependent than the negative freedom approach is.

These considerations may, at first glance, appear to be rather distant from the nitty-gritty of practical policymaking in the field of food and hunger. But foundational questions are ultimately quite central to the acceptability of particular policy analyses. While the tendency to avoid facing these foundational questions is quite common, it is more a reflection of escapism than a demonstration of uncanny wisdom. Ultimately policies have to be justified in terms of what is valuable and how various policies may respectively enhance these valuable things. There is no escape, therefore, from considering both the question of what is fundamentally valuable and the question of what instruments enhance these things best. It is indeed the combination of the intrinsic considerations and instrumental analyses that can lead the way to an adequate examination of what should be done and why.

While these conceptual and theoretical discussions can be carried further—I have tried to discuss some of these further issues elsewhere[10]—I shall devote the rest of this lecture to rather practical matters, dealing with actual policy disputes in the field of food and hunger.

OPULENCE AND LIVING STANDARD

A preliminary point first. The process of economic development is often seen in terms of the expansion of the material basis of well-being and freedom that people can enjoy. This approach has a rationale that is easy to understand, since the positive freedoms that we can enjoy and the well-being levels that we can achieve are both dependent on the commodity bundles over which we can establish command. This clearly is the sense behind assessing economic development in terms of the progress of real gross national product per head. On the other hand, freedom and well-being depend also on the *use* that is made of the opulence of the nation. Income distributions can vary. No less importantly, the command that people enjoy over essential food, health services, medical attention, etc., depends crucially on the delivery system for these commodities. A public distribution system geared to the needs of the vulnerable sections of the community can bring the essentials of livelihood within easy reach of people whose lives may remain otherwise relatively untouched by the progress of real national income.

Table 1 illustrates the point. Oman or South Africa may have a gross national product per head that is a great many times higher than that of China or Sri Lanka, but each of the former has under-five mortality rates (covering infants and children) that is two or three times higher than those prevailing in the poorer economies. The life expectancy at birth in Oman and South Africa lingers around the

TABLE I. Opulence, Life and Death

	GNP Per Head (Dollars) 1985	Life Expectancy at Birth 1985	Under-5 Mortality Rate (Per Thousand) 1985
Oman	6,730	54	172
South Africa	2,010	55	104
Brazil	1,640	65	91
Sri Lanka	380	70	50
China	310	69	48

Sources: *World Development Report*, 1987; *The State of the World's Children*, 1987.

mid-fifties, while China and Sri Lanka have achieved longevity rates reasonably close to those prevailing in Europe and America.

This is, of course, a well-known point, but it is worth emphasizing in the present context, since the demands of agricultural policy in general and food policy in particular are often seen primarily in terms of expanding the material bases of well-being and freedom. Indeed, as we shall presently see, there is an important policy issue related to this question even in terms of the recent economic reforms in China. The point to note here is that the positive freedom to lead a long life may well be typically enhanced by expansion of material prosperity, but the relationship is far from a tight one, and indeed it is quite possible for the freedom to live long to go down, while the level of economic opulence goes up. The shift of focus from the national product to the freedom enjoyed by members of the nation can bring about a major reexamination of the requirements of economic policy.

The freedom to live long is, of course, only one of the positive freedoms that may be thought to be important. It is a freedom that is particularly valued since our ability to do other things is, obviously, conditional on our being here, and it is not surprising that the option of living longer is very rarely refused. This is, of course, the reason why longevity, which is an *achievement,* can also be seen as an important indicator of the *freedom* to live long (we tend to exercise this freedom, in most cases, to the maximum extent we can), and the metric of life expectancy is, thus, a fairly basic indicator of a foundational positive freedom. There are, however, other important positive freedoms as well, e.g., freedom from hunger and undernutrition, freedom from escapable morbidity, freedom to read and write and communicate. Indeed, the list of important freedoms must be seen to be a long one in any accounting that aims at some degree of comprehensiveness. While any practical analysis may have to confine attention to only a few indicators, the need to have a wider informational base for a more definitive analysis has to be borne in mind.

Often these indicators move in the same direction (e.g., life expectancy, avoidance of morbidity, and literacy frequently tend to be highly correlated), but this is not invariably the case. For example, in the contrast between different states in India, Kerala comes out as having very much higher life expectancy and literacy than any other Indian state, but in terms of morbidity rates, Kerala does not seem to have this advantage. Indeed, measured in the metric of reported illnesses, Kerala's morbidity rate is much higher than that of many other Indian states.[11] Some of that difference may undoubtedly be due to the fact that a more literate population, with access to medical attention and health care, is likely to report illnesses more thoroughly. But it is possible that even after these corrections are made, there is some dissonance between Kerala's performance in the fields of literacy and life expectancy and that in the prevention of morbidity.[12] The conflicts between different indicators may not, of course, always be serious, but the general possibility has to be kept in view in interpreting results of empirical analysis based on one or a few indicators. In this sense, analyses of the kind pursued in this paper must be seen to be tentative, even though it can be argued that even a preliminary move in the direction of indicators of certain basic capabilities and freedoms can bring out aspects of economic policy in general and food policy in particular that tend to be overlooked in the more traditional concentration on national income in general and food production in particular.

CHINA AND INDIA

The comparison of the performances of China and India in dealing with problems of well-being and elementary freedoms has been one of the subjects of great interest in the field of comparative economics. In terms of achievements of GNP per head, China's performance would seem to have been better than India's, even though in terms of standard estimated figures, the Chinese GNP per head of $310 is only about 15 percent higher than India's $270, for 1985. Since Simon

TABLE 2. China and India

	China	India
GNP per head ($) 1985	310	270
Calorie consumption per head 1985	2,602	2,189
Life expectancy at birth (years) 1985	69	56
Under five mortality rate (per thousand) 1985	50	158
Famine mortality (millions): Chinese famines 1958–61	29.5	
Excess Indian "normal" annual mortality (millions) 1985		3.8

Sources: World Bank, *World Development Report 1987* (New York: O.U.P., 1987); UNICEF, *The State of the World's Children, 1987* (New York: O.U.P., 1987); B. Ashton, *et al.,* "Famine in China 1958–61", *Population and Development Review,* 10 (1984).

Kuznets'[13] estimate of GNP per head for China and India were about comparable, with a "product per capita" 20 percent higher in China, in 1958, it is tempting to think that China's and India's performances in terms of production have been roughly comparable. In fact these figures underestimate the relative performance of China vis-a-vis that of India, and if more comparable figures are used, China would seem to be further ahead than India in terms of national product and national income per head.[14] Nevertheless, it would appear that judged in this perspective, while the Chinese have done noticeably better than what has happened in India, the Chinese performance in this field is not tremendously superior to that of India. Furthermore, some of the advantages that China now enjoys compared with India as far as national product is concerned relate to the high growth rate of the Chinese economy in very recent years, since the economic reforms of 1979. More on this later.

In terms of calorie consumption per head, the Chinese picture is considerably better than India's, as Table 2 reports. Here again, a big part of the difference has arisen only in recent years through the rapid expansion of agricultural output in general and food output in particular since the economic reforms.

If we look, instead, at the indicators of basic freedom to avoid premature mortality, i.e., life expectancy at birth, China's performance would seem to be of a different order of magnitude altogether from that of India. Chart 1 presents the respective time series of life expectancy in the two countries. Beginning with life expectancy

Chart 1

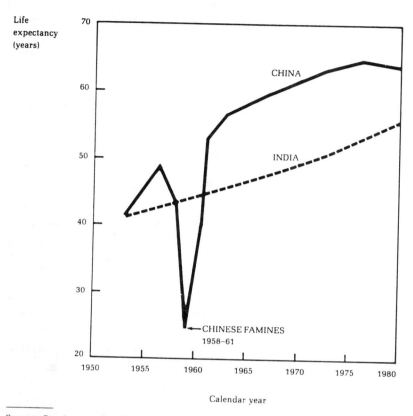

Source: See Amartya Sen. *Hunger and Entitlements* (Helsinki: WIDER. 1987).

figures quite close to each other—not much above 40 years—in the early 1950s, the Chinese have been able to raise the life expectancy figure to close to European standards, while India lags behind by a big margin. The difference in the achievement of a life expectancy close to 70 years and that in the mid-fifties is very large indeed, as we know from the history of life-expectancy changes in different parts of the world.

FAMINES AND PREVENTION

One of the interesting features in the comparison of life expectancy of China and India is the remarkably sharp drop that the Chinese figure has around 1958–61. These are the years of the Chinese famines following the failure of the Great Leap Forward. At one stage life expectancy had fallen to the mid-twenties. While the Indian progress of life expectancy has been slow, it has not undergone fluctuations of this kind at all. Indeed, it must be recognized that in the field of famine prevention, India's record is distinctly superior to that of China.

I have tried to argue elsewhere[15] that India's success in eliminating famines since Independence is not primarily the result of raising food output per head, as it is often thought to be. Indeed the increase in availability of food per head in India has been fairly moderate (as it had also been in China up to the economic reforms[16]) and the ratio of food to population has remained lower in the post-Independence period than it was in the late 19th century, when India had several famines. The main difference has been brought about by an administrative system which compensates the loss of entitlements as a result of such calamities as droughts and floods by providing employment —often at cash wages—giving the affected population renewed ability to command food in the market. The process is further helped by using substantial stocks held in the public distribution system which can be brought in, to supplement what the creation of income does in regenerating lost entitlements.

This administrative system does, in fact, have its roots in the Famine Codes formulated in British India in the 1880s. However, these Codes were often invoked too late, and intervention was often not a high priority item for the then government. In some cases, most notably in the notorious Bengal famine of 1943, no famine was ever officially "declared", in order to avoid the necessity of taking actions required by the Famine Code (as Governor Rutherford of Bengal explicitly put it in an intra-government communication).[17] The situation is now altogether different given the nature of politics in post-Independent India. No government at the center—or at the state level—can get away without extreme political damage if it fails to take early action against famines. The presence of active opposition parties and a relatively free news distribution system provide the political triggering mechanism that the Famine Codes in their original form lacked.[18] The availability of food in different parts of India has often fallen greatly *below* those prevailing in Ethiopia, Sudan, or the Sahel countries (see, for example, Table 3) at the time when they had their worst famines.[19] Indeed, even the normal availability of food

TABLE 3. Famine, Averted Famine and Cereal Production:*
Sahel and India

	Gross Production Per Head			Net Availability Per Head		
	Sahel	India	Maharashtra	Sahel	India	Maharashtra
1971	102	96	51	101	84	55
1972	75	92	46	76	84	57
1973	78	83	27	85	76	46
1974	115	88	62	120	82	73

*100 = 182 kg. per head per year.

Source: Jean Dreze, "Famine Prevention in India", WIDER Conference Paper, to be published in J. Dreze and A. Sen, eds., *Hunger, Economics and Policy,* to be published by Oxford University Press.

per head for India as a whole is not decisively higher than that of Sub-Saharan Africa, as Table 4 shows (India coming halfway down the list of Sub-Saharan economies, with less food availability per head than many countries with persistent famines).

The Chinese experience in this respect has been quite different. There was, of course, a very remarkable drop in food output per head after the Great Leap Forward (though not more than in some parts of India in different years, e.g., in Maharashtra in 1973), but there was no major revision of economic policy, no alert anti-famine relief operations, and not even an official recognition of the existence of famine for a number of years. The famine in China raged on for three years, and it is now estimated that the additional mortality because of the famine amounted to about 29.5 million.[20] It is quite remarkable that a famine of this magnitude could continue unrecorded without bringing about a major policy shift, and this failure is certainly one connected closely with the absence of a relatively free press and the absence of opposition parties free to criticize and chastise the government in power. It may, thus, be argued that the massive deaths connected with starvation and famine during 1958–61 relate closely to the issue of freedom and information and criticism.

CHINESE ECONOMIC REFORMS

While the progress of food production in China was relatively moderate until the economic reforms, things have moved very fast indeed after 1979. Table 5 presents the gross value of agricultural output (including food output) between 1979 and 1986, as reported

TABLE 4. Comparative Food Availability Per Head 1983:
India and Sub-Saharan Africa

Country	Daily Calorie Supply Per Head
Less than India	
Ghana	1,516
Mali	1,597
Chad	1,620
Mozambique	1,668
Benin	1,907
Kenya	1,919
Zambia	1,929
Guinea	1,939
Zimbabwe	1,956
Burkina Faso	2,014
Nigeria	2,022
Cameroon	2,031
Angola	2,041
Central African Republic	2,048
Somalia	2,063
Sierra Leone	2,082
India	2,115
More than India	
Sudan	2,122
Zaire	2,136
Botswana	2,152
Togo	2,156
Ethiopia	2,162
Malawi	2,200
Mauritania	2,252
Niger	2,271
Tanzania	2,271
Rwanda	2,276
Uganda	2,351
Liberia	2,367
Lesotho	2,376
Burundi	2,378
Congo	2,425
Senegal	2,436
Ivory Coast	2,576

Source: *World Development Report 1986*, Table 28.

TABLE 5. China Since 1979 Reforms (Indices)

	Index Gross Value of Output		Index Death Rate	
	Industry	Agriculture	National	Rural
1979	100	100	100	100
1980	109	104	102	101
1981	113	111	102	102
1982	122	123	106	110
1983	135	135	114	120
1984	154	159	108	105
1985	181	181	106	104
1986	197	210	108	105

Sources: People's Republic of China, *Statistical Yearbook of China 1986* (in English); 1987 (in Chinese).

in the *Statistical Yearbooks of China*. It would seem that the agricultural output has doubled in the seven years since 1979, and the rate of growth of agriculture, which is typically much lower than the industrial growth rate, has in fact been exactly comparable. That the economic reforms permitting greater freedom to earn profits based on economic calculations have been a success from this point of view can scarcely be denied. It is possible to question some of the figures, and it has sometimes been argued that there were incentives for understating the agricultural output in the pre-reform period, but even when these corrections are made, the performance of Chinese agriculture since the economic reforms must be accepted to be altogether exceptional.

On the other hand, judged in terms of the freedom to avoid escapable mortality, the picture is much muddier. Even in Chart 1, one notices a slight tendency for the life expectancy to decline in the period following the economic reforms. This is brought out also in Table 5 in terms of the index of death rates, which goes up—rather than down—in the post-reform period. While the peak increase in death rate is now well past, the last reported death rates in China are still *higher* than that in the pre-reform period. Questions can be raised about the acceptability of these official mortality statistics, and it must also be recognized that the Chinese death rates were very low indeed by the time the economic reforms began. But it is still remarkable that rather than the increase in material prosperity pushing down the death rate, what has happened is some *increase* in mortality rates along with the policy package that has characterized the economic reforms.

TABLE 6. Barefoot Doctors in China

	Total		Female	
	Numbers (Millions)	Index (1975 = 100)	Numbers (Millions)	Index (1975 = 100)
1970	1.218	78	n.a.	n.a.
1975	1.559	100	0.502	100
1980	1.463	94	0.489	97
1981	1.396	90	0.443	88
1982	1.349	87	0.410	82
1983	1.279	82	0.371	76
1984	1.251	80	0.356	73

Sources: World Bank, *China: The Health Sector* (1984), for (1970–81): *Statistical Yearbooks of China* 1985 (for 1983 and 1984); *Zhongguo tongji nianjian 1985* (for 1981–83). *The Statistical Yearbooks of China* from 1986 onwards do not give the numbers of barefoot doctors any more.

This policy package has included some radical changes in the distribution of health care in the rural areas, e.g., a withdrawal from the strategy of using "barefoot doctors" (Table 6), and a general shortage of public funds for communal health care under the new privatized "responsibility system". Whether the increase in death rate is firmly connected causally with these policy changes remains to be further investigated, but there is a serious question mark here concerning the post-reform economic policies which must be addressed.

It is remarkable that the enormous expansion of life expectancy in China, from a figure close to 40 years to one close to 70 years, took place in the pre-reform period with only a moderate increase in food availability per head but with a radical expansion in the delivery of health care and food to different sections of the population. Since the reforms, food availability per head has gone up radically, but the delivery system has undergone some changes, including contraction in some respects, and there seems to have been some decline from the previously achieved peak of high life expectancy and low death rate. While the Chinese economic reforms must be praised for what they have achieved—the increase in production has been altogether remarkable—there is need to reassess the policy lessons of the Chinese reforms, especially when attention is shifted from production, GNP and output per head, to the basic indicators of the freedom to live long and the related positive freedoms. While the Chinese experience of famines in 1958–61 raises one type of issue relating food to freedom (in that case concerning freedom of information and opposition), the post-reform experiences of China raise another type of question concerning that relation (involving in this case freedom to avoid premature mortality as an indicator of success, as opposed to the size of production and output).

ASSESSMENT OF SRI LANKA'S ACHIEVEMENTS

Another country in which the enhancement of life expectancy has received much attention is Sri Lanka. As Table 1 indicated, Sri Lanka has a remarkably high life expectancy in comparison with its relatively low GNP per head. This achievement has been seen as being closely related to the policy of public intervention in Sri Lanka.[21]

The role of public intervention in Sri Lanka in enhancing the positive freedom to live long has been questioned in a number of contributions in recent years, leading to some lively controversies. For example, based on comparing Sri Lanka's performance since 1960 with other countries, it has been argued that Sri Lanka has not been an exceptional performer.[22] Unfortunately, the period chosen for this comparative assessment, beginning with 1960, has made these comparative studies quite misleading. Extensive public intervention in Sri Lanka began in the early 1940s, and this was indeed accompanied by a sharp reduction in death rate, which went down from 20.6 per thousand in 1940 to 8.6 per thousand in 1960. By 1960, when the now-famous international comparative studies begin, the death rate in Sri Lanka was within hitting distance of more advanced countries in Europe and America. It is not surprising that the progress since then has been relatively slower, especially compared with other countries which had more scope for reduction in mortality rates. Also, as it happens, the period beyond 1960 has been one of some fluctuation of public intervention, and some of the major planks of public intervention used in Sri Lanka to enhance the quality of life have undergone, in fact, some decline in the 1970s. The policy of free or subsidized distribution of rice which was introduced in 1942, has suffered from reductions in the later decades, and even the expansion of health services which was very fast during the 1940s and 1950s, has slowed in the later periods, with a *reduction* in the number of doctors and other medical practitioners in the decade of

TABLE 7. Sri Lanka

	Public Distribution of Food	Number of Medical Personnel	Death Rate Per Thousand
1940	No (Introduced 1942)	271	20.6
1950	Yes	357	12.6
1960	Yes	557	8.6
1970	Yes (Reduced 1972, 1979)	693	7.5
1980	Yes	664	6.1

the 1970s. Table 7 presents some of the relevant figures. The fact that the enhancement of life expectancy and related indicators has not been very fast since 1960 says very little about the alleged lack of effectiveness of public delivery systems in the expansion of life expectancy in Sri Lanka. By the time the comparative studies begin much of the dramatic reduction in death rate in Sri Lanka had already taken place, and the comparisons also suffer from concentrating in a period in which there was nothing like the steady rise in public delivery arrangements for food and health care that had taken place in the earlier period, when mortality rates had indeed crumbled at a dramatic rate.

PERIODIZATION AND BRITISH MORTALITY DECLINE

The issue of periodization, which proves to be central in appraising Sri Lanka's achievements, is in general an important question in assessing the effectiveness of different policies in the enhancement of life expectancy and in the decline of mortality. Even in Europe sharp reductions in premature mortality have been closely connected with expansion of public delivery of basic essentials of living, including health care and medical attention, and it is possible to move towards the identification of the relevant causal connections by distinguishing between different periods in which mortality reductions have been fast or slow.

Table 8 presents the extension of life expectancy at birth in England and Wales during the first six decades of this century. It can be seen that in every decade the life expectancy at birth went up

TABLE 8. Extension of Life Expectancy at Birth: England and Wales, 1901–1960 (additional years)

Between	Men	Women
1901–1911	4.1	4.0
1911–1921	6.6	6.5
1921–1931	2.3	2.4
1931–1940	1.2	1.5
1940–1951	6.5	7.0
1951–1960	2.4	3.2

Source: S. Preston, N. Keyfitz, and R. Schoen, *Causes of Death: Life Tables for National Populations* (New York, 1972). See also J.M. Winter, *The Great War and the British People* (London: Macmillan, 1986).

moderately—by between one and four years—with two exceptions. In the decades between 1911 and 1921 and between 1940 and 1951 life expectancy increased by nearly seven years. These were, of course, the war years, and the improvement is to a great extent, recording the impact of public distribution systems that came in with protecting the general public from the possible effects of war. Public provision of food rationing and distribution, expansion of health services (including the introduction of the National Health Service in the 1940s), and other expansions of the involvement of the state in distributing food, health care, medical attention, etc., made a radical difference to the entitlements to these vital commodities enjoyed by the population at large, including its most vulnerable sections. The enhancement of life expectancy reflects these results of public policy, and it would be a mistake to think of the increase of life expectancy in Britain as the result entirely of enhanced overall economic opulence (or a general increase in GNP per head). Once the issue of periodization is appropriately faced, it is hard to escape the fact that even in the history of a country such as Britain, it is the delivery system of food and health care—over and above increases in economic opulence—that has played a strategic part in crucial periods of expansion in the elementary freedom to live long and live well.

INTRINSIC AND INSTRUMENTAL ROLES

In assessing the relevance of freedom in the making of food policy, both the intrinsic and the instrumental perspectives have to be kept very firmly in view. The instrumental perspective is often invoked in the context of emphasizing economic incentives in the expansion of national output in general and food production in particular, and there is undoubtedly much to be said for taking adequate note of this question, as the experiences of the Chinese economy in particular have sharply brought out in recent years. At the same time, the instrumental perspective has to be extended from the freedom to earn profits to freedoms of broader kinds, including political freedom in the form of freedom of opposition, freedom of information, and journalistic autonomy. We have seen that these freedoms can be quite crucial in the delivery and use of food.

The instrumental perspective is, however, inherently limited, since freedom can be seen as having intrinsic importance as well. In assessing economic development and social progress, it is natural to think of the enhancement of basic positive freedoms to avoid premature mortality, to escape morbidity, to eliminate undernutrition, and so on. While freedom is a complex notion, various aspects of it can be usefully studied in terms of statistical information of a kind that is frequently available and which can be made more easily accessible if the perspective of freedom is taken seriously by public policymakers.

The importance of this perspective arises partly from the fact that the metrics of gross national product, real income, etc., may often be quite misleading about the extents of freedom that people do enjoy and can build their lives on. Even in such elementary matters as avoiding premature mortality, the statistics of national products (including those of food output) can hide more than they reveal. It is possible for the national product per head and the food availability per person to go up sharply without reducing mortality rates, sometimes accompanied by increased mortality, as seems to have happened in China since the economic reforms of 1979. Once the process of economic development is reassessed in terms of the important indicators of elementary freedoms, a different light altogether may well be cast on economic policy changes that call for adequately broad evaluation. The Chinese economic reforms have been undoubtedly extremely successful in terms of raising production and enhancing income, but since the post-reform period has also seen an increase—rather than a reduction—in death rates, there is room for asking searching questions about the nature of the policy package that has gone with the economic reforms, and about variations to this package that can be considered from the economic point of view. The remarkable success of the Chinese economy in raising life expectancy at birth, from a figure close to 40 years just after the Revolution to a figure close enough to 70 years just prior to the economic reforms, was built on paying particular attention to public delivery systems involving food, health care, and related necessities. It is this aspect of the Chinese success that is in some danger of going out of focus— with possibly serious consequences—if the understandable concern with raising output and income distracts attention from the problem of delivery and public distribution.

Freedom is not a remote consideration in policymaking. This applies just as much to the making and assessing of food policy as it does to many other fields of policymaking in social and economic matters. Indeed, the inclusion of freedom as a consideration—both at the intrinsic and at the instrumental level—has the effect of appropriately broadening the concepts that must be invoked in the formulation and execution of food policies. The need for that broadening has been one of the main contentions I have tried to put across in this lecture.

The perspective of freedom, with its diverse elements, is much too important to be neglected in the making of food policy. Food and freedom are both central concerns in human life, and they have links that are both crucial and diverse. These links demand our attention. The elementary freedom to live long and live well for a great many million people is at stake.

ENDNOTES

[1] Isiah Berlin, *Four Essays on Liberty* (London and New York, Oxford University Press, 1969)

[2] See my "Well-being, Agency and Freedom: The Dewey Lectures 1984," *Journal of Philosophy*, 82 (April 1985).

[3] James Buchanan, *Liberty, Market and the State* (Brighton: Wheatsheaf Books, 1986), and Milton Friedman and Rose Friedman, *Free to Choose* (London: Secker and Warburg, 1980). I have discussed this contrast, among others, in my "Freedom of Choice: Concept and Content", Alfred Marshall Lecture to the European Economic Association, Copenhagen, August, 1987, *European Economic Review, 1988*.

[4] John Stuart Mill, *On Liberty* (London: 1859; republished, Harmondsworth: Penguin, 1974); John Rawls, *A Theory of Justice* (Oxford: Clarendon Press, and

Cambridge, MA: Harvard University Press, 1971); Robert Nozick, *Anarchy, State and Utopia* (Oxford: Blackwell, and New York: Basic Books, 1974).

[5]K. Marx and F. Engels, *The German Ideology* (1845–46; republished, New York: International Publishers, 1947), p. 22.

[6]Peter Bauer, *Equality, the Third World, and Economic Delusion* (Cambridge, MA: Harvard University Press, 1981).

[7]P. Streeten, et al., *First Things First: Meeting Basic Needs in Developing Countries* (New York: Oxford University Press, 1981); Morris D. Morris, *Measuring Conditions of the World's Poor* (Oxford: Pergamon, 1979); F. Stewart, *Planning to Meet Basic Needs* (London: Macmillan, 1985).

[8]A.C. Pigou, *The Economics of Welfare* (London, Macmillan, 1920; sixth enlarged edition, 1952).

[9]Paul Streeten, *Development Perspectives* (London: Macmillan, 1981).

[10]Sen, "Well-being, Agency and Freedom: The Dewey Lectures 1984", *Journal of Philosophy,* 82 (April 1985); *Commodities and Capabilities* (Amsterdam: North Holland, 1985); *On Ethics and Economics* (Oxford: Blackwell, 1987).

[11]P.G.K. Panikar and C.R. Soman, *Health Status of Kerala* (Trivandrum: Center for Development Studies, 1986); B.G. Kumar, "Poverty and Public Policy: Government Intervention and Levels of Living in Kerala, India," D.Phil. dissertation, Oxford University, 1987.

[12]The relatively low nutritional intakes in Kerala may have some effect on the prevalence of some illnesses, even when mortality is prevented by an extensive system of medical care.

[13]Simon Kuznets, *Modern Economic Growth* (New Haven: Yale University Press, 1966), pp. 360–1.

[14]Dwight H. Perkins, "Reforming China's Economic System," Harvard Institute of International Development, forthcoming in *Journal of Economic Literature;* Subramanian Swamy, "Chinese Price Structure and Comparative Growth Rates of China and India", Harvard Institute of International Development, 1986, to be published.

[15]Amartya Sen, "Development: Which Way Now?" *Economic Journal,* 93 (December 1983), reprinted in *Resources, Values and Development* (Oxford: Blackwell, and Cambridge, MA: Harvard University Press, 1984). See also N. Ram, "An Independent Press and Anti-Hunger Strategies—The Indian Experience", WIDER, 1986, to be published in J. Dreze and A. Sen, eds., *Hunger: Economics and Policy,* Clarendon Press, Oxford, and O.U.P., New York, forthcoming. Note that political and journalistic pressure is less effective in preventing high levels of "normal" mortality than in countering deaths from open starvation which are more visible and easier material for news reporting and for political pressure. See footnote 20.

[16]See Carl Riskin, "Feeding China: The Experience Since 1949", WIDER, 1986, to be published in Dreze and Sen, *Hunger: Economics and Policy,* cited earlier. See also his *China's Political Economy* (Oxford: Clarendon Press, 1987).

[17]See my *Poverty and Famines* (Oxford: Clarendon Press, 1981), p. 79.

[18]On this see my "How Is India Doing?" *New York Review of Books,* 21 (Christmas 1982), reprinted in Dilip Basu and Richard Sisson, eds., *Social and Economic Development in India: A Reassessment* (New Delhi, London, Beverly Hills: Sage, 1986).

[19]On this see Jean Dreze, "Famine Prevention in India", WIDER, 1986, to be published in Dreze and Sen, *Hunger: Economics and Policy,* cited earlier.

[20]B. Ashton, *et al.,* "Famine in China 1958–61", *Population and Development Review,* 10 (1986). While this figure of famine mortality is exceptionally high, it should also be noted that normal mortality rates in China are now very low. Indeed, if India had the mortality rates prevailing in China, there would have been 3.8 million less deaths in India *each year* around the middle 1980s. That is, every eight years or so more people die in India in excess of Chinese normal mortality rates, than died in China in the biggest famine of the century. India has no more reason to be smug than China has.

[21]Paul Isenman, "Basic Needs: The Case of Sri Lanka," *World Development,* 8 (1980); Amartya Sen, "Public Action and the Quality of Life in Developing Countries," *Oxford Bulletin of Economics and Statistics,* 43 (1981).

[22]Surjit Bhalla, "Is Sri Lanka an Exception? A Comparative Study in Living Standards," in T.N. Srinivasan and P. Bardhan, eds. *Rural Poverty in South Asia* (New York: Columbia University Press, 1987); S. Bhalla and P. Glewwe, "Growth and Equity in Developing Countries: A Reinterpretation of Sri Lankan Experience," *World Bank Development Review,* 1 (September 1986). See, however, the rejoinders of Amartya Sen to the former volume, and those of Graham Pyatt and Paul Isenman in the latter journal, 1 (May 1987). See also Martin Ravallion, "Growth and Equity in Sri Lanka: A Comment" mimeographed, Australian National University, 1987; and Sudhir Anard and Ravi Kanbur, "Public Policy and Basic Needs Provision: Intervention and Achievement in Sri Lanka", WIDER Working Paper, 1987, forthcoming in Dreze and Sen, *Hunger: Economics and Policy.*

Comments on Article by Amartya Sen

AMARTYA SEN: These are some remarks based on my paper "Food and Famine," the text of the Sir John Crawford Memorial Lecture given at the World Bank in 1988.*

It is useful to see economic development as a process of expansion of the positive freedom that people enjoy. The focus here is primarily on the

---

*To be published in *World Development.*

freedom that a person actually has to lead one kind of life or another. It takes the form of valuing freedom as intrinsically important—not just instrumentally so. Also, the concentration here is primarily on what you are positively able to do or be (if you so choose), as opposed to freedom in the negative form, namely, what others prevent you from doing. The issue of freedom in this broader positive form is central to development economics. Indeed, it is what development economics is all about.

To illustrate, one of the most elementary freedoms is that of being able to live long and avoid premature mortality. This is generally accepted as a goal that people like to pursue, and the freedom to do so is of utmost importance. It is for this reason that this can be a good index of development, supplemented by other important related freedoms important for the quality of life.

There can be considerable dissonance between per capita real income and life expectancy (and similar other indicators such as health, nourishment, and education). Opulence, in the form of per capita gross national product, which has served for a long time as the main criterion of development, may be a very poor indicator of the freedom to live long and well. A country like Oman may have twenty times the income per head as China or Sri Lanka but a much lower life expectancy. Even if we take a country like Brazil, with great success in achieving fast economic growth, we will find that though its income per head may be five times higher than that of China or Sri Lanka, its life expectancy is still lower.

In comparing China with India—a comparison with much economic and political interest—the perspective of income per head is not very enlightening. The difference of GNP per head is not very great ($300 for China, $290 for India). Yet, in life expectancy comparison the Chinese lead is very large indeed. Though they started with similar life expectancies in the early 1950s (a little over forty years in each country), China has a figure now close to seventy years and India, a life expectancy of around fifty-six years.

It is particularly interesting to note the Chinese experience since the economic reforms of 1979. It is now estimated that up to 1979, the Chinese expansion of GNP in general and of agriculture in particular was quite slow. Not much higher in agriculture than that of India, probably just about the same. But since the economic liberalization, we see a dramatic development—near doubling of agricultural output between 1979 and 1986. There are some who doubt the figures, but all agree that the jump upward in terms of agricultural output has been quite dramatic.

On the other hand, the picture over time is quite different in terms of life expectancy. The Chinese reduced their mortality and expanded their life expectancy extremely impressively before the reforms—through better delivery of health care, education, and sanitary developments (despite not being able to raise their agricultural and food output very much). Exactly the opposite has happened since then. Along with greater agricultural output since the reforms, we also find an increase in death rate. Also, life expectancy fell after the reforms rather than rose. Official Chinese statistics show this, and they are confirmed by the detailed calculations of Judith Banister for the period from 1979 to 1984. The increase in infant mortality in particular is especially striking.

While agricultural output doubled between 1979 and 1986, there has not been a single year in this period after 1979 when the official death rate has not been considerably higher than that before the reform. It confirms the general argument that successes measured in terms of GNP per head can be very misleading indeed.

To understand the fuller story, one has to look at the changes in the public health distribution system, which was the backbone of the Chinese expansion of life expectancy. The number of village-level medical workers (including—but not only—"barefoot doctors") has fallen sharply. The proportion of population covered by cooperative medical services related to production brigades has dropped dramatically. Why this kind of reduction in the Chinese health distribution system has come about is a subject of considerable interest. In some part it is connected with the general withdrawal from the collective sector toward private enterprise that has been so successful in creating greater agricultural production. It emphasizes a contrast often seen in the world: cooperative public action in the field of health and education is typically much more successful than it is in agriculture. A general withdrawal from both can create problems in one field even when it raises productivity in the other. I think we see this in the Chinese case. To some extent, it is also a financing problem; the change from the earlier cooperative system of agricultural production to the new individualist "responsibility system" makes the financing of cooperative public health facilities that much more difficult. There is a resource crisis for cooperative health activities in the Chinese rural economy. And of course there are also the compulsory birth-control measures (including the policy of the "one-child family"in some regions). These policies as well as the general crisis in rural health services have hit the female children hard, and the rural mortality picture has much worsened for girls vis-à-vis boys, given the pro-male bias in Chinese rural society.

To move to a different issue, I would emphasize another general point about the contrasts between commodity production and the quality of life. The availability of food and GNP may have very little to do with famine. India is often praised for solving the problem of famine through a revolution in food production. The story is attractive, but I fear not true. Food production and food availability per head have not gone up greatly in

India—the increase has been moderate. But it *is* true that India has had no famine since its independence in 1947 (the last famine was the Bengal famine in 1943, in which about 3 million people died).

In terms of calories per head, India lies about halfway in the range of sub-Saharan African countries, but some of the countries that have more food and more calories per head also have had famines. The absence of famines in India has little to do with food output per head or with GNP.

It has to do with its public distribution system, which is alerted into action whenever the food command of any substantial section of the population is threatened by a flood, or a drought, or anything else. The relief mainly takes the form of employment creation, and wage incomes help regenerate the lost purchasing ability. Having a large stock of food grains in the public distribution system also helps. There have been big droughts or floods in different parts of the country (in 1967, 1973, 1979, 1987, for example), but there has been no famine, thanks to quick regeneration of lost entitlements of the affected population through counteracting public action.

The triggering of quick preventive action ultimately relates to politics. In a system with opposition parties and independent newspapers, tremendous pressure is generated in India for the state to act whenever there is a threat of famine. It is very hard for the government to get away with nonaction when large-scale starvation threatens. The situation is very different in many African countries, with little opposition and a heavily controlled press. Not, of course, in all African countries, but the ones with freer politics and freer newspapers have also tended to be, in general, more successful (for example, Botswana and Zimbabwe). Indeed, even the Chinese famines of 1958–1961, in which it is now estimated that between 16 million and 30 million people died, would have been, I believe, impossible if the then Chinese government had had to work with opposition parties and a freer press rather than being able to continue its disastrous policy without serious change for three years.

On the other hand, the interest of opposition parties and newspapers in endemic nonextreme hunger (that is, undernourishment rather than open starvation) is limited, and the continuation of regular deprivation in India has not become "politicized" in the way famines have. In this respect, the political commitment of the Chinese government has been a greater source of protection for its population than political plurality has been for India's. A not-easily-observed low level of nutrition is hard to politicize and not easily made newsworthy, even though it does raise morbidity and mortality rates. I believe India's future will depend a lot on the activism of its journalists and political parties in making endemic deprivation as embarrassing for the governments as famines have become.

There are important policy issues in the perspective of freedom. Positive freedom is of great importance in itself. Negative freedom too can be important, even in the context of development. They may have an important instrumental role—a role that newspapers and political parties play in preventing famines and can potentially play in other types of deprivation. This is one of the cases in which civil rights and liberties and press freedom, rather than being luxuries for developing countries, have a vital role to play in generating a better living standard.

The diverse experiences of India and China bring out many interesting issues. The contrasts between them go in different directions—for example, the Indian success in eliminating famine, despite continued undernourishment and endemic deprivation, vis-à-vis the Chinese success in encountering undernourishment and deprivation and in raising longevity, despite probably the largest famine in recorded history. There are also significant contrasts over time, especially in China since the economic reforms, with a sharp rise in output and food availability and a fall in life expectancy.

In studying economic development, there are many interesting issues concerning freedom. They involve the intrinsic importance of freedom as well as its powerful instrumental role. Development is all about freedom in the broadest sense.

GELIA T. CASTILLO: Amartya Sen's analysis is refreshing and persuasive. The fourfold classification of freedom—positive, negative, intrinsic, instrumental—in relation to food, health, and medical services is a liberating concept. There is no freedom without food. In a recent study done by an NGO, instead of going through the lengthy process of getting data on income, the villagers were asked, Who are the poorest households in this village? All knew. When asked, Why do you consider them the poorest households in the village? they replied, "Because when they wake up in the morning, they don't know where they are going to work." And why do they want to work? "Because they want to get food."

In a very recent analysis of household behavior in farming systems, it became evident that household food security is a crucial operational strategy for all low-income households. One way to use the household perspective in viewing production and consumption is to see what is revealed in diversified household strategies. It is not rice, corn, vegetables, livestock, wage labor, or remittances, but all these. Sometimes in minuscule amounts but always in unimaginable combinations. It is not just the men, not only the adults, but also the women and children who participate in the production and decision-making process. And all of this is aimed to provide food for the family.

With these realities before us, perhaps we ought to shift our goal of increasing farm income to talk about resourceful households. We might shift our goal from increasing farm income to improving food security at the household level throughout the year. We have seen time and again that household food security is a major preoccupation of resource-poor households.

I like very much Sen's remarks on freedom of information. During the Marcos years, there was not much freedom of information. One of the things we wanted to ask the Department of Natural Resources to do was to release a map of the Philippines, showing who had control over the public natural resources. This was said to be impossible. Anyway, when the new government came, we repeated the request, and this time the information was released. It came in the form of corporate names. We could not learn who the people involved were, so we are asking for another list. I suspect it will be a bit more difficult to get!

LINCOLN C. CHEN: Amartya, you link freedom, politics, and public policy. I wonder if you would also give some reflection to a cultural interpretation. India and China are very different cultures in terms of normative attitudes toward information exchange, criticism, and public policy—in both pronouncement as well as acceptance of public policy. Sino culture is monolithic, and edicts move from top to bottom, irrespective of the political inclination. Indian culture is pluralistic, at times chaotic, with much diversity and bubbling from below. Are there not some cultural explanations in addition to political factors?

NANCY BIRDSALL: Amartya Sen's remarks are fascinating but in some ways troubling too. They suggest that there is no trade-off between food and freedom, that freedom, in an instrumental sense, advances the likelihood that you will have enough food, and food does give you more freedom. But when you come to the case of China and life expectancy, the freedom to exercise entrepreneurial rights, the freedom to earn profits or whatever, there is a trade-off. It raises the question whether there is not some legitimate trade-off—for example, between the freedom not to die prematurely and the freedom to exercise certain other human capacities. China seems to be an example where a very authoritarian approach—and some would say the same is true of Cuba—purchased this very high life expectancy. It raises the question whether one would want to be a Chinese peasant in 1970 or an Indian peasant in 1970. If I may add one footnote, another good example in terms of freedom of information is what happened during the emergency in India, the population policy, the vasectomy push. The negative reaction was rapid. In China, by comparison, it took years for local unhappiness with a very stringent policy of population control to take hold; even today, it is not at all clear that people have freedom in terms of family planning. On the other hand, people would say that the family-planning policy in China contributed greatly to the increase in life expectancy.

ARTHUR KLEINMAN: Continuing with Nancy's point, I also would like to hear more discussion of the China example, of the reasons for the decline in mortality. To draw the right conclusions, the organization of work units in the cities and the organization of the communes would need to be considered in any study of the the decline in mortality. And, in the reform period, the breakdown of the commune system, and again the lessening of its coercive power, would need to be taken account of.

Plenary Session

DAVID E. BELL: The title of this plenary session, "The Future Prospects of Development," seems artfully ambiguous to me. It requires us to think about the meaning and the concepts of development, how they have changed and where they are headed. The title also requires us to think about the real world, development in the sense of active occurrences, things that are going on.

Four of our number have been asked to lead off this plenary session. Edmar Bacha is an economist; McGeorge Bundy, a political scientist. Both Dr. Bacha and Dr. Bundy have participated extensively in public responsibilities in their own countries. Gelia Castillo, a rural sociologist, has been active internationally in development enterprises of many kinds; Clifford Geertz, an anthropologist, has had rich experience overseas, especially in Indonesia and Morocco.

EDMAR L. BACHA: The question that I would like to address is why, when we compare this conference with the way development economics started in the postwar era, there seems to have been a total change in the issues that interest development theorists and practitioners. There are three possible causes to explain what appears to be a change of heart, a change of direction.

The first possibility has to do with the shift from Pax Americana to Pax Niponica. The United States is not what it used to be, certainly not in the beginning of the development era. The second arises from the fact that development no longer lives exclusively in the house of economics. There is a tendency to run away from the more technocratic outlook on development policy, to see it more as a political process. So, basically, economists are out; political scientists are in. Finally, using Amartya Sen's terminology, we appear to be moving away from an instrumental view of development. We worry less about material content and are inclined to look more at human content. Amartya Sen made a very strong point when he said that development economics is about freedom.

As Paul Krugman's paper suggests, development economics was originally a chapter in the history of transfer theory. It dealt with the international aspects of transfer theory.

Developing countries are today a much more differentiated group than they used to be, especially in their relationships with the developed world. Some export manufactures; some cause financial problems; some continue to rely on the production of primary products. Because U.S. hegemony no longer exists, the major U.S. approach to all these matters has to be different. It has got to be articulated with the policies of America's allies, and even more with those of Japan, much more so than in the past.

We see today a growing internationalization of the national economies; with it, a growing importance of specific groups of developing countries. We cannot teach international trade at this time without dealing with the developing countries. We cannot teach international finance, or finance itself for that matter, given the fact that banks are now international entities, that they are so heavily involved in developing countries, without treating the developing countries. We cannot teach macroeconomics the way we did in the past, concerned as it is with the interactions of developed countries with one another but also with interactions with developing countries. Bright scholars a generation ago would have looked down at development economics; today they are very much concerned with the issues that constitute development economics. As practitioners in fields of international finance and international trade, they are obliged to be concerned.

Also, and very importantly, what used to be specific to developing countries we now realize exists also in industrial countries. Problems of health, education, women, and the like are paramount in the developing countries; they are no less preoccupying to specialists in the developed world. In a sense, development economics has become mainstream economics, macroeconomics, concerned with trade, money, and finance. It has also moved sideways into sectoral economics, into health, education, and the like.

What does this imply for the future? Perhaps an attrition in the number of those who call themselves development economists and a growth in the number of those who are health economists and the like. We may also find many more area specialists. If one wishes to split developing countries into differentiated groups, the regional bases must be recognized. They need to be regarded as integrated political, social, historical, and economic entities. This suggests that you will have area specialists and sector specialists. Who, then, will be obliged to look at the big picture? It will not be development economics; it may be something new called development studies, which will incorporate the insights of economists and social scientists.

MC GEORGE BUNDY: This has been an extraordinarily interesting two days for me. It is a return to a subject with which I was actively concerned in earlier years in a variety of ways, to which I have not been giving the kind of attention that all the other participants have in the last decade. I have found myself battered by conflicting reactions, and happiest when I heard Lincoln Chen say that in India the glass was half full and half empty, because all of the glasses seem to me to be in that condition.

It was right to begin, I think, with the contemplation of catastrophe; it was comforting to be told that it is neither inevitable nor the only possible way of thinking. It was also right to be reminded that the contemplation of catastrophe was a very large part of what got this whole enterprise going in the years after World War II. There is no doubt, for example, that the entry of the Ford Foundation into the field of international development owed much to a visit to a newly independent India of high-minded, intelligent, disinterested, and idealistic trustees—all men in those days—who reached the conclusion that if the foundation's concern was with human welfare, which its charter explicitly said it was, the foundation could not be absent from this extraordinary and dangerous adventure, the adventure of Indian independence.

The glass seems to be half full, not only with respect to individual countries, and half empty too, with respect to the performance of donors, but also with respect to the record of analysts, with respect even to the hypothesis of a conservation of catastrophe. Nothing in this mixed record, in my view, changes the correctness of the perception that to be concerned with these matters is not only deeply interesting in terms of human engagement and intellectual adventure but deeply correct in a moral sense.

The second proposition that seemed to come across in a wide variety of ways was the inescapable role of politics in all this. We are talking about problems that very often yield to understanding best when we have an economist with us, but the choices over and over again are political. They are political for institutions; even more so, for governments. Even if the political failure of Africa was not the fault of General de Gaulle—and I come from an American generation that was in the habit of thinking that if you could blame General de Gaulle, you had always solved the problem—even if that was not so, and I am inclined to think it was not, the problem of the quality of the polity is clearly of the first importance, whether you see it from the perspective of the political scientist or from the point of view of the development analyst. It has always required political support within both the developing and the grant-making country to get this enterprise under way.

We should not, therefore, be surprised that there was a connection from the beginning between the dominant phenomenon in the international relations of the United States—the Cold War—and the American concern for development. David Bell and I can remember arriving in Washington and deciding in the White House that we needed to change the name of the development agency to AID so that it would sound helpful. I remember being visited by Averill Harriman, who said that we were crazy. You will never get a dollar for that, he said; why do you think we called it mutual security? The same challenge, the same mixture of motives,was in our heads when we properly, and fairly, I think, baptized our adventure in hope in this hemisphere, an Alliance for Progress, to link the American continents. The leaders in that enterprise were not only Americans but what we used to call anti-Communist democrats in Latin America. These forces existed, and they were very important.

I have been much struck by the inconclusive but energetic discussion of the way in which the United States might go about these matters in the future. I do not think it is wrong that there is no disagreement among us about the imperfection of recent performance. I regret to say that I think it is correct to start from the premise that the performance of the American government in this area will rarely rise above whatever standard is set by the occupant of the White House. This is a subject which requires effective interpretation to the American people. It also requires, and this is something that I saw firsthand with two presidents, that the president learn to engage himself with the subject.

Fortunately for those who were staff officers at the time, both JFK and LBJ, in their entirely different ways, were deeply engaged in the development question. Johnson's method was harder to understand. I remember the time when he refused to act on repeated and increasingly insistent memoranda; he would simply return the memoranda without a mark. These memoranda argued that it was time to get food exports moving to India. Eventually, it became clear that what he was waiting for was a chance to talk to Subramaniam, the Indian minister of food and agriculture, and that he wanted to talk to Subramaniam before he released the food exports rather than later. We concluded that Lyndon Johnson had decided to give a lecture on self-reliance in his most earnest and intense way, a lecture that would be remembered precisely because the prize would be delivered at the end and not at the beginning. In later years Subramaniam used to say that the largest contribution that the Americans had ever made to the agricultural self-sufficiency of India was the speech that he got from Lyndon Johnson. Well, that was cheap aid.

What that particular episode reflects is a triple combination of shared political interest, a common and mutually trusted intent, and the ability of both players to keep their ends of the bargain. Now, to get the president into a position where he can have that kind of influence in the international process requires that he have the resources. That problem was relatively easy in the case of food because, as we all know, readiness to export food has been a political reality in the United States, and the means for making cost-free exports of food had been written into law years earlier. Lyndon Johnson was the sort of man who knew how to count up his powers and abilities and make the choices that would allow him to go into action.

In an entirely different way, the same kind of engagement became stronger and stronger with JFK, and let me remind you that these were not the first and second presidents who became deeply engaged. They were the third and fourth, because the Point Four program was a White House invention in Harry Truman's time. There was no president who more insistently and repeatedly made clear to the Congress that, given a choice, he would rather have dollars for economic assistance than dollars for his military forces than Dwight D. Eisenhower. So when we talk about executive leadership, we are not talking about something that has never happened. We are talking about something that highly successful presidents have practiced; they have not been removed from office by an angry public for their foolish attention to people far beyond our shores.

I believe myself that the raw materials for a new national consensus are here. I think that we desperately need to have the leadership of a proven politician. I think that there is a requirement, as there was in the beginning with the Marshall Plan, for a prior engagement of congressional forces, so that there is bipartisan presence both at the takeoff and at the landing. I think there needs to be a reconciliation and reassertion both of our interests and of our obligations. There is no conflict here.

It is true, and it is important for us to understand this truth, that it is not right, if it ever was, for an American program to be framed only in terms of what the United States can do. It is clear that the countries with the resources are more numerous now. Some of the resources in other countries are now larger, or at least less encumbered than our own, so there will be a new coalition of donors. It is also true that the standards that were set in earlier years for this or that kind of assistance and the ways of thinking geographically are today different. I strongly share the view that regions are different and that regions need to be treated as regions. There is unfinished political business in the relationship between Japan and the regions that would naturally qualify for Japanese economic support and attention, but that business, in my judgment, ought not to be attempted without the Americans.

I am always reminded when I come back to Harvard of how much this extraordinary institution—we are outside it, but we are near enough to think of it as here—how much this institution has changed. Only as recently as the time of James Bryant Conant the assumption made was that the university had reached its full growth. What a mistake! It took 300 years to build the constituency that has made Harvard possible. I used to think, when I was working for Harvard, that the only way to be a great university was to have started 200 or 300 years before. That is not true, but it does take time, and it does take a constituency, and it takes a sense of what you are about and a confidence that you are free in your society to go about that business. These are not easy things to get. I think perhaps what I carry away from this meeting most poignantly is the feeling that there is no more important task than the one that Soedjatmoko sketches, that there should be a national research university of the first rank in as many countries as possible. Indeed, that challenge will be with us a generation from now and beyond that.

So, I say we have a half-full and half-empty record. My feeling as I listen to competing emphases is that they are usually both right, that there is work ahead for both the developed and the developing, that there is great importance in macro analysis and in large-scale action but also in the understanding of the village and the family—that Gandhi and Nehru are at least half right, both of them. Things are both economic and politic; they are both public and private; they require action and thought; they need the lender and the borrower. They need elites but not elitism; they need democracy but not demagoguery, and all of them must be undergirded by moral imperatives. I cannot fully agree with Amartya Sen that the best test of success is long life. It appears to me that there is such a thing as enough life and that there are very many other things that one wants. I would side with those who would want less life of higher quality if forced to the choice. I certainly feel that it is right for people who have reached the age that David Bell and I are scraping against to be glad that the problems of making the national government work on these subjects will now properly fall into other hands.

GELIA T. CASTILLO: One issue that we have not discussed sufficiently is that of sustainability, not only in the physical and social sense but also in the economic. If we are to be concerned with sustainability, we must return to the population problem, which we have not discussed sufficiently. It remains unresolved; we need to return to it in a more vigorous way.

We have to deal also with the problem of scale—large, small, and medium. We have to deal with the issue of time. It is amazing how little attention we have given to that subject. What is the time we use to measure the things we do? I used to say that a project is judged a success because it has not had a chance to fail, and a project is deemed a failure because it has not had a chance to succeed. Sometimes we do not know which is which, because we never give the experiment a chance.

Then, there are the problems of social urbanization, the problems of institutional development. We have not lacked good ideas during the last forty years, but somehow we never paid sufficient attention to the question of institutional development, which takes time, which is so often difficult to get our hands on. Side by side with institutional development is the issue of human capital development. A lot of donors now say that we have resolved that problem. I doubt it. We need continuing investment, more creative ways, certainly, of considering this question. Whatever macro policies we have, dealing with finance and the debt crisis, we need always to trace back what impact it is likely to have at the micro level. We seldom do that. Most people are divided into macro specialists or micro specialists; they rarely get together. I think we have to take a look at this if we want to look at the human dimensions of development policies.

CLIFFORD GEERTZ: I think the reason I was asked to comment briefly was that I was accidentally present at the creation of the Old Testament times that Frank Sutton talked about. I went out, as some of you may know, on an MIT project of anthropologists to Indonesia in 1951, under the auspices of the as-yet-unformed, though forming, Center of International Studies. It seemed to me at the time there was a rather characteristic course of development for economists going to Jakarta. When they first arrived from MIT or wherever, they were extremely technically minded. After a time, it became apparent that they did not quite know whom to give their advice to. The political structure was somewhat different than it appeared to be. Inevitably, they began to become a little interested, beyond their technical economic concerns, with how the political system worked or did not work in Indonesia. After gaining some sense of that, they became intrigued with the fact that the society from which the people manning that system came was different from any they were used to. They did not understand how the class system worked, how education worked, the intellectual background of most of the ministers with whom they were dealing. So they began to be interested in how society, at least at the upper echelons, worked. Then, finally, as they became even more bewildered, they noticed that people perceived them with quite different cultural assumptions, that they were dealing for the most part with Javanese, that Javanese were not exactly the same as Sumatrans, and so on. They began to be concerned with this, having started off with strictly economic perspectives.

At this point, they were confronted with three choices. Some simply went back to MIT and a clean, well-lighted room, where they could build their models and not have to worry about all this messy reality. Others went more or less out of economics altogether and started investigating child naming or searching for the mystical quality of the mysterious East. Some of their work was interesting, some not, but it tended to exclude them very quickly from the development economics community. The best hung in, trying to relate their expertise to a foreign setting, culturally, socially, and politically, making pragmatic adjustments as best they could. This is the group out of which was built development economics, as Frank Sutton described it, with all its strengths and weaknesses. It was pragmatic, policy oriented, and a bit ethnocentric. A good deal of public learning took place.

The question is what has happened to it since. Like McGeorge Bundy, I have been away from it for quite a while. My impression of what has passed is that not all that much has changed, though there have been some changes. One change has to do with a greater interest in distribution issues. Another is that some of the numbers today come from surveys, in Indonesia at least, that are not the work of the state bureaucracy. Those who were anthropologists in the field in the beginning saw how bureaucrats "gathered" their figures and why they gathered them that way. The politics of numbers has become much more clearly recognized, and that's a net gain.

On the other hand, it seems to me that despite protestations to the contrary, and the obvious example of Japan, not to speak of the newly industrialized countries (NICs), you have still pretty much the freeway, lots of entrances but only one exit, a view that sees all change as going in one direction. It is now broadened into modernization, into the notion that the movement is toward a situation fundamentally like our own. The differences are recognized now, but they are still rather marginalized. Thus, for example, the new interest in the institution of Confucian capitalism.

There is today a greater sense of the diversity of the Third World; it was always there, but it is now recognized. Singapore, Chad, India, and Costa Rica do not make much of a set. There has been a useful pluralization of interests on the one hand, but this has led also to a certain amount of country-itis on the other. Area studies were just starting up when I first went to Indonesia. Now, we have built up a cadre of area specialists. There are real questions about how you get overall integration.

My impression from these two days is that development thinking has not changed nearly as much as the objects to which it is applied. The political-economic interconnection, for example—the first hurdle that my friends had to overcome—still remains very troublesome. For all the realization of its importance, it is still not as well handled as it might be. I think most development people are still more comfortable talking about technology than they are talking about power. As an example, consider the role in the NICs of what might be called authoritarian liberalism. It seems to me that in many countries, not all in the Third World, but some—Indonesia certainly and others as well—you are getting the rise of a combination of a Smithean idea of how to get rich with a Hobbesian idea of how to govern. This phenomenon, I think, has not been sufficiently reflected upon.

Yesterday, someone mentioned that the state's main objective in most places is not economic development, whatever it may say; its main objective, which needs to be brought back into our theories, and which has always been present, is to preserve the system that brought it to power, that gives it power and keeps it there. Developmental matters need to be assessed in terms of their contributions to those purposes. The elites' concerns are with matters such as stability—not as an abstract necessity for development but stability for stability's sake. There has not been enough concern with the fact that the local interests of a political elite and the general ones of economic development are not necessarily coincident.

The result of this political imperative—and I think we must be made aware of it—is that it makes development something that is judged in terms of stability by such people. The result of that, increasingly, at least in Morocco as I know it, is the desire to disconnect the politically disturbing effects of development from the welfare-creating effects, somehow or other to get the rewards of development without any of the unpleasant side effects. The appeal of the political elite, in Indonesia, Malaysia, or Morocco, is to an authoritarianism combined with fidelity to a technocratic, economic elite, which is given a good deal of free play in economic matters.

The result, in some cases at least—I do not argue that this is entirely general—is that economic effectiveness, rationality if you will, increases substantially, even marginally, while political rationality does not. The political capacity of the mass of people at the village and small-town level, or even among the urban masses, remains undeveloped in a quite literal sense of that term. In both Indonesia and Morocco, and I think this is true of many other countries, there is a deliberate policy effort to keep it that way.

When I first went to Java in 1951, economic rationality was hard to find, locally or centrally. The level of economic literacy was very low and economic fantasy very high. But the political capacity, especially at the local level, where I knew it very well, was often quite astounding. Local government in Indonesia at that time was perhaps better on average than it was in the United States. Now, as some of you know, I went back a year ago. The situation is now reversed. Economic rationality is widespread. The economy is highly commercialized; in ideal Western terms, it makes sense. Political life, especially locally, is stunted and, in fact, in some degree of disintegration. One finds a disjunction between marked economic advance (more in Indonesia than in Morocco) and equally marked political stasis.

So, I do not see that people in development communities are giving much thought to this sort of problem, the long-run implications of increased economic rationality coupled with political centralization, authoritarianism, or whatever. Yet, as Professor Chowdhry's paper brought out, local sophistication, if that is indeed the word, is critical, even to central government activities, if they are to be effective.

The civil rights issue, as I see it in the United States, for example, rests on the fact—surprising to most people and certainly surprising to me—that there was such a very high level of local political leadership among blacks in small southern towns, mainly centered in the church. That was why the federal government could do something to displace reactionary local white elites, why indeed it could be moved to do so. I think that if we were still waiting for the federal government to move without pressure from that direction, we would still be waiting today.

The point I want to make is that the working of politics on the local and regional levels is as important as the working of politics on the national level. The disjunction of the two is proceeding in at least some of the new states. It is something that we ought to think about rather more than we do.

Another area where I think Old Testament thinking has not changed enough concerns what I choose to call the tunnel-vision view of development problems. We still tend to divide things up conceptually in terms of our own particular academic genres and to stay within those artificial confines. This is of course partly necessity, which cannot be avoided if specialized professional skills are required. Some, however, is caused by calculated blindnesses or, at least, serious omissions. Allow me to cite a number of examples to illustrate this, dwelling principally on education, because it has been much discussed here, but realizing that matters are similar for health, trade, and other areas as well.

It is apparent to everyone, or at least should be, that the school system that has emerged almost everywhere in the Third World is the main mechanism of the system of social stratification. The older mechanisms—birth, family associations, and cultural style—have all greatly weakened. The main sorting mechanism is now education. That is the principal reason for the fierceness of the dispute over education's distribution, why schools proliferate so, and why the system tends to be the cockpit of social conflict. Yet the discussion of education tends to proceed in purely "cognitive capacity" terms, with almost no analysis of the other, what I think to be its dominant, function. There is too little discussion of stratification systems, how they work, particularly or generally, and the problems they pose when the educational system is at the center.

The result is a somewhat unrealistic cast to the discussion. What is at stake and what is going on have to do with status and power—privilege, to put it bluntly—and not a simple yearning for knowledge, for greater cognitive capacity. It is not out of a sudden upsurge in the thirst for knowledge that East Java, one province in Indonesia, has now 300 universities. Morocco has a university in virtually every city in the country. Something is going on there that involves a struggle for power and status.

My point is not that cognitive capacity does not matter, or that it is not what an educational system should be about, but that attempts to understand why this or that system is shaped in this or that way is not going to get us out of the tunnel view of the matter. The multifunctionality of social institutions and the tendency for secondary functions to displace primary ones—as I think has happened in this instance—is almost a sociological cliché. Yet I cannot see that the cliché has entirely sunk in. I use education as an example. Health and trade are very similar.

Well, I could go on, but I had better not. That we have today a more differentiated notion of the Third World countries is incontestable, but a thorough-going reflection on the implications of that differentiation for developmental theory is still uncommon. Everyone says that it is the case, but issues of comparison—what sort of comparisons need to be made—appear to be more settled than they in fact are. Their difficulty is enormous, especially to someone like me who is trying to compare the apples and oranges of Indonesia and Morocco. The role of general theory, the lack of it, and the problem of differential change in various parts of the single system—all these things seem to me to be not sufficiently reflected upon.

Having been away from development for a few decades, and now listening to our debates, I do not argue that development thinking has not changed, only that though it has changed, it has done so less than I had imagined it had. It still seems that we reach out of technical economic matters toward politics, beyond them to social structure, and beyond that, to cultural issues. This reaching out remains as it was in the 1950s, tentative at best; it is still a very nervous-making enterprise for development people. Old Testaments die hard.

GEORGE ZEIDENSTEIN: I want to rise to the point that Gelia Castillo made, that there has been insufficient attention paid to population concerns. Why has the subject been so thoroughly omitted from the papers, the program, our discussions? Is it because we think the problem has gone away? After all, what some people today think of as the heyday of population concern coincided with different fertility rates. In one sense, one can say that the globe is witnessing a fertility transition; therefore, there is less need to talk about it. Or, turning it the other way, is it that the problem is just too intractable? Does it resist any sort of policy intervention, simply going its own way? If, in fact, fertility has gone down, can the people who have been working on population problems claim credit for that? It may be due to all sorts of other factors.

Or, is our omission of the subject a comment on the large proportion of economists among us? In many economic models, fertility change is often taken as an externality. It is one of the givens from which we leap off and design the things we wish to do; therefore, there is little reason to talk about it. Or, again, is it an extreme reaction to what in some quarters is thought to have been the extreme stridence in the past by those who were concerned about population issues? I do not know, but I admit to some perplexity.

Here we are in this session talking about the future of development, and I am certain that few in this room would disagree that rapid population growth in very poor countries—moreover, mostly among the poorest of the poor—is very much ahead of us and is going to be an important factor in reference to all development efforts. Why, then, the silence?

Even the point about the global downturn of fertility does not hold up very well when you think about sub-Saharan Africa, the Middle East, northern India, Pakistan, or Bangladesh; even China has a problem with somewhat rising fertility. However strident the population field may once have been, it is not very strident today. All in the population field today would agree that population is one of the sectors of development, but only one. Many accept that development in itself is not the best contraceptive but also that contraception is not the principal way to development.

All that being said, part of the problem, I think, is that professionals in other sectors of development do not pay much attention to population, even though first-rate social-science-based research has demonstrated that among the determinants of fertility are some of the things that population professionals in education and rural and industrial development have something to do with. There are different ways of spending development dollars in various sectors that can have better or poorer fertility outcomes. I think it should be a matter of concern to all of us that we think of ways to involve professionals in other sectors, not at the expense of objectives that are primary for them but with the idea of putting the issues in front of them, asking them to think about population on a regular and consistent basis. Professionals in the population field are much more interested today in the relationship between population and health, especially in the health of women and children. As Nancy Birdsall has pointed out, family-planning programs are one of the major inputs in primary health care today; they are especially useful in improving the health of women and children.

As we talk about development for the future, one of the things we need to be concerned about is that health professionals, especially on the ground, pay so little attention to family planning. Their curative training and their curative outlook lead them to emphasize other things. It is vital that professionals in all the other sectors of development, whose activities clearly have an effect on demographic behavior, should recognize that they are having that effect and should, in some systematic and consistent way, pay attention to it.

CRANFORD PRATT: One of the main points that Professor Geertz made seemed to me to contradict one of the few generalizations that I am comfortable with as I reflect on Third World politics. This disagreement has to do with the favorable treatment that he gave to the political system that he called authoritarian liberalism. Against that, I have the strong conviction that there is evidence of widespread disillusionment both on the Left and the Right with authoritarian shortcuts, whether it be the decline of confidence in the single-party state in Africa or in bureaucratic authoritarianism in Argentina, Chile, and Brazil. Professor Sen argued convincingly for the importance of political liberties and a free press in explaining India's sensitive responsiveness to the challenge of famine. We have widespread evidence on the Left of a declining faith in vanguard parties. All this adds up to the generalization that there is today an increasing skepticism about authoritarian shortcuts. Professor Geertz has not convinced me to surrender this generalization.

CLIFFORD GEERTZ: One of the things about the Old Testament, as I said yesterday, quoting Albert Hirschman, is the notion that all good things go together, that economic development, democracy, and so on in some way coalesce. I think we are seeing in many places—not everywhere—a kind of division between authoritarianism in the political realm and a more open market, something that would have been thought, under the old dispensation, a natural monster. But both seem to last; they are not transitional. I think this sort of thing has become more attractive precisely because of the increasing attraction of political stability for these beset countries. It is not so much attraction to authoritarian shortcuts in planning—that, I think, may indeed be somewhat less popular than it was—but attraction to the idea that a good kind of world is one in which the government keeps things extremely stable, in which there may in fact be a great deal of political constraint. I do not myself, of course, applaud such sentiment; I simply argue that it is there. The economy is run by technocrats; indeed, there is a war between two kinds of technocrats, those who are essentially economists and those who, trained as technical experts—especially engineers—believe in high technology. There is a notion abroad that you can bring these two things together. I do not say that there has been a general regression to authoritarian regimes in the Third World but that belief in the notion that authoritarianism can be combined with market economics has increased.

CRANFORD PRATT: My suggestion, if I may make it in one sentence, is that there is a declining confidence in intellectual and concerned circles in the Third World in every kind of authoritarianism.

CLIFFORD GEERTZ: Well, that is possibly so, but it does not make much difference, since intellectuals do not run the Third World.

ABIOLA IRELE: There is a reaction against authoritarian governments in Africa. That I can affirm with confidence. Nobody believes what the government says.

ROBERT A. LE VINE: I would like to say something about the fluctuating romance between development policy and education. I do not believe that development economists have ignored education; it is just that they have gone through various phases, considering whether it is the prime solution or only part of the problem. Certainly there was a phase when it was in favor as the great solution for the development of human capital. Then it was seen as producing unemployment on a large scale. Still later, perhaps associated with the 1980 *World Development Report* from the World Bank, it was seen as increasing agricultural productivity, reducing fertility, and increasing health. Primary education was the panacea. I think the real lesson to be learned is that education as an answer to problems is embraced by economists when it can be demonstrated that it affects quantitative indicators that they care about. On the other hand, a lot of the criticism of the proliferation of education and the decline in the quality of life having to do with the social and psychological impact of education and the spread of schooling everywhere is something that does not enter into development thinking because it is not part of the kinds of things that economists can quantify or deal with in policies.

DWIGHT H. PERKINS: I am interested in the nature of political development and who is really responsible for dealing with such issues. While this has been a relatively civilized session, without too much bashing of economists, when I look at the various social science disciplines and what they are contributing to the field of development, I see political science as having basically gone off, given up on political development. Anthony Low's paper was wonderful; it would have been even more wonderful if it had reflected a tremendous body of work done by political scientists instead of one man's thoughts based on his experience. In fact, political development as a field of inquiry has died.

Economists may not be dealing with these issues, but they are dealing with some others when they talk about education. Why are not psychologists contributing in a way that relates to this? I have a somewhat different view of what is happening in political development. I do not consider myself in any way an expert on that subject, but when I look at what is happening in Asia, in China, and while I am prepared to buy some of Cliff Geertz's views of what is happening in Indonesia, I do not buy the free-market view of how the economy works. It is a very bureaucratic economy, as are most developing economies. The Adam Smith view simply does not begin to describe the way these economies are run, and that is why an authoritarian system can work. The political development in certain parts of Asia is bleak, but the political development in Korea, where I have been, is actually quite vigorous. In China, where the word *totalitarian* had real meaning until very recently, you have a very different world. It is not democratic in any sense, but there are not strong institutions growing up of a new kind.

The economists cannot handle these things. Who is one to turn to, able to help? I do not see it in the academic world today. Anthropology, for example, does not deal with these issues for the most part.

JUDITH TENDLER: My perception of the way the field is going is in a certain sense just the opposite of what other people are saying. Whereas Bacha and others describe development economics as getting more institutional, more concerned with distribution problems, I see the opposite happening. As a development economist, I find the field less concerned with these issues today than it was even in the 1950s, let alone in the 1970s. In the 1950s, when one used the word *structural*, it meant rigidities in the economy caused by, among other things, distributional inequities, particularly in land tenure patterns. Today the word *structural* has a totally different meaning, particularly when you find an economist talking about structural adjustment, getting prices right, and so on. The reason why this is an issue, why economics has become more narrow, why people do more economist bashing—which I suffer just as much as Dwight Perkins does—is that economists, as opposed to other people in the development studies field, have power. Anthropologists, political scientists, sociologists, and historians do not have power.

Economists, particularly today, not only hold sway through powerful institutions like the World Bank and the International Monetary Fund but also hold commanding heights in government in Third World countries. One has only to look at the economics journals today to see a much narrower economics than one saw in the 1960s and particularly in the 1970s, when income distribution and poverty were real concerns of economists, not just other social scientists. A vivid and sad manifestation of the problem today is that at MIT I have students who come to me from the economics department who are hoping to secure doctorates in economics, who are concerned with development issues, want to work on subjects of poverty and income distribution, but feel they are ostracized. Such studies are not considered respectable; they are thought to be "soft," even though they excel in the "hard" skills.

PETER D. BELL: I have been reflecting on this business of the glass being half empty and half full, and whether we are optimists or pessimists. I think that I am an optimist according to my favorite definition of the term, which I probably learned from someone here, and that is that an optimist is one who believes that the future is still in doubt. To be optimistic in that sense means that we have to take advantage of that doubt with a certain amount of force, with energy and ideas, and that is a need, certainly, if international cooperation is going to continue to be part of development. If there is going to be a future for international cooperation, it is very important, as some have said earlier, that it be infused with moral force. For development cooperation to have a future, it must be disciplined by the purpose of supporting people who are poor, marginalized, vulnerable, within what we call developing societies. What is needed is a reexamination of that commitment; it has become diffused over time. We still really do not know how to support the development of poor people on an appropriate scale while we maintain humane values with regard not only to purpose but also to process. This, I believe, is at least as much a political as an economic enterprise.

KENNETH PREWITT: Before the Industrial Revolution, the wealth of what today we call the developed world and what we call the less developed world was roughly equal. In the early stages of the Industrial Revolution, the developed countries were twice as wealthy as the less developed. This ratio became three to one in the late part of the nineteenth century and four to one by the early part of the twentieth century. It is now estimated at eight or nine or ten to one. This global inequality will continue to grow unless serious intervention takes place. A major part of the intervention finds its home in the multilateral and bilateral aid agencies. But the social sciences have let us down by not drawing attention to the emergence of new international development aid structures and analyzing what these structures can and cannot accomplish. It is shortsighted to talk about development today without giving attention to the political economy, even the ethnography, of the World Bank, WHO, UNICEF, UNDP, and the large bilaterals. In the last quarter century, we have rearranged the institutional structures through which development does or does not take place, is interfered with, or is accelerated, and we have not reflected on what this has meant.

ALFRED STEPAN: While I accept that there has been a rather disturbing withdrawal from the development field in political science, I believe that there are some areas of hope. When you subdivide the field, for example, looking at areas of dire poverty, especially in situations of authoritarianism, investigators are searching for new forms of empowerment, forms of resistance, ways for the poor to organize themselves. There has been a growing literature dealing with local organizations, neighborhoods, women's groups, and the like. This has been a major focus for many people working in Latin America, for example, not least in Brazil.

I think there has been a good advance also in the area of "regime theory," especially in the study of international organizations. While I do not think regime theory is focused enough on the regulatory environment or on the possibility of creating new major world organizations and development facilities, I think it is going to move in that direction very quickly. On the question of national political economies, at the moment political scientists seem more interested than economists. The literature on the problem of democratic consolidation is also of interest to development theoreticians and practitioners. The most urgent problem, in my view, is to find individuals who will capably and enthusiastically teach what we used to call development economics.

JOHN D. GERHART: I want to respond to Judith Tendler's question of why people are not working on the economics of poverty. There are three reasons, I think. First, there is a form of technology bias that gives increasing attention to technique over substance; it applies across the board but is particularly evident in economics. The data base in the developing countries does not exist to allow the student to demonstrate his mastery of the quantitative techniques that are demanded for an advanced economics degree. I believe that students are being discouraged from choosing a development topic because of this type of technology bias.

Second, there is a decreasing number of supervisors in economics departments who themselves have firsthand experience in the Third World and who would encourage a student to take on such a topic. Many graduate departments have no one with residential overseas Third World experience; there is no possibility of close and constant supervision.

Finally, there is a lack of funds to do overseas field research for the eighteen months or two years that would be required for a topic that is solid. Again, this applies across the board but is particularly evident in economics where there is a lack of funds for American or foreign students to do overseas dissertation research. We frequently see foreign students being told to use state of New York data, Oklahoma data, whatever is available. They can then do their work, get it done quickly, and go home. A priority should be to encourage empirical fieldwork overseas.

DWIGHT H. PERKINS: The social sciences have their own intellectual logic of development; there are topics that come along and excite students and faculty at particular times. In the economics field today, the ideas that have excited the brightest graduate students and economists generally have been areas like that of rational expectations, certain kinds of mathematical general-equilibrium theory, open-economy macro theory. Much of that may end up in some very arid type of scholasticism that will never go anywhere, but some of it has already been productive. The open-economy macro, for example, has clearly been an important contribution to understanding real-world problems.

These things happen, and they are not simply controlled by money or by problems; they are controlled by a logic. I assume that this is what has happened in anthropology—why development anthropology is not very interesting to most anthropologists—and I expect that this is true also of other fields.

Now, the question comes back, can this be changed? Real problems do help bring it back if the real problems are big enough and if people throw money at them. All that helps, certainly. But it does not necessarily solve the intellectual problem. The problem is particularly hard for a young social scientist thinking about doing a thesis. The problem is multidisciplinary. To understand the economics, you have to understand the politics. To understand the politics, you have to understand the culture, the society, and so on. Well, you tell that to a Ph.D. student who wishes to get his thesis finished so that he may find a job, and you do not immediately persuade him. You tell it to a senior experienced person who has been doing research for many years, and you are not wholly convincing. There is a long, long history of the failure of multidisciplinary work. Personally, I think that one of the ways you approach the situation is to look at real problems that require solutions, to work on policy-type problems precisely because they are inherently multidisciplinary. If people will indeed focus on trying to solve a particular problem together, you may achieve something. That may not be the only or the most effective way of doing it, but I know that it is not just a matter of throwing money at a problem.

LINCOLN C. CHEN: I would like to share some reactions regarding what "development" represents to different people and three key challenges facing the field today. Some perceive development as an academic field, involving primarily the social sciences but dominated by economics. After all, isn't economic growth the goal of development? At another gathering, many technocrats—agronomists, doctors, engineers—would have spoken of another perspective, about their work on farm fields, health clinics, and bridges and dams. For others still, development is social justice, in the way one culture relates to another but also how people within society treat each other. Human rights abuse might have dominated the discussion. And then, there are the artists concerned about the conservation of rich cultural heritage while promoting artistic expression to reflect contemporary challenges.

After nearly two decades abroad in Bangladesh and India, I returned recently to learn what others think of the development field in which I as a practitioner was engaged. In India, we worked with local colleagues on the problems of environment, poverty, health, economic and political relations, and culture and the arts. We worked with voluntary agencies, development institutions, government bureaucrats, academics in the universities, and journalists and artists. We were concerned with political commitment and social constraints, new and adapted technologies, and improving the performance of social organizations.

Returning from overseas, I now see that our work was part of a much larger international enterprise. The conglomerate is highly diverse with many agendas and even "takeovers" of various groups. It demonstrates only a small part of the development field as I saw it in India and Bangladesh. Here our preoccupations are with transnational relations, the debt crisis, America's foreign policy, East-West tensions, North-South relations, and so forth. These issues, of course, are critically important to the world, but somehow I can't help register a note of concern over the self-interested purposes of many of these concerns as well as the dehumanization of the development experience through their abstraction of problems faced by people in all sorts of desperate circumstances.

For the future, three questions are critical to the development field. First, from where will the next generation of bright young people come, and how are we going to attract them to the field? How will we fill an auditorium like this with the best from all societies, the Indias and the United Stateses? From where will we find the young men and women who want to be engaged in these problems—as academics, problem solvers, and practitioners?

Second, where are the leaders, social institutions, and financial resources that will be needed to promote and support the field? We are in the midst of an institutional crisis in development. The old rationale and support bases have been gradually fading away; new ones are emerging but have yet to be clearly delineated. Many factors are involved here, but they primarily relate to the decline of America's world dominance in an interdependent global system in which all sorts of horizontal transactions are evolving. One-way transfer of technical advice and foreign aid is a declining element of this process. Needed is a search for mechanisms of coequal exchange and joint approaches to commonly shared problems.

Finally, where are the constituencies for building the future organizations and attracting the financial-resource flows? What is happening to American public attitudes and opinions and to our national leadership, in the White House and elsewhere? How does the development field cut through its Gordian knot, in which foreign assistance has so many purposes mixed into its mandate, and so many strings, that it has lost its effectiveness?

I would urge us all to address these questions. They are important for the development field. The challenge is fundamentally moral and ethical, only secondarily academic, with all sorts of practical dimensions of how we and others live in an increasingly smaller world community.